You already know her. It is she
who moves you in your dance.
She is the music of your life.
Do you need to ask her name?

—The Goddess Path

If you have never encountered the goddess outside your own heart, *The Goddess Path* will awaken you to her many names and faces. *The Goddess Path* offers you a creative, individualized approach to spiritual discovery and worship that will develop your inner resources and gently challenge your willingness to change.

Use this book to invoke twenty different aspects of the goddess, to create meaningful rituals that honor her feast days, and to foster growth in neglected or blocked areas of your life. Wherever you are on the goddess path, this book holds spiritual treasures for you.

❧

About the Author

Patricia Monaghan, Ph.D., is one of the pioneers of the women's spirituality movement and the author of several books on spirituality, including the classic encyclopedia of mythology *The New Book of Goddesses & Heroines.* Currently living in Chicago, Patricia is a member of the Resident Faculty of the School for New Learning at DePaul University, where she teaches science and literature.

To Write to the Author

If you wish to contact the author or would like more information about this book, please write to the author in care of Llewellyn Worldwide and we will forward your request. Both the author and publisher appreciate hearing from you and learning of your enjoyment of this book and how it has helped you. Llewellyn Worldwide cannot guarantee that every letter written to the author can be answered, but all will be forwarded. Please write to:

Patricia Monaghan
℅ Llewellyn Worldwide
P.O. Box 64383, Dept. K467-7
St. Paul, MN 55164-0383, U.S.A.

Please enclose a self-addressed stamped envelope for reply, or $1.00 to cover costs. If outside U.S.A., enclose international postal reply coupon.

Patricia Monaghan

The Goddess Path

Myths, Invocations & Rituals

2000
Llewellyn Publications
St. Paul, Minnesota 55164-0383, U.S.A.

FIRST EDITION
Third Printing, 2000

Cover design by Anne Marie Garrison
Cover photo © Shigeru Tanaka/Photonica
Editing and book design by Rebecca Zins
Illustrations by Nyease Sommersett

Library of Congress Cataloging-in-Publication Data
Monaghan, Patricia.
    The goddess path: myths, invocations & rituals / Patricia Monaghan.
        p.   cm.
    Includes bibliographical references and index.
    ISBN 1-56718-467-7 (trade paper)
    1. Goddesses.   2. Goddess religion.   I. Title.
BL473.5.M665   1999
291.2'114—dc21   99-11387
                                                      CIP

Llewellyn Publications
A Division of Llewellyn Worldwide, Ltd.
P.O. Box 64383, Dept. K467-7
St. Paul, MN 55164-0383, U.S.A.
www.llewellyn.com

Printed in the United States of America

Other Books by Patricia Monaghan

The Office Oracle: Wisdom at Work
(Llewellyn, 1999)

Magical Gardens: Myth, Mulch & Marigolds
(Llewellyn, 1997)

The New Book of Goddesses & Heroines
(Llewellyn, 1997)

O Mother Sun: A New View of the Cosmic Feminine
(The Crossing Press, 1994)

Seasons of the Witch (poetry)
(Delphi Press, 1992)

Winterburning (poetry)
(Fireweed Press, 1990)

The Goddess Companion
(Llewellyn, 1999)

Forthcoming

Wild Girls
(Llewellyn, 2001)

To Nancy Mostad,
publication goddess

Contents

The Goddess Defined

The Goddess Revealed

The Goddess

Defined

Finding the
Goddess

The goddess path is within you . . .
that is where she lives, even when you forget to look for her.
Look for her there, and you will always find her.

Somewhere in Asia at this moment, a woman is opening her palms to the statue of a naked dancing goddess, her throat ringed with skulls.

Somewhere in Africa at this moment, a man is sounding a deep drum pulse, calling the village to offer morning prayers to the goddess of earth.

Somewhere in America at this moment, women in a circle are closing their eyes, gripping each others' hands, and humming quietly.

Somewhere in the town where you live, a woman today will enact a ritual that honors the goddess. Perhaps she will do so unconsciously: decorating a tablecloth with an ethnic design showing the plant goddess surrounded by her heraldic animals, or baking a special holiday pancake that keeps the winter goddess at bay. Or perhaps she does so consciously, meditating as she watches a candle flicker, calling out the name of the goddess whose power she wishes to bring forth. Hera, she sings, or Aphrodite, or Artemis, or Brigid—names spoken like sighs or promises.

Somewhere in the town where you live, a man today will honor the goddess. He will do it, perhaps, unconsciously: cutting the hedges as his grandfather taught him, with respect for the plant's life, or caressing his lover's cheek with tender care. Or he will do it consciously, calling out to the feminine force in the universe and within himself. Oshun, he sings, or Kuan-Yin, or Isis, or Kali. Familiar names, unfamiliar ones, ringing though his heart's chambers.

Perhaps that woman is you. Perhaps that man is you.

Or perhaps it could be.

Across Europe and America today, on television programs and in book clubs and during weekend workshops, women and men talk about finding the goddess. Yet, in truth, she has never been lost. She has never died; she is still vividly alive. Across the world, many religions still honor her in ritual and prayer. And even in religions that seem to exclude her, the goddess has found ways to survive, as saint or bodhisattva or revered leader. She lives too in dreams and in art, illuminating our lives with her multiple meanings, leading us into deeper connection with ourselves and with the earth we inhabit.

The goddess has never been lost. It is just that some of us have forgotten how to find her.

But the path to her is there. In many lands, it remains a vital thoroughfare, traveled by ordinary people as they make their way through life. But in much of the western world, the goddess path has become virtually invisible, overgrown through centuries of neglect of the rituals that restore and refresh her. That path is being cleared today by scholars and artists, ritualists and poets, dancers and drummers. Men and women alike are seeking and finding ways back to the realm of the Great Goddess who is life and death, love and growth, dance and nature's cycles.

There is no one way to follow the goddess path. There is no one true church of the goddess, no pope of the goddess movement. There is no one ritual that unites all believers. There are no dogmas, no doctrines, no creeds. There is no university that can give you credentials to honor the goddess, in your heart or in public. There is no Bible that tells you everything you need to know and that limits what you can do.

There is only you.

You, and others like you, who have joined to create a religion that honors the feminine force in nature and in ourselves. Some say that this is an old religion, come back like a fruitful tree that has been too heavily pruned but which nonetheless survives. Yet even if the roots are old, this is new growth, new flowering, new fruit.

You, and others like you, walk the goddess path. How many are you? It is impossible to say, for this journey is so individual that no statistics can capture it. There are those for whom the goddess is a private intellectual search, who read about her and speculate on her meaning in culture and in myth. There are those for whom she is an emotional construct, a way of understanding the varying voices of the emerging self. There are those for whom she is a part of everyday ritual, honored in meditation and in prayer.

There are those who seek out others to join in invoking her, and those who honor her privately. There are those who find themselves creating altars of stones and feathers on tabletops, who do not even have a name for what they do. There are those who pause in the garden on an overcast day and remember—but who cannot find words to explain what they remember.

All are on the goddess path.

Wherever you are on this path, this book holds treasures for you. If you have never encountered the goddess outside your own heart, this will introduce you to some of her manifestations. If you have long been on this path, this book will provide prayers and rituals to stimulate your celebrations. If you are somewhere between those extremes, you will find much to illuminate your way as you continue your journey.

This book is not the path; it is only a signpost on the road. The goddess path is within you. To walk it, you must develop your inner resources and strengths. Information and insights will come to you from others. Evaluate them in light of the truths of your own heart. For that is where she lives, even when you forget to look for her. She is always there, providing the love and strength and power you need. Look for her there, and you will always find her.

~

Basics of Goddess Spirituality

She is the very power of feminine essence in the universe.
She is both an expression of what we know about our human world,
and she is a power far beyond our expression.

Religious ritual and practice are usually described as being based in theology, a word derived from Greek roots that means the study (*logos*) of the ways humans understand god (*theo*). Among goddess scholars, the parallel study is called thealogy: the study of the goddess (*thea*) and of the meanings we find in her image. This chapter will examine several basic thealogical questions, in order to establish a groundwork for the rituals and prayers and invocations that make up the later chapters.

There are many questions that concern thealogians today, questions that are complex, provocative, sometimes even disturbing. They ask whether the presence of a goddess empowers the women of a culture, or whether religion can praise the divine feminine while institutions oppress real women. They ask what are the connections between spirit and body in goddess religion, and whether its vision differs from that offered by religions based on male gods. They inquire as to whether goddess worship can be incorporated into traditional monotheistic religions like Christianity, or whether such a change would destroy the very basis of such religions.

This book is not designed to examine all of the controversies of contemporary thealogy. And, just as churches every Sunday are filled with reverent believers who do not need to be theologians to worship, so you can honor the goddess without knowing the thealogical answers, or even all the questions. But there are two questions we cannot avoid, for it is difficult to honor the goddess without knowing who she is. These primary questions are: Is the goddess inside us, or outside? And is the goddess one, or many? Examining the possible answers to these questions equips one to employ the image of the goddess in ways that most fulfill inner needs.

The Goddess Within, the Goddess Outside

Where is the goddess?

Is she inside us? Or is she outside, in the universe that surrounds us?

Or is she, perhaps, both?

The question of whether divinity is immanent (within us) or transcendent (outside us) is one that is argued in many religions. Both visions can be held simultaneously in the same religion, or even within the same worshiper. Among Christians, for instance, the Society of Friends primarily argues for an immanent godhead, while many individual Quakers believe in a universal divine force. Similarly, most Calvinist Protestants locate god outside humanity, in heaven presumably, but also allow for the presence of the divine in each believer. The old man in the white beard whom many of us as children envisioned to be god is a classic description of transcendent divinity. The "still small voice" of conscience is a classic depiction of immanent deity.

Because the goddess path is an evolving religion, there is no single final doctrine on this subject. Various speakers and writers hold dramatically different views. To some, the goddess is essentially an inner experience. To others, she is a vast force in the universe, utterly beyond human imagining. Yet others see her as both transcendent and immanent, with the inner goddess being mystically connected to the external. Let us look at each of these visions of the goddess in turn.

An immanent goddess appeals to many, for one can feel a tremendous and consoling intimacy with such an interior goddess. Goddess studies, in such a framework, usually become a part of psychology—although, as we will see, archetypal psychology bonds the inner and the outer goddess. Books that discuss the connection between the goddess and women's emotional lives generally assume an immanent goddess, as do workshops and teachers who encourage us to connect with the goddess strength within in order to better our lives. One of the most appealing aspects of this vision of the goddess, in fact, is its immediate application to daily life. Locating within ourselves the steely energy of Athena, for instance, can be useful in helping us through professional difficulties. Finding the soft spot in our hearts where Aphrodite dwells can prepare us to receive passionate love.

The immanent goddess does not exist outside the forms that embody her. These need not be human: many cultures have seen goddess energy as immanent in nature, with each plant having its own resident spirit who lives and dies with that tree or flower. Mountains, boulders, stars—each can be seen as occupied by a unique goddess spirit. Such a completely immanent goddess is not immortal, except insofar as goddess energy always exists in innumerable forms. But each individual goddess, like so many wood nymphs, is mortal.

The immanent goddess did not create the rose; she *is* the rose. She does not take care of you; she *is* you.

Great power exists in this image of the immanent goddess. For women, finding a connection to a divinity within themselves can be transformative, enlivening, empowering. For men, the connection to an inner goddess can both help sustain a connection to real women and heal social wounds brought on by the crippling of the feminine in our culture.

But a vision of the goddess only as immanent presents some problems to her worshipers. For those brought up in religions with a transcendent god, a goddess who exists only in the mind and heart somehow seems unreal, not truly divine. Queenly Hera seems less powerful when she only can be found in shards, here and there, in the souls of women struggling to make sense of their complex lives. Calling on the mercy of Kuan-Yin can seem less comforting if we cannot envision her as a being truly outside ourselves and therefore able to offer help.

Thus many are drawn to the image of the goddess as transcendent, as a force of nature existing outside of us. This goddess is frequently seen as the universe itself: Mother Nature, the Great Goddess, the Great Mother. Vast beyond words, powerful beyond measure, timeless and immortal, she can never be trapped in a single time or space.

There is a certain appeal in the picture of a divinity who is so totally separate from us. We become children of the universe, happy in our knowledge that, somewhere, unceasingly, a Great Mother is taking care of us. There is also a moral and ethical dimension to the comfort transcendent divinity offers. We need only follow external demands—what some religions call commandments—to know that our actions are appropriate and right, rather than making each decision through an arduous process of inner search.

But, as with the immanent goddess, there are negative aspects to the image of the goddess as transcendent. Such an overwhelmingly powerful goddess may seem too separate from her tiny creations. We may feel that nature is an impersonal force with no particular interest in any of her many creatures. Such a goddess faces the same difficulties as the sky god who was forced to reassure his children that not a single sparrow fell from the sky without his knowing, for the truly transcendent goddess can seem distant, even uncaring.

These two descriptions define the extremes of thealogical thought on this subject. But in practice, most travelers on the goddess path today perceive divinity as both immanent and transcendent. They find the goddess within themselves, a power to be called on for strength and vision in facing life's challenges. But they believe as well that the feminine force of the universe is larger than themselves. They believe that she can be found suffused throughout nature—but that she also is a force beyond individual plants and animals and persons.

Archetypal psychology offers a vocabulary for discussing the connections between the inner and the outer goddess. An archetype is an elusive concept, with perhaps as many definitions as there are archetypal psychologists. First articulated by the great psychologist Carl Jung, the archetype is like an energy template, a form into which the forces of the universe naturally flow. As natives to this universe, we are hard-wired to recognize these patterns when we encounter them. Thus the Great Mother is an archetype that both expresses and contains the universal force of mothering. We instantly recognize this force when we encounter it in dreams, in myth, in our waking lives.

Archetypal psychology, then, gives us a vision of a transcendent goddess who is also immanent. The goddess exists, in this framework, as something like an endlessly divisible hologram: every fragment is completely her, but no one fragment can be said to contain all of her. This is the framework most often employed in the discussions of goddess meaning in the following chapters. To the question "Where is she? In here, or out there?" this book answers "Both." She is universal nature, eternally creating and changing, unknowable and vast, a force beyond our limited comprehension. But she is just as much within our hearts and our bodies; she is the force of sexual attraction and of motherly affection, of righteous fury and steely intelligence.

She is all, she is everything. She is around us, and she is within us. We cannot be without her, and we can never encompass all of her.

One Goddess, Many Goddesses, and the Question of God

People talk about "the Goddess," implying that there is just one. Then they start singing about "Isis, Astarte, Diana, Hecate" and issue encyclopedias listing thousands of goddesses.

Which is it?

Is there one goddess, a single overarching universal power? Or are there many goddesses, each with their own powers and talents and domains? How can we honor the goddess when she seems to have so many names, identities, stories? Are there separate prayers for every one? Do we need to remember to invoke everybody or will we be punished, like the fairy-tale princess Briar Rose, for forgetting to invite someone to the goddess party?

And what about god? There are many religions where there is a god but no goddess. Does believing in a goddess similarly mean that one cannot believe in a male divinity?

We will begin with the second question first. For the question of god is deeply related to the question of singular or multiple goddesses. It is a historical fact that no monotheistic goddess religion has ever been known. Monotheism—religion based on the worship of one god only—exists in several forms, all of which have spread far beyond their original homelands. Christianity and its ancestor, Judaism, both come from the eastern Mediterranean; Islam comes from the same area of the world. Buddhism, which in its theistic (god-centered) form is focused on a male or neuter divine figure, emerged from the Indian subcontinent. These religions have spread far beyond their areas of origin, so that Christianity is found in South America and Islam in Indonesia. And all have in common a belief that there is a single divine being, not seen as female.

But, although there have been goddess religions on every continent save Antarctica, there has never been a similarly monotheistic goddess religion. Traditional goddess religions are polytheistic; they express divine reality through many goddesses—and many gods as well. Hinduism and Shinto are the only polytheistic religions left today with great numbers of adherents; in tribal or geographically delimited areas, other smaller polytheistic religions exist, too. Otherwise, throughout the world today, monotheism rules.

For those who grew up in a monotheistic framework, it is emotionally difficult to understand how polytheism works. It can seem like there isn't any "real god," any definitive divine power. It can appear as though the universe is some vast bureaucracy, with many shuffling divine figures in a warren of cubicles, fulfilling their tiny duties. It can appear to lack the stern focus of monotheism.

And so some on the goddess path have embraced a belief in a monotheistic goddess, one who rules all, like the god of their childhood did. Some women exclude the male divine—for reasons we explore further in the section on Artemis. In doing so, they diverge from the mainstream of goddess worship for millennia. For traditional goddess religion, throughout historical times, not only encouraged belief in male divinity, it required it.

As to whether the goddess is singular or plural, the answer is the same: in traditional societies, she was seen as multiple. In some cases, the same goddess passed through several phases of her life, as did the Greek Hera; in other cases, multiple goddesses "ruled" different aspects of life, as the Japanese Amaterasu for the sun and Toyome-himi for water. The question we have just examined, of immanence or transcendence, comes into play here too, for the multiple goddess was often immanent in forms of nature, such as trees and streams.

Many thealogians believe that, beneath this multiplicity, the goddess was always seen as one—all goddesses being ultimately united in one Great Goddess whose domain was all of life, death, and rebirth. In such an argument, the goddesses are one just as Father, Son, and Holy Ghost are one; Christians invoke them separately but nonetheless believe in the ultimate unity of the trinity.

Like the question of immanence and transcendence, the proper answer to the question of whether there is one goddess or many may well be: both. She is both multiple and singular, she is young and old and middle-aged, she is fat and she is slender, she is black and brown and red and olive and pink. But she is also all of those at once, the very power of feminine essence in the universe. She is both an expression of what we know about our human world, and she is a power far beyond our expression.

∾

Images of the Goddess

Is she virgin or mother or lover? Is she ancient as time itself,
or young as spring? Is she human or animal or vegetative?
Is she the earth or the sky, the moon or the sun?

This goddess—this immanent/transcendent, singular/multiple archetypal force—has been pictured in so many ways throughout human history that her image can seem like a ceaselessly changing kaleidoscope. Is she virgin or mother or lover? Is she ancient as time itself, or young as spring? Is she human or animal or vegetative? Is she the earth or the sky, the moon or the sun?

Because of the dizzying array of possible goddess images, it is helpful to have some kind of framework to approach her study. Many students have found a route to understanding her complexity through study of a single culture. Often, it's their culture of origin. This can bring special pleasures, as when Lithuanian women discover they know more about the goddess than they had realized because family traditions echo ancient rituals. Similarly, followers of the goddess from Irish or Japanese or Native American backgrounds are often pleased to discover vestiges of goddess lore they had imbibed almost virtually with their mother's milk.

There is no blood quota test for goddess study, however. Many are drawn to the power and beauty of the Greek myths, for instance, which have no known biological connection to the eastern Mediterranean. Artemis, Athena, Hera: their stories and images speak to us, move us, transform us, over centuries and continents. The study of goddesses from cultures other than that of our family of origin can be enormously helpful in introducing us to the variety of ways in which the feminine has been pictured.

When studying other cultures, however, it is important to be aware of the ideas and desires of current participants in those cultures. Those interested in studying Native American goddess traditions, for instance, should become knowledgeable about the disempowerment that actual Indian people have experienced over the last two centuries on this continent, and how this affects relations among Indians and non-Indians in terms of spirituality. While some Indian leaders willingly share spiritual knowledge with those from outside the culture, others have begged non-native individuals not to worship using traditional Native American symbols and divinities, in order to respect what little is left to Indian people of their original heritage. Similarly, practitioners of the religious traditions that emerged in the Caribbean and other parts of the Americas when enslaved Africans encountered the indigenous religions of the area may not always welcome participants from more culturally privileged backgrounds.

Spirituality is not a drugstore; don't automatically assume you can fill your cart with whatever you find appealing. Listen carefully to the varying voices you'll hear, and don't flinch from examining your own motives for pursuing a certain course. You may find that your calling is pure and unavoidable, or you may be forced to admit it's mere spiritual greed. Finding yourself pulled to a certain religious tradition may challenge you in more ways than you expect. Keep yourself open to all the learning you'll be asked to do.

Beyond culture and ethnicity, some students of the goddess have found it helpful to find an abstract framework that supports their study of her diverse images. A calendrical approach works for some; studying the goddesses of winter during that dark time connects lived reality with ancient myth. Similarly, studying goddesses associated with a specific life phase can be extremely meaningful as one passes through that period—witness the popularity of the crone goddess among women of middle age. Finally, studying goddesses of various cultures who are connected with a specific domain—gardening goddesses, for instance, or goddesses of art—can be personally meaningful to someone whose passion includes that area of life.

Frameworks for Goddess Imagery

In addition to these approaches to the diverse images of the goddess, there are several theoretical frameworks that have been used to analyze her. One of the most familiar is the triple goddess, who usually appears as Maiden and Mother and Crone. Such goddesses are found in ancient art: the Celtic Brigid and the pre-Greek Hera, for instance, were seen as triform goddesses. Three is a sacred number in such cultures, and the triplicity of goddesses reinforces, and is reinforced by, that sacredness.

There is much to commend the use of the triple goddess as a framework for goddess study. But as Cybill Shepherd complained in one memorable episode of her television series, *Cybill*, "Maiden, Mother, Crone" leaves something out. The comedian found her own name for the missing aspect, invoking the goddess as "Maiden, Mother, Cheerleader, Crone." In doing so, she put her finger on what is left out in the conventional triple goddess series: the vision of the goddess as sexually active. (No reference to the activities of current, former, or potential cheerleaders is hereby intended.)

Shepherd's tongue-in-cheek commentary on goddess symbolism intentionally or unintentionally reflects another analysis of the multiple images of the goddess. Originally articulated by Carl Jung's brilliant follower Toni Wolfe, then elaborated by psychoanalyst Anne Ulanov, it divides "the feminine" (the Jungian term for the archetypal energies connected with the goddess) into four parts. Wolfe, and Ulanov following her, named these the Mother, the Amazon, the Hetaira, and the Medial Woman. Like most Jungian analysis, this four-part schema further subdivides into polarities or oppositions. On the personal pole is the Mother, who relates to her children or surrogate children warmly but without distinguishing their individual uniqueness; opposing her is the Hetaira, whose name derives from that of ancient Greek courtesans and who relates individually and often sexually to those she meets. On the impersonal pole we find an opposition between the Amazon, a woman who connects to ideals rather than to people, and the Medial Woman or Medium, who connects to the transpersonal or spiritual realm.

Followers of Wolfe and Ulanov ask women to determine which of these figures express their major and secondary identification; the opposite figures are then considered to be submerged or "shadow" energies, less available and potentially troublesome to the individual. A woman with a very active Hetaira force, for instance, may have an equally strong shadow Mother, so that she unconsciously smothers her lovers. A woman with a strong Mother, conversely, can have a powerful unconscious Hetaira who seduces and entraps her children.

Outside of the therapeutic relationship, this four-part division of the feminine is useful in other ways, especially for discussing goddess imagery. It includes the three parts of the traditional goddess trinity: Mother, Maiden (Amazon), and Crone (Medial Woman). And it adds the missing cheerleader, the Hetaira. There are, however, several problems with simply adopting these words as labels for goddess energies. Firstly, the Maiden is not always Amazonian; that word, which derives from the hypothesized female warriors who invaded Greece, isn't appropriate for a maiden goddess like Persephone, who is ravished away from her loving mother and who has no way to fight back. Similarly, the Crone is not quite the same as a Medial Woman; as a queen, for instance, she may make decisions based on abstract values, but that seems to fall short of the spiritual grandeur of the medium. Even more questionable is the use of the title of Hetaira for the love goddess. While the goddess Aphrodite was once praised for being "Porne"—one of her titles, which means "whore," and was intended as a title of great love and regard—the equation of female sexuality with prostitution is not, for most women today, a positive one.

Using the four-part framework, we therefore will refer to the goddess as Mother, Daughter, Lover, and Crone, and will examine images of the goddess in those forms as well as their relevance to women's life cycles. It should be noted that these energies are available to women throughout their lives. Many girls are deeply in touch with spiritual realities, participating thus in the Crone energy; many older women have much of the youthful Daughter in them. Although there is a cycle of aging and development implied in the names for these goddess figures, in fact we can engage any of them at any point in our lives. For men, the cycle can be experienced in two ways: through the women around them, passing through life's stages; and through the development of these archetypal energies within the self, as parts of what Jung calls the anima, the feminine aspect of the male.

The Mother Goddess

Sometimes the term "mother goddess" is used of any important goddess, but in this section we will examine those figures directly connected with woman's sacred ability to give life—and to take it.

Mother goddesses can be found in all cultures. The most ancient goddess images known represent the goddess as mother—as a woman able to bear and nurture life. Figurines and cave paintings from the European Paleolithic era (the Old Stone Age about 24,000 years ago) show a big-breasted and big-bellied woman, robust and of uncertain age. She is usually shown alone, not with a child, but she looks pregnant or as though she had recently given birth. Found painted inside huge caves, or carved from bone or stone, she often has no face, although frequently she has a fairly elaborate hairstyle suggesting braids or coils.

This figure represents the oldest divinity humankind ever knew. Some interpreters believe that the faceless figures represent the earth, not specifically the human female. In this interpretation, Paleolithic people regarded the earth as their mother—just as we still, today, refer to Mother Earth. According to such arguments, the full-bodied goddess figures represent the abundance of natural food the earth provides for us. Without her bounty, we would starve and die.

But many ancient cultures did not employ what is known as either/or logic, using instead what we call both/and thinking. Thus the figurines and paintings from ancient times may represent both the earth as our mother and the tribal mothers who were fertile enough to conceive and give birth. At a time when life was much more chancy than it is now, human beings would have been happy to worship an abundant-bodied woman who represented both the fertility of the land (thus, food for her human children) and the fertility of human females (and thus, more food-gatherers for the tribe).

This mother goddess appears as the mother of plants and animals as well as of human beings. As the first, she is often depicted as a plant herself, rising from the ground, her hands shoulder-high and wide apart. As mother of animals, she is shown with wild beasts by her side, leaping to her upraised arms. Some figures show the goddess as both mother of plants and lady of beasts.

In addition to the sculptures and paintings of the goddess alone, we also find many representations of her holding offspring. Sometimes this child is clearly female, a new smaller self born to the mother goddess. Even more often, the child is male. This represents the goddess's power of conception and birth at its highest point—not because the male god is more powerful than the female, but because the goddess thus shows herself able not only to create a duplicate of herself but to bring forth a being completely different than herself as well.

Although obviously connected with birth, the mother goddess is also connected with death. As a literal mother, she gives birth to our death even as we are born, for bringing a child into this world guarantees that one more death must occur. And as a cosmic mother, the goddess rules over both the transition from non-life to life and the transition from life to life-beyond. Sometimes the images of the goddess as death are attractive and sympathetic, as is the case with Egyptian Hathor, the love goddess who rested in a tree at the edge of the horizon, offering the deceased their first taste of immortal food, or Lithuanian Saule, who similarly rests in a cosmic tree, hanging the souls of the dead like fruit on its branches.

But other images of the mother goddess as death are fearsome, even frightening, as is the Hindu goddess Kali. She is shown with necklaces of human skulls and earrings of leg bones; she bears a sharp knife with which she dismembers living beings; she dances in the graveyard, surrounded by her flesh-eating minions like the rat and the dog. Not, perhaps, a pretty picture of the goddess—but certainly a powerful one. Repellent as such images appear to those outside the culture that creates them, the deep truth they convey is that death is inescapable, part of life's processes. A philosophy or religion that ignores death is partial at best. In some of the greatest poetry of India's Middle Ages, worshipers of Kali sang love songs to her—love songs to their own eventual deaths. Thus the mother goddess is honored as the goddess of death as well, completing life's great cycle.

The Daughter Goddess

Among ancient goddess images, we find many that show a youthful, self-contained figure—the goddess as a young woman. She is usually young and relatively slender; her demeanor is calm and somewhat static. The earliest such image is the Paleolithic Venus of Brassembouy, which shows the goddess as a pubescent or pre-pubescent girl with small features and an unlined face.

The goddess as Daughter refers to that time in a woman's life when she is sufficiently well-grown to be articulate and self-reliant, but before she begins to become sexually active. She may be fully developed as a woman; the Greek Kore statues, which show the maiden goddess, reveal her firm breasts and rounded hips. She may be physically mature enough for childbearing, but the Daughter goddess is not yet involved in selecting a mate. Rather, she is at the cusp of full womanhood. Her attention is still directed inward; often the statues show a self-absorbed expression, as though the girl is thinking deeply and feeling just as deeply. The Greek Artemis is the most fully developed goddess figure of this stage—free, surrounded by other girls (her servant nymphs), and uninterested in romantic relationships.

In addition to appearing simply as a Daughter, the goddess in this aspect reveals herself as an athlete and a warrior. The Daughter goddess is not always static and self-absorbed. Often she is depicted in movement—Artemis, for instance, running through the forests, quiver over her back, surrounded by her hunting hounds. The Daughter moves athletically and entirely for her own pleasure, not to attract another's gaze. She may be dancing or doing acrobatics, she may be running or swimming, but she is centered within herself.

In some cultures, we find the Daughter armed and armored—as with the Greek Athena, for instance. Warrior goddesses appear in many cultures, and they are generally depicted as young women without children. The maiden as warrior shows us that the Daughter need not always be protected by another; she is strong enough to protect herself, and her city or tribe as well. Psychologically, the Daughter within is vulnerable and in need of protection; recognizing this, we sometimes wear more armor than we need. Part of the wisdom of the Daughter is to permit us to defend ourselves without making her energies too remote to be accessed.

The Lover Goddess

Among the world's goddesses, some of the most beloved have been those whose domain included human love. Such goddess were—and are—popular simply because people of every era and culture long for and appreciate the joys that love can bring. But the Lover goddess means more than simple physical pleasure. She is the force that brings us together, whether that be with others, with ourselves, or with the divine. She is the force of attraction and of connection.

The Lover goddess rules, obviously, sexual attraction, binding people to each other through intense shared pleasure. Of the various goddess images we've considered, it should seem that the Lover goddess would be the one most alive in contemporary culture. After all, doesn't it endlessly promote sexuality, with billboards and advertisements of people in alluring poses? Yet look closer: that curvaceous model is selling a car, not connection with another human being; that waif-like girl is selling tobacco, not a night of pleasure. (Of course, the implication that sex might follow from the purchase of said car, or from the use of said tobacco product, is implicit in the advertisements.)

Far from promoting and glorifying human sexuality, such advertisements imply that sex is a secret world of pleasure available only to beautiful people with lots of possessions. If this were truly the case, the human race would have died out eons ago, for only a small proportion of the world's population is ever beautiful and rich. In fact, tender and passionate sex has been one of the greatest pleasures the goddess has brought to all her children—whether they are beautiful or average or even ugly, whether they are brilliant or slow, whether they live in a castle or in a mud hut.

Beauty is connected to the Lover goddess, true. But love comes before, rather than after, beauty—for whatever we love seems beautiful in our eyes. This does not necessarily only involve sexuality, for who has not had a precious souvenir, broken or defaced, which still evokes memories of a special place and time to us, while others just see the surface and disregard it? Just so, the lines of a beloved spouse's face grow more beautiful with the years, though Hollywood might never admit it.

In addition to encouraging us toward love and tender connection with each other, the Lover goddess also grants us inspiration and ecstasy. Thus the artist and the maenad are connected with this aspect of the goddess: the artist, because she connects us with beauty in the form of words or music, dance or color; the maenad, worshiper of the god of intoxication, because she offers us an opportunity to forge a personal and primal relationship with the divine itself. For the Lover goddess is, at base, about connection. Whatever helps us find connection with ourselves, with each other, and with the universe around us falls within her domain.

The Crone Goddess

The final face that the goddess wears is that of a distinguished, usually kindly, older woman. Hers is the face of wisdom, for she has lived long enough to have observed the results of human endeavors and desires. She, like the Daughter, looks inward—but hers is a gaze of meditative pondering, for as an older woman she stands on the cusp of the greatest mystery, that of death.

Many ancient Crone goddesses were demoted, when their people were conquered or converted, into hags, evil stepmothers, forest-dwelling witches, and other villains of fairy tale and legend. Thus we often find Crone goddesses appearing as evil or threatening figures. And the power she represents can still be threatening today to those who are uncomfortable with women of power.

Two variations of the Crone image are the queen and the priestess. In some cultures, these roles were melded so that queens led their people religiously as well as politically. The image of the woman as a powerful head of state, and the corresponding image of her connecting directly with the divine, have in common the aspect of service to the community. For the Crone does not seek power for herself, but for what she can do for her people. Similarly, she does not seek connection with the divine just to enjoy the ecstasy it provides; rather, through that connection, she can assist her people. Thus the Crone is an especially noble and selfless form of the goddess image. She represents ideals of social harmony and cooperation, as well as the strength and wisdom to attain such harmony.

Using Goddess Images and Narratives

The visual appeal of goddess images is very strong, especially to women who have grown up surrounded by religious icons of subservient women and by cultural icons of apparently sexually available women selling expensive objects. Similarly, the narratives that make up goddess myths are very appealing to women who have lived their lives among limited options, either in the context of religion or in literature and other media. For men, goddess imagery counters the commercialization of women's sexuality in the media, offering strong, positive images of women at every stage of life.

Goddess images and narratives can become part of everyday life, thereby sending messages to the deep mind that the power of the feminine is active and alive and cherished. Placing small pictures or sculptures of the goddess where you will see them daily is a good way to begin this process. Establishing altars with images of the goddess and her symbols is a pleasurable activity; when the altar is completed, it serves as a constant reminder of that goddess's power. Altars need not be elaborate tables full of significant objects. A little sculpture next to a vase of fresh flowers is quite sufficient. The point of establishing altars is to impress upon the deeper levels of the mind how powerful and dynamic feminine energy can be.

Similarly, the narratives of the goddess—the stories that surround and depict her—can become part of your life in numerous ways. They can be used to spur creativity, as patterns for action in original stories and poems and paintings. They can be analyzed and discussed for the human wisdom they encode. They can be used to design rituals or other celebrations. The remainder of this book will assist you in bringing the goddess into your daily life through such creative activity and ritual.

∾

Ritual and the Goddess

If the goddess is a verb, she is best honored in action—
by moving and dancing and enjoying and yes, even lamenting.
And for most people walking the goddess path, this means ritual.

God is a verb, argued the great thealogian Mary Daly in one of her early books. Implicit in this statement is another, hidden one: that god is not a noun. God is not a person, place, or thing, not something static and changeless. God is action and essential being.

In the same way, the goddess is not a noun. She is not just an image in art or sculpture; she is not simply an eternal, distant presence. Whether we see her as a feminine presence permeating the universe or as our soul's inner truth, the goddess moves—and dances and enjoys and laments.

If the goddess is a verb, she is best honored in action—by moving and dancing and enjoying and, yes, even lamenting. And for most people walking the goddess path, this means ritual.

Ritual: the word may conjure up unsettling (or intriguing) images of women dancing naked under a full moon. But ritual can be far more ordinary than that. We practice ritual constantly, for it is simply action undertaken with a specific intention. Each morning, we brush our teeth with the intent of keeping away tooth decay (even an action with a scientifically proven basis can be a ritual). In a larger framework, we serve the same foods at holidays and perform the same expected activities, intending to create a happy space for friends and family. If you doubt the hold ritual has over those who claim to disdain it, imagine the consternation if you put up a Fourth of July tree or went door-to-door for eggs at Easter.

Thus goddess ritual can be as simple as lighting a candle or as complex as creating a rite of passage for a woman entering her croning years. It can be as brief as a gesture, as long as a play. It can be as timeless as a vision or as ordinary as a shared meal.

Even though ritual is part of our everyday experience, the deliberate employment of ritual to honor goddesses can feel uncomfortable even for those dedicated to following the goddess path. Those brought up in traditional monotheistic religions have been warned since childhood about "worshiping false gods." For such people, it may seem dangerous to act on goddess knowledge. Even those far from their church of origin may feel a shyness or discomfort at the idea of practicing a goddess religion instead of, or in addition to, their conventional religion.

There's a reason for this sensation: those warnings derive from a time when monotheistic god-centered religions were struggling to eliminate vestiges of goddess worship. Those "false gods" were usually goddesses.

Even those not burdened with such hesitations may feel awkward taking their first steps on the ritual side of the goddess path. Grown people playing dress-up—isn't this all, well, a bit juvenile? Others may be eager to practice, but don't know how to find others with whom to share their enthusiasm. Still others may fear the reaction of family members or neighbors who might witness and condemn un-orthodox behavior.

Each person must find his or her own level of ritual comfort. For some, inner prayers and readings can suffice. For others, verbal invocation—the repetition of names or prayers or significant words—that take place in private can be satisfying. Consciously dedicating to the goddess such womanly activities as craft work or cooking can bring inner and outer realities into alignment.

But there are times and occasions that virtually demand a formal ritual, whether created singly or with a group. The year's major turnings, significant rites of passage, bondings and dissolvings—these external events call for more than simple silent prayer. It is for these occasions that all religions provide their own significant rituals.

Among those following the goddess path, there are two major approaches to rit-ual. There are those who follow written, often published, formulae and a rigid rit-ual structure. At the other extreme are those who create ritual spontaneously, changing the structure to suit the group's needs and mood. The first could be called a liturgical approach, the latter a creative one. Most groups and individuals fall between these two extremes.

There are important philosophical differences between the liturgical and the creative approaches to goddess ritual work. Liturgical ritual usually stems from a belief that there is some exterior source of truth; creative ritual usually claims that the source of truth is within the individual. The latter is more appropriate to the goddess path, for just as no one can definitively claim to be the leader of the god-dess movement, so no one ritual can be held up as the authorized and authoritative one. Creative ritual encourages you to find the sources of truth within yourself. The immanent goddess reveals herself in that search.

Using this Book

This book provides information on twenty goddesses from various cultures. At the beginning of each chapter is an invocation or prayer to that goddess from the orig-inal culture but put into contemporary language. A retelling of the goddess's myth follows, together with information about how she is usually interpreted. A section on symbolism gives ideas for creation of altars, art, and other artifacts to that goddess; a list of the goddess's major feasts follows, together with information about how she was traditionally honored. Another section gives suggestions for rituals honoring the goddess. Most are based on actual rituals performed by that goddess's earliest worshipers; some reenact the story of the goddess herself. Other suggested rituals are inspired by resonance between everyday life problems and the powers of the goddess.

At the end of each chapter is a list of questions and activities that expand upon the material presented. These can be used in any way that is productive to you. You may gather a group to work through the chapters and their activities; you may do so in a solitary fashion; you may pick and choose among the activities. Many of the questions are good jumping-off points for journal entries; you may wish to keep a special *Goddess Path* journal as you engage in this quest.

Each of the rituals is written as a series of suggestions rather than instructions. They are intended as a basis for your own creative interpretation rather than as a precise pattern for duplication. Most of the rituals can be used singly or with others, and in mixed or single-sex groups. They derive from no specific church or other organization's framework, so they can be employed by Unitarians and Dianic witches as readily as by Catholic nuns and eclectic pagans.

This book is not a daily missal, nor a cookbook. You won't find precise measurements or required activities here. But the ingredients are here for our own creative spirits to engage. Do so, and the rituals you create will express the goddess within and without you.

A Goddess Index

The goddesses in this book come from a variety of cultures and represent different aspects of feminine reality. Because of their familiarity to many readers, a significant number of goddesses from the classical tradition have been included. To assist you in designing rituals appropriate to yourself or your group, use the indexes below.

Mother goddesses	Amaterasu, Brigid, Demeter, Gaia, Hera, Saule
Daughter goddesses	Athena, Artemis, Inanna, Kuan-Yin, the Muses, Paivatar, Persephone, Saules Meita
Lover goddesses	Aphrodite, Hathor, Inanna, Isis, Oshun, Pomona
Crone goddesses	The Cailleach, Kali
European goddesses	Aphrodite, Artemis, Athena, Demeter and Persephone, Gaia, Hera, the Maenads, the Muses (Greek); Brigid, the Cailleach (Irish); Saule and Saules Meita (Lithuanian); Pomona (Roman); Paivatar (Finnish)
African goddesses	Hathor (Egyptian), Isis (Egyptian); Oshun (Yoruba)
Asian goddesses	Amaterasu (Japan), Kuan-Yin (China); Kali (India); Inanna (Near East)
American goddesses	Oshun (African diaspora)

The Goddess Year

The goddesses in this book can be invoked at any time, but certain divinities traditionally had specific seasons and festivals associated with them. They are described in this book:

January

1   Roman Strena, feast of abundance; see Gaia.

February

Mid-month   Chinese festival of Kuan-Yin's birthday; see Kuan-Yin.

New Moon   Indian Ratanti Puja; see Kali.

2   Imbolc, Celtic feast of fire; see Brigid.

2   Ancient feast of hag-goddess; see Cailleach.

3   Japanese feast of Setsubun, "closing the door of winter;" see Amaterasu.

5   Spanish Feast of St. Agatha; see the Cailleach.

14-15   Roman Lupercalia, festival of Juno Februa; see Hera.

26   Lesser Eleusinian Mysteries; see Demeter & Persephone.

March

1   Roman Matronalia, festival in honor of Juno's motherhood; see Hera.

3   Egyptian Blessing of the Fleets; see Isis.

3   Japanese feast of Hinamatsuri, girls' doll festival; see Amaterasu.

8   International Women's Day; see Hera.

15-25	Greek and Roman festival of dying-god Attis; see Aphrodite.
19	Roman Quinquatrus, feast in honor of Minerva; see Athena.

April

Full Moon	Mounichion, ancient Greek lunar feast; see Artemis.
1	Veneralia, Roman feast of love; see Aphrodite.
3 and 4	Romans honored Cybele; see Gaia.
13	Roman Ceralia, dedicated to Ceres; see Demeter & Persephone.
22	Earth Day; see Gaia.

May

1	Beltane, Celtic feast of spring; see Aphrodite.
1	Romans honored Fauna, goddess of fertility; see Gaia.
15	Marriage of Hathor; see Hathor.
24	Feast of Thracian goddess Bendis; see Artemis.
25	Arbor Day; see Pomona.
31	Roman Sellisternia, festival of Isis as Stella Maris (Star of the Sea); see Isis.

June

1	Roman feast of Juno Moneta; see Hera.
24	Lithuanian Ligo, summer solstice celebration; see Saule.

July

12	Adonia, Greek feast of love; see Aphrodite.
17	Egyptian Night of the Cradle; see Isis.
18	Egyptian Night of the Drop; see Isis.

August

Full Moon	Greek festival to protect harvest; see Artemis.
Full Moon	Women's foot-races; see Hera.
7	Egyptian Feast of Inebriety; see Hathor.
15	Greek Panathenea; see Athena.
15	Roman Nemoralia, feast of women and light; see Artemis.
21	Roman Consualia; see Gaia, Pomona.
25	Roman Opiconsivia; see Gaia, Pomona.

September

Full Moon	Agrotera, goat-sacrifice to huntress goddess; see Artemis.
17	Egyptian celebration of Hathor's birthday; see Hathor.
21	Major Eleusinian Mysteries; see Demeter & Persephone.

October

Full Moon	Strenia, Greek festival; see Demeter & Persephone.
Mid-month	Chinese festival of Kuan-Yin's assumption as bodhisattva; see Kuan-Yin.
3	Egyptian Feast of Lamentations; see Isis.

11	Greek Thesmophoria, all-women's ritual; see Demeter.
16	Egyptian feast of Opening the Bosom of Women; see Isis.
Varying dates	Indian Kali Puja; see Kali.

November
Dark Moon	Chalkeia, Greek feast of weaving; see Athena.
12-14	Mysteries of Egypt; see Isis.

December
1	Roman feast of Bona Dea; see Gaia.
21	Winter Solstice; see Amaterasu, Paivatar, Saule.
25	Roman Saturnalia, sacred to Ops; see Gaia.

About the Invocations

The prayers and invocations that begin each goddess's section derive from a variety of sources: ancient liturgies and scriptures, folk songs and tales, epic poetry, drama and tragedy. They represent more than a dozen original languages; I have translated some directly from the original languages into these versions, while others are derived from English translations published in the sources cited in the bibliography. Some prayers are taken from relatively well-known works, such as the Irish epic cycle *Tain bo Cuailgne,* or from Greek dramatists such as Euripides; in such cases, several translations have been compared to create this rendition. Other prayers derive from a single source; they were recorded by a folklorist or anthropologist doing fieldwork among a specific people, or by an indigenous artist capturing the intention of a culture's ritual and prayer to the goddess.

In casting these into contemporary language, I have not in general attempted to remain within the bounds of a specific poetic or linguistic form. These are not, in that sense, translations at all, but rather adaptations of the original prayers. In addition, I have altered phrasing that would have been instantly intelligible to the early listener embedded in her culture but which is generally meaningless to the modern reader. Thus when the Homeric Hymn to Aphrodite tells us that the goddess went to Cyprus and entered the Paphos temple, her ancient worshipers would have immediately recognized the references to a Mediterranean island and to a renowned temple of love. But to modern readers, such references are more puzzling than illuminating; thus they have been changed to make their meanings clear. Similarly, where the cultural significance of a reference is not generally known to the average reader, a few words of explanation have been added. In the same hymn to Aphrodite, for example, not all contemporary readers would recognize the Graces as the goddess's handmaidens, so the adaptation here defines them as such.

In creating these adaptations, I have focused on the reverence, delight, joy, and devotion that peoples of the goddess have shown toward her. The images, the metaphors, the relation of speaker to divinity, the emotional content—all remain the same as in the original. There is an old Italian joke that puns on the similarity of the words, in that language, of translator and traitor. It is devoutly hoped that these adaptations do not betray their originals, but capture the love for the goddess encountered in the sources. As you use these prayers in your own life, please honor not only the divinity within and without yourself, but the original speakers and singers of these magnificent invocations as well.

∾

The Goddess

Revealed

Gaia

Abundance

Of Gaia I sing . . .
Queen and goddess, I invoke you:
you are all-powerful and my needs are so small.

1

Of her I sing, the All-Mother,
old and rock-hard and beautiful.

Of her I sing, the nourisher,
she upon whom everything feeds.

Of Gaia I sing. Whoever you are,
wherever you are, she feeds you

from her sacred treasury of life.
Bountiful harvests, beautiful

children, the fullness of life:
these are her gifts. Praise her.

2

The wide blue sky wants to penetrate the earth.
The earth longs for utter union. Look: it comes!

Rain falls. Rain falls as sky meets earth.
Rain falls. Earth bubbles with life.

Life springs forth from the damp soil:
flocks of sheep like clouds, oceans of wheat.

All gifts for earth's children. And one more:
peace. Peace that blossoms in a rain of love.

3

Earth, holy mother, source of nature,
you feed us while we live, hold us when we die.

Everything comes from you, everything returns to you.
What else could we call you but Our Mother?

Even the gods call you that. Without you
there is nothing. Nothing can thrive, nothing can live

without your power. Queen and goddess, I invoke you:
you are all-powerful and my needs are so small.

Give me what I ask and in exchange, I will give you
my thanks, sincere and from my deepest heart.

∼

Myth and Meaning of Gaia

Gaia goes back to the beginning. So said the Greeks, who probably adopted this earth goddess from the people who lived in Attica before they migrated there. She owned a great mountain shrine, where a serpent named Python lived. At that prophetic site, the sybil—named Pythia after the great snake—inhaled sulphurous fumes before speaking in magical phrases about the future. The most famous oracle of the ancient world, Delphi was Gaia's long before it was overtaken by the interloping god Apollo.

They might overtake her sanctuary, but the Greeks could not eliminate Gaia nor her worship. And so they did what conquerors usually do with unconquerable supreme gods and goddesses: they incorporated her into their own mythology, naming her as the most ancient of goddesses, the one who existed before anything or anyone else. Gaia was thus praised by the singer of the Homeric Hymns, source of the first invocation, and hundreds of years later by the dramatist Aeschylus, from whose otherwise lost drama *The Daianads* the second invocation survives. In Rome, Gaia was assimilated to a native earth goddess, Tellus Mater; the third prayer was offered to her there.

It is impossible to say what Gaia's original worshipers believed, but here is her myth as the Greeks told it. In the beginning, they said, there was only formless chaos: light and dark, sea and land, blended in a shapeless pudding. Then chaos settled into form, and that form was huge Gaia, the deep-breasted one, the earth. She existed before time began, for Time was one of her children. In the timeless spans before creation, Gaia existed, to herself and of herself, alone.

But finally Gaia desired love, and for this purpose she made herself a son: Uranus, the heaven, who arched over his mother and satisfied her desire. Their mating released Gaia's creative force, and she began to produce innumerable creatures, both marvelous and monstrous. The jealous Uranus hated Gaia's other children, so the primeval mother kept them hidden from his destructiveness by keeping them inside her.

Eventually, however, her dark and crowded womb grew too heavy to endure. So Gaia created a new element: gray adamant. And from it she fashioned a new tool, never known before: a jagged-toothed sickle. With this Gaia armed her son Chronos (Time), who took the weapon from his mother's hand and hid himself.

Uranus came, drawing a dark sky-blanket over himself as he approached to mount his mother/lover. His brother/son Chronos sprang into action, grasping Uranus's genitals and sawing them off with the rough blade. Blood rained down on Mother Gaia. So fertile was she that the ash-tree nymphs, the Meliae who were humanity's ancestors, sprang up from that blood. Thus we ourselves are grand-children of earth and sky, according to the Greeks.

After Chronos's success against Uranus had ended heaven's role as earth's husband, Gaia did not cease in her prodigious productivity. She had dozens of children by as many fathers. She birthed the Giants after mating with Tartarus, her son and the ruler of hell; she was mother of the Fates, those spinning goddesses who control our destiny, by her son the ocean. And even without mating, she bore other children, including the Python, and another dragon named Ladon. Gaia was stupendously fertile, even managing to carry to term a child conceived when an eager god ejaculated on the goddess Athena's thigh and she, ever the virginal one, brushed it off onto the earth.

Gaia was a powerful creator goddess, a parthenogenetic mother who could create the entire world without assistance. She was all-knowing, as her temple at Delphi attests, for she knew the future as well as the past. There is perhaps no goddess in Greek literature with the sheer raw power of Gaia, who stands equivalent to the Hebrew Jehovah, from whom the Christian high god descends. Although we cannot know how much of her myth, as recorded by the Greeks, reflects the beliefs of her earlier followers, it is likely that Gaia was a strong and fertile force to them as well.

In contemporary science, there is a theory that the earth—soil, water, atmosphere, and living creatures, all together—is a system so intricate and self-regulating that it can be seen as an enormous, conscious, living entity. The articulator of the theory, James Lovelock, has called it the Gaia Hypothesis. How fitting that, three thousand years after her worship was suppressed in her homeland, this goddess's name should re-emerge to indicate an intuition that the earth is alive. Alive, and full of enormous generative energy. Alive, and still as creatively productive as in her primeval youth.

Symbols of Gaia

Only one symbol of the ancient cosmic mother survived the displacement of her original worshipers: the snake. In her myth, Gaia is served by the great snake Python, who was resident in her shrine at Delphi. The snake is often misinterpreted by casual readers today, who often read serpents in light of the Judeo-Christian Eden myth. There, the snake appears only to tempt the primeval parents away from the sky god's single commandment. But to our foremothers, the snake—with its ability to shed its skin and thereby seem to be reborn—was not a symbol of evil. The connection of the ever-renewing serpent with the goddess of earth would, to them, have seemed quite fitting.

When the Greeks worshiped Gaia, they left her offerings of honey and barley. Both are symbols of feminine abundance: honey, because of its rich sweetness and its connection with the matriarchal bee; and barley, a seed that looked to the ancients like a tiny vulva, with its conch shape and little central slit. Both are appropriate to employ today in calling down the beneficence of great and fertile Gaia.

Feasts of Gaia

Just as her symbols have disappeared, so has any record of Gaia's feast days. Thus we can honor her on any day we choose. And what would be more appropriate than Earth Day, April 22? The day dedicated to honoring the living earth is a good choice for a ritual aimed at calling down Gaia's abundance on her children. Participation in activities designed to draw attention to the potential dangers to Gaia's health and safety would be an excellent contemporary substitute for lost rituals to ensure the planet's health.

The celebration of Earth Day in springtime also makes it appropriate for an invocation to Gaia, for many earth goddesses are honored in that season. The Romans showered statues of their Great Mother, Cybele, with rose petals on April 3 and 4. Also in Rome, women gathered on May 1 to honor Fauna, goddess of fertility, in rituals celebrated by the vestal virgins.

But spring is not the only time to ask for blessings from the abundant earth. Winter, too, has its own rituals of this sort. On December 1, Roman women invoked Bona Dea, who was also called by names signifying abundances: Richessa, Abundia, and Satia. Ops, the goddess from whom we get our word *opulent*, was honored as part of the Saturnalia in late December, when the Lord of Misrule reigned and the populace celebrated in the most raucous way; other festivals to Ops, both celebrated at harvest time, were the Consualia on August 21 and the Opiconsivia on August 25. Finally, at the feast called Strena on January 1, Romans offered friends and neighbors fruits macerated in honey to wish each other a plentiful new year.

Suggestions for Invoking Gaia

How many of us grew up with an attitude of scarcity—the idea that there is not really enough to go around, whether the commodity in question is love or money or intelligence or even popcorn? How many of us still, today, act in fear that we'll find ourselves lacking—that we'll be short of money, desperate for love, dejected and rejected and abject, seated in a darkened theater without something to munch on?

For those on the goddess path, it is important to function instead from a sense of abundance, from a belief that the universe can provide for us and for all her other children. Failure to believe in an abundant universe is a recipe for becoming stingy and self-centered. For how can we be generous to others when we fear that we, ourselves, won't have enough?

But how can we believe in an abundant universe when so much that we hear seems to point the other way? How can the universe be abundant, you may ask, when there is starvation in many parts of the world? How can it be so, when there are homeless families begging at the entry to Disneyland? Where is Gaia's abundance, that this can happen?

But such poverty is rarely the earth's fault. For more than two decades, wealth in the United States has increasingly found its way to the hands of a small privileged class, while many others have been forced into poverty or near-poverty. And just as a disproportionate amount of the nation's wealth is consolidated in the hands of a few, so a widely disproportionate percentage of the world's resources goes to maintaining an extraordinary standard of living in a few developed countries—of which the United States leads the pack.

Gaia is not in charge of the distribution of her resources. She creates wealth, whether it be emotional or financial. She gives to all who ask. So there is enough. It's most often human greed that makes it seem that there isn't.

If you have grown up poor or working class in the United States, it is easy to mistake social arrangements for emotional realities, and to imagine that the world is a hard and withholding place from which we have to scratch our meager living. (The Eden story supports this interpretation of life's challenges.) For those who grow up in a family where love is not readily shared, it is similarly easy to believe that love is a rare commodity and that we must compete for what little exists. Again, Gaia—who gave birth to and nursed innumerable offspring—is not the cause. There is love in the world, ample love for all the creatures who live here. Without the confidence to ask for love, however, it grows less likely that love will be offered you.

Thus, invoking Gaia regularly should be part of an overall effort to begin to believe in the universe as a place of abundance—and to manifest that abundance in your own life. Abundance, in this sense, does not mean excess. You are not asking for more than you need. You don't have to have ten homes; you only need one. You don't have to be adored by the entire world; you only need good friends and a loving companion. You don't have to have a hundred pairs of shoes—just enough to live your life in comfort and success.

Thus the counterweight to Gaia's abundance is simplicity, for it is much easier to believe in an abundant universe when we ask only for what we really need.

For women today, one of the most painful areas in this struggle centers on food. Food—simple nourishment of our bodies—in our culture has taken on a great deal of extra meaning, because women are constantly barraged with the demand that they be slender. There are important sociological features to this cultural message, for weight is inversely associated with wealth and status to us today. Rich equals thin, we are constantly told. And thin equals loved.

In other cultures and at other times, an ample body was associated with personal wealth, because only those with ample means would have enough food and leisure to be large. But eating little and exercising a great deal—the typical life of, say, an Irish peasant in the nineteenth century—is now the lifestyle of the rich and famous. As a result, women—especially young women—worry compulsively about how much they eat and how much they weigh, to the exclusion of many other concerns.

This social concern with women's weight serves several purposes that should be noted. Firstly, it encourages women to become consumers; the diet industry accounts for billions and billions of dollars of income, so there is a strong incentive for those connected with it to encourage women to pursue ever more elusive ideals of body size, even to the point of the ever-more-common surgery. And, perhaps more importantly, excessive concern with appearance keeps women busy worrying about their weight rather than demanding daycare and other benefits for themselves and their children. More women run for weight control than run for office. An incredible amount of woman-energy, incredible hours of woman-time, are spent focusing on physical appearance. This may be a realistic reaction to the world's messages, but does it really serve women's spiritual interests?

How does one invoke the goddess of abundance under these conditions?

The most appropriate way is through a ritual involving food. Because it is a highly-charged experience for most women today, consciously and thankfully eating the food that Mother Gaia provides can be an astonishing experience. Such sacred eating is the basis of communion services in all cultures. Eating the food of the mother goddess means, symbolically, allowing ourselves to be nurtured by her. It also means thanking her for providing that nurturing. It is this gratitude that is, ultimately, the most transformative.

Thus the best way to invoke Gaia is through a feast. Ask each participant to bring an especially meaningful dish—perhaps one prepared by a mother or grandmother for a special holiday, or one that has other emotional resonances. Assemble this feast on a table and, gathering around it, use the invocations above to call down the goddess. Then, in turn, ask in your own words for an increased sense of abundance in your life.

Then eat. Eat freely and thankfully. Neither stint yourself if you want more, nor gorge on the plentiful food. Both are reactions that deny abundance. Rather eat, concentrating on the joy of feeling fed and cared for. As you share this feast, each participant can explain the emotional significance of the dish she has prepared. You may also discuss areas of your life where you feel especially full and ample. Make sure to keep the dinner conversation pleasant. Do not allow negative comments, including such common ones as "I shouldn't . . ." and "I just can't resist . . ." Praise the food in honest terms, and enjoy it openly and zestfully.

After you have finished, invoke the goddess again, and this time ask her to make all her creatures aware of her bounty. Make a pledge to help in some way, however small, to share your own bounty with others. Finally, thank the goddess for all she has given her children and will give us in the future.

≈

Questions and Activities

1. What was your childhood like, in terms of experiences of abundance? Were you encouraged to believe that life will provide what you need, or were other messages louder and clearer?

2. What do you hunger for most? How can you satisfy that hunger?

3. What do you most deeply believe you should not want? Where did you get that idea?

4. What are your reactions to other women who seem to have more than you do? Are these reactions different from your reactions to men who have more?

5. How easy do you find sharing? What do you resist sharing? What do you find easy to share?

6. If you could have anything you wanted for dinner, without concern for health or weight, what would it be? What memories are associated with that choice? What does this tell you about yourself?

7. What are you most afraid that you will never have enough of in your life?

8. Gather some magazines and newspapers and read through them with this question in mind: What messages are you being given, through these media, about abundance and women's right to it?

9. During one day, pay attention to the inner dialogue you have about abundance. What messages are you giving yourself on this subject?

10. Every day for a week, leave some money in a place where a stranger will find it. What are your feelings in response to these actions?

Athena

Strength

Grey-eyed one, I sing of you, wisest and most beautiful,
relentless Athena, protector of cities, strong-armed and fair.
Hail to you, Athena, may I never live
without the shield of your protection.

Grey-eyed one, I sing of you, wisest and most beautiful,
relentless Athena, protector of cities, strong-armed and fair.

From his head the great god birthed you,
dressed in golden armor and bearing a sharp spear.

The holy mountains shook when you were born,
and the earth quaked, and the sea's dark waves broke
    against the land.

Even the sun stopped in astonishment at this sight,
this goddess, fresh-born and strong.

Hail to you, Athena, may I never live
without the shield of your protection.

Myth and Meaning of Athena

This Homeric Hymn honors a goddess who, coming to the Greek mainland from her original home in Crete, became ruler of the primary city of the ancient world while maintaining many symbols of her ancient identity. Greek myth tells of a contest between Athena and Poseidon, blue-skinned god of the sea. Both wanted to rule the Greek city, and neither would give way to the other. Finally, a vote was called, and the citizens—men and women alike—gathered to cast their ballots.

Not surprisingly, the men voted for the god, the women for the goddess. The odds were in Athena's favor, for there was one more voter on the women's side. And so the city became Athens, city of the goddess.

The men accepted the ballot's results rather bitterly. They struck back at the women by passing three new laws: they barred women from voting, stripped them of citizenship, and gave children the father's name rather than the mother's. Athena, too, they altered beyond recognition, making up a story of her motherless birth from the head of the chief god. In this now-familiar story of Athena's genesis, she appears completely male-identified. But another story exists that shows the goddess in a different light. Athena, it says, was the daughter of Pallas, a winged giant who tried to rape his virginal daughter. She killed him, then tanned his skin to make a shield and cut off his wings to fasten to her feet.

However she came by her fierceness, Athena never consorted with men, remaining forever a virgin. Oddly, she did have a son, an enigmatic offspring named Erichtonius, a snake-shaped boy born of an attempted rape that the virgin goddess escaped. Semen fell on her thigh from her over-excited assailant. When she brushed it off, it fell to the earth and became a child, who was then hidden forever from sight. This apparent anomaly in Athena's virginal life history may well point to an earlier serpent identity, for she is also associated with snake-haired Medusa, whose visage Athena wears on her goatskin cloak. Similarly, the massive snake that reared up beside her statue in the Parthenon, her major temple on the Athenian Acropolis, suggests that the snake was an early and primary symbol of the virgin goddess.

Athena—her name is so ancient that it has never been translated—was originally a household goddess, possibly related to the bare-breasted Cretan goddess depicted embracing snakes or holding them overhead. This original Athena was the essence of the family bond, symbolized by the home and its hearth—and by the mild serpent who, like a household cat, lived in the storehouse and protected the family's food supplies against destructive rodents. As household goddess, Athena ruled the implements of domestic crafts: the spindle, the pot, and the loom. By extrapolation, she was the symbol of the community itself, the larger social unit based on countless homes.

With the Greeks arrived a maiden goddess called Pallas; she was a warrior, protector of her tribe. To connect her with the already-resident city protector Athena, a story was invented that Pallas was a maiden killed by Athena, who then took the girl's name as her own. The goddess also armed herself, not with snakes but with a sword, the better to protect her newly rich city-state. Thus the hearth-loving maiden became the warrior goddess of classical times, whose enormous helmeted statue towered over visitors to her main temple in Athens, the Parthenon.

Symbols of Athena

Athena is most vividly symbolized by the snake which, in the famous statue in her main temple, rears up beside her, taller than any human viewer. Snakes are generally misinterpreted by contemporary western viewers conditioned by the story of Eve and her apple to see the serpent as evil and dangerous. Freud didn't help matters, associating the snake (and lots of other things) with male genital equipment. What a protective virgin goddess is doing in the company of a huge snake seems now a bit questionable, if not suggestive.

Yet the snake had other meanings to the people who originated this image of the goddess. First and foremost, it was a symbol of protection, for without serpent assistance, grain stored for winter would have fed mice, not men. In addition, the snake's well-known ability to shed its skin and emerge, apparently reborn, gave rise to an association with rebirth. The statue of a goddess standing by her snake familiar, then, would have been a powerful message of protective strength and hope to those who entered her temple.

Armor and weapons are also among Athena's symbols. She was frequently sculpted wearing a helmet, carrying a shield or spear. It has often been noticed that, with the rise of private property, previously pacific mother goddesses began to appear as goddesses of war—for when the rich fields were commonly held, there was no need to fight for their use. As land began to be owned by the wealthier citizens, the goddess took on a new role as defender of the city's wealth and safety.

Apparently opposite to the imagery of the sword and shield, Athena also is envisioned as the goddess of the loom and the spindle. A weaver, she once turned a woman into a spider for claiming to have greater skill than her own. But there is, in fact, little contradiction in her imagery, for textile production was an important part of each home's economy, and therefore of the richness of the city as a whole. Without such wealth, there would be no need for her strong arm of protection.

Finally, the most charming of Athena's symbols is that of the owl, which appears on early Athenian coins as an alternative image to the goddess in human form. In some statues and paintings, an owl sits on the goddess's shoulder, while in others it flies in the air above her. Still recognized as a symbol for wisdom, the owl suggests that Athena's power is so strong that it needs to be held in check by careful consideration and judicious concern for the outcome of any endeavor.

Feasts of Athena

Each year at midsummer in Athens, a splendid image of Athena was taken from the Acropolis, the hill on which her temple stood, and borne ceremoniously down to the sea. (It is to be assumed that this was not the huge marble and gilt statue, but a smaller one designed for the occasion.) There the goddess was carefully washed and, renewed in strength and purity, was decked in a robe newly woven by the city's best craftswomen.

This festival, the Panathenea, was the most popular of all the goddess's rituals. Preceded by games and followed by feasting, the procession recognized Athena as a matron of the city and all its residents. To honor this goddess, then, a festival on her ancient feast of August 15 is appropriate.

Preparations for this feast went on year-round. On the dark of the moon in November, Greek women celebrated the Chalkeia. On that day, the looms on which Athena's new chiton would be woven were stretched with their warp threads. An invocation or ritual would be appropriate on that day to honor crafts and craftworkers.

In Rome, the goddess associated with Athena was Minerva, one of the three most important divinities of the empire (the others being Juno and her consort, Jupiter). Minerva's principal feast was the Quinquatrus on March 19. Called "the day of craftspeople," the festival was especially celebrated by artists, artisans, and schoolteachers.

Suggestions for Invoking Athena

The warrior strength of Athena is not based on aggression. Rather, she represents defensive strength, the ability to stand one's ground and not be moved. Yet the distinction between aggression and defense is an extraordinarily difficult one to make. It has been said that all wars are waged for defensive reasons; no nation will admit it intends to steal land or wealth (the usual reasons for wars) and so concocts a "threat" that makes invasion necessary. Similarly, individuals are rarely honest about their intentions to steal from or harm others emotionally. A raped woman "asked for it" by wearing provocative clothing; a battered woman "asked for it" by not cooking the right dish for dinner. Aggression disguises itself as defense in the interpersonal as well as the international arenas.

Thus Athena's wisdom is extremely important in learning to use defensive strength appropriately. Even the Athenians themselves were not always true to their goddess in this regard, their invasion of Sicily in 415 B.C.E.—which provoked the women of the city to castrate all the male herm-statues to signify their opposition—having been launched on a trumped-up rumor of Athens' danger from the distant island. In following the path of this goddess, developing the insight to distinguish one's own motives is extraordinarily important.

The ancient Panathenea can serve as a model for development of a contemporary ritual in honor of this goddess of defensive strength. Celebrants from the Church of All Worlds in Nashville, Tennessee, have occasionally staged reenactments of the festival in that city's own replica of the Parthenon. A visit to this little-known American treasure can be a very powerful experience for those following the goddess path. Not only is the building itself complete (as the actual Parthenon is not, the splendid sculptures of the pediments having been removed to become the Elgin Marbles of the British Museum), but the interior is graced by a contemporary version of the statue of Athena that once stood in the original temple. Known now only from miniatures, the ancient statue was long ago destroyed; the Greek temple now stands vacant. In Nashville, however, the stunning and enormous replica statue stands within the temple, permitting a glimpse of what ancient Athenians saw when they entered their primary shrine. A visit to the Nashville Parthenon is an unforgettable experience for anyone who honors Athena.

To reenact the festival of Athena in your own home, you will need a statue of the goddess and a location where it will spend the next year. The location can be an altar, prepared with symbols of the goddess. Or it can be a shelf or niche that will represent the temple of the goddess until the next festival in her honor.

Similarly, your statue need not be life-sized or larger, as the original was likely to have been; it can be a relatively small statue of the goddess. Although it is possible to purchase a statue of Athena for this festival, it would be more in keeping with her rulership of crafts to create one yourself. Artistic perfection is not the point here (although Athena would be best honored by something that at least vaguely resembles a human figure), for the essence of art is process, not product. Images of the goddess can be constructed out of any material, including wood (or twigs), found objects, cloth, or clay. It is not known whether the original was robed or not, but Athena's famous modesty suggests that a simple shift should cover her body, and her warrior nature suggests that a helmet should be her headgear.

A chiton—a sacred robe for the goddess—is also necessary. If this is your first reenactment, you will need two robes, one to discard to signify the end of one year, another in which to dress the goddess after her ritual bath. Again, it would be easy to purchase a pretty bit of cloth for the garment, but hand-weaving or hand-decorating it is more in keeping with the goddess's energy. She is, remember, the goddess of crafts, not of shopping. Knitting or crocheting, embroidery, fabric painting—all these are possible ways to make or to decorate the chiton. Images of owls or snakes, stylized into spirals and meanders, are especially fitting to deck the goddess's mantle. If you are celebrating with a group, decorate small squares of cloth with similar images for mementoes of the occasion; if this is your second or later ritual, plan to cut up the old robe at the end of the ritual.

When the preparations have been completed, the festival proper can begin. Prepare a bath for the goddess. Traditionally, Athena was bathed in the sea below her city. An outdoor setting near a stream, river, lake, or ocean would be ideal for a reenactment of Athena's rite, but a barrel or tub of water will also serve. An empty basin, with some pitchers of water, is another possibility. In any case, the bath should be somewhat separate from the site of the ritual itself, to suggest the distance between the temple and the sea.

As Athena is a virgin goddess, men should not look on her statue during this ritual. If men participate, they should turn and form a protective shield between the ritual and the door. As the ritual takes place out of their sight, men can reflect on any feelings of exclusion, imagining how many women feel in such circumstances. They can also experience the special role they can play in sustaining and protecting women during private times. After the bath and re-robing of the goddess, male participants can join in the remainder of the ritual.

Carry the garbed statue to the bath. There, invoke the goddess with the Homeric Hymn. Then, ceremoniously, take the old chiton from the statue, praying for the wisdom to discard old ways and old attitudes in your own life. Bathe the statue as you pray for purification and inner strength. Dry the statue carefully, then dress it in the new chiton. As you do so, invoke the strength to combat oppression in your life, to defend yourself against those who would injure you. Imagine yourself being girded again to do the goddess's battle against those who would take what is rightfully yours—emotionally, spiritually, and intellectually, as well as physically.

Carry the statue back to the space you have designated as its temple for the year. As you place the newly garbed goddess in her place, invoke her power again. Hold within yourself the image of the goddess. Women's skill has made her garment, just as your own skills provide a basis for defense against any who would take from you. Catalogue for yourself the defensive skills you possess. Pledge to use Athena's wisdom to distinguish which of your actions are undertaken in defense, and which are overreactive and aggressive. As you conclude the ritual, pass around squares of cloth from the goddess's old chiton so that you may each have a reminder of the shield of Athena, offering strength throughout the year.

⁓

Questions and Activities

1. Find, or imagine, a picture of a woman in the military or in armor. What is your reaction to that image? Where did you develop your ideas about women and power?

2. As a child, how did you react when threatened or challenged? How do you react today? If there is a difference, when did you begin to change—and why?

3. In what ways were you physically active as a child? Are you still physical in that way? If not, when did you begin to change—and why?

4. Take the following list of words and write down your responses to them: fierce, angry, defensive, strong, powerful. Which words would you feel uneasy about if they were applied to you, or to a woman you care about? Why?

5. Have you ever attempted to protect yourself and failed? How did it feel? How did others react to you?

6. Have you ever been physically assaulted? Were you able to protect yourself? How did others react to you when you told them about the assault?

7. Have you ever taken a martial art form for self-defense? If so, how did it make you feel? If not, why not?

8. Have you known women friends or relatives who have suffered physical assault? How did you react to their situation?

9. In your work life and your personal life, are there areas where you feel frequently invaded or beaten? What do you do to stand up for yourself? How could you be more effective?

10. Are there times when you have hurt others, either physically or through words, because they provoked you? How did you feel afterward? How do you feel about the event now?

Hera

Dignity

Let us sing now of Hera, the women's goddess;
Let us sing now of Hera, child of earth;
Let us sing now of the queen of gods.
Let us sing now of the most beautiful goddess.

Let us sing now of Hera, the women's goddess,
she who rules from her throne of gold.

Let us sing now of Hera, child of earth,
daughter of that most ancient of goddesses.

Let us sing now of the queen of gods.
Let us sing now of the most beautiful goddess.

There is no one more beloved than you,
womanly Hera, no one we honor more.

There is no one more revered than you,
queenly Hera, no one more blessed.

Above all others, you are the most honored.
Above all others, you are the most beloved.

∽

Myth and Meaning of Hera

She's the only goddess who appears weekly as the villain of a television drama. A generation of young Americans now have a vivid vision of Hera, an evil stepmother if ever there was one, constantly sending that kindly hunk Hercules off to perform some impossible feat or to torment some poor nymph whose only crime was dallying with her husband Zeus. And all this just because Zeus had too good a time with Hercules's human mother! When Hera appears on the small screen, her cow eyes peeking through peacock feathers, even Hercules shudders in fear of what she'll demand next.

It's a wildly inaccurate, to say nothing of insulting, portrait of the chief goddess of ancient Greece. But we can't fault the scriptwriters for this slanderous depiction of the ancient goddess of womanhood. For the image of Hera presented weekly in *Hercules: Legendary Journeys* is pretty much the same one painted by the Greeks themselves: Hera is vicious, spiteful, arrogant, but very powerful. Married to the highest god, she does nothing but rage about his infidelities, persecute nymphs, and—and, oh yes, invent tortures for Hercules, whom the Greeks saw as muscular like our contemporary hero, if not nearly so endearingly thoughtful and sweet.

What you won't learn from television is that Hercules is the Roman translation of the Greek name Heracles—"glory of Hera," an ancient hero who originally served a much different goddess, founding shrines to her all across the land that became Greece. This erased goddess was the dark-eyed sky queen we call Hera, although that title means only "Our Lady" and was probably not the goddess's original name.

Long before Zeus entered Greece, the people there had their own chief divinity. She was their queen and ancestral mother, and she ruled alone, needing no king to back her up. (Television viewers should note that Hera was, among many other duties, goddess of winds, a job stripped from her by the Hellenic invaders and given to a newcomer, Aeolus—Hollywood Hercules's companion-at-arms.)

Ancient Hera needed no consort. But one was on his way. When the patriarchal tribes of the north descended into Hera's land, they brought with them their sky god, Zeus. Because Hera's religion was too strong to utterly destroy, a marriage of convenience was forged between the two predominant divinities. From this forced joining of the pre-Hellenic goddess of women with the newly arrived thunderbolt wielder, the Hera of classical times emerged.

This new Hera was not a very attractive figure, a jealous and petulant wife who hounded her unfaithful husband and his lovers. Of course, the myth admits, Hera never wanted the marriage to begin with—in this, apparently reflecting the political realities of that turbulent time. For one thing, Zeus was her brother; the Greeks had revised Hera's history to create this relation. But even here Hera's earlier sovereignty was revealed, for she was born third—after Hestia, the fire goddess, and Demeter, the earth mother—while Zeus was born last of the Olympians.

In spite of Hera's objections, Zeus so desired the statuesque goddess that he transformed himself into a cuckoo—the bird for which Hera had a special fondness—and flew bedraggled into her lap. Soothing the pitiable bird, Hera suddenly found herself being raped by Zeus. Shamed by the violation, the goddess agreed to restore her dignity by joining in marriage with Zeus. She gave birth to several children: the smith Hephaestus, the war god Ares, and the maiden Hebe. Some sources say that all three were born parthenogenetically, which would be in keeping with Hera's earlier identity as a goddess who needed no husband.

And Zeus didn't really need, or want, a wife. It wasn't long before he was off again, looking for other goddesses to rape. With Leda he pretended to be a swan, with Semele he turned into a shower of gold—and the goddesses generally wound up diminished, if not pregnant with an unwanted godling. Here again, scholars detect political reality disguised as myth, with the elimination of various goddess cults appearing as the seduction or rape of the central divinities, and the goddess's parthenogenetic children assigned proper fathers.

Finally, the myths tells us, Hera wearied of Zeus's ceaseless pursuit of other goddesses and organized a heavenly revolution against the tyrant. She and the other Olympians tied him to his bed—his favorite place of work—and gathered to mock him. Working himself free, Zeus took his revenge on the instigator of the palace revolt by stringing Hera from the sky, her wrists tied to golden bracelets and her ankles weighted by anvils.

Once freed from this humiliation, Hera resumed her persecution of Io, Semele, and other paramours of Zeus, siding against him in the Trojan War and otherwise making a mythic nuisance of herself to the father figure of the patriarchy. Eventually, little remained of the ancient threefold goddess of dignified womanhood except the insistence, within Greek mythology, on the periodic retreat of Hera into solitude. This bit of lore makes little sense for the figure of Hera in classical times, but it was vital to the ancient goddess, representing the last stages of her development.

The ancient Hera passed through three life stages: youth, prime, and age. First, she was the maiden Hebe or Parthenia, called virginal not because she avoided intercourse but because, having no children, she was free of responsibility. In this stage, she was also called Antheia ("flowering one"), symbol of both the flower of human youth and the budding earth. Next, she revealed herself as the mature woman, Nymphenomene ("seeking a mate") or Teleia ("perfect one"); she was the earth in summer, the mother in the prime of life. Finally, she showed herself as Theira ("crone"), the woman who has passed through and beyond maternity and lives again to herself.

In all these stages, Hera represented the epitome of woman's strength and power. Far from being spiteful and malicious, she was generous and self-assured. The ancient Hera was sufficiently beloved that, even after being recast in such a negative way, she was still worshiped and revered. Symbolizing the inner essence of feminine development, Hera is a goddess who never deserved the indignities heaped on her. Had she not been so powerful and beloved, she would have simply been raped and discarded. As it was, she was demonized—but still she lived on.

Symbols of Hera

Hera has three symbols, which can be connected with her three ancient phases. The first of these is the cuckoo, the bird whose form Zeus assumed in order to rape and disempower the goddess. As her myth shows, Hera had a tender spot for the cuckoo, a bird that was depicted atop her scepter in ancient times. At Mycene, a Cretan colony on the Greek mainland, miniature temples mounted with cuckoos have been found buried in the rubble along with statuettes of a naked goddess holding the same birds on her arms. As Hera's worship goes back to that period, these statues may represent her most ancient worship.

It is not known what the cuckoo represented in Hera's original religion, but birds generally refer to a union of body and soul, for the bird can walk on land or fly into the sky. As the great archaeologist Marija Gimbutas has pointed out, the bird is one of the greatest ancient symbols for the heavenly goddess. The cuckoo is, in many places, connected to the springtime, so this bird may indicate Hera in her youngest phase.

The peacock's meaning is connected to that of other birds, with the additional symbolic meaning of its blue color. Because blue is the color of the sky, many peoples have connected it with the divine. A blue bird, being the color of the sky where it can soar, is like a multiplied heavenly symbol. Both these images reinforce the connection of Hera with the heavens, of which she was queen. In addition, the peacock is often associated with summer, and therefore this bird may symbolize Hera's second phase.

Her third phase, as the crone of autumn, is symbolized not by a bird but by a fruit: the pomegranate, which she shares with Persephone. She is often depicted holding the pomegranate, but there is no reference in her myth to its significance. Ripening late in the year, the leathery-skinned pomegranate, so full of juicy seeds, is a marvelous image for the woman in her late years. The deep red juice of the pomegranate was often likened to blood and, in some areas of Greece, was designated as food for the dead; it was the fruit of the underworld in the myth of Persephone, heightening the connection of this phase of the great Hera to age and death. However, in the hands of these gentle goddesses, the symbol of death was also a promise of resurrection, for both were regularly reborn in spring.

Another symbol, although less frequently used for Hera than these three, is the cow. She was said to have cow eyes and disguised herself as a cow in one myth; cows were often sacrificed to her. Other cow goddesses are associated with celestial phenomena, as is the case of the sun goddess Hathor in Egypt. Thus Hera's cow identity shows her to be a heavenly goddess, ruling the celestial vault and its luminaries.

Feasts of Hera

In honor of the three phases of Hera, the ancient residents of Greece celebrated the Heraea, a competitive festival that dates to earlier times than the Olympics. Every four years—and later, on the full moon of August, every year—women came to a field near Hera's town of Argos for the 160-yard races. They ran, bare-breasted and with hair unbound, in three age groups to honor the goddess's three stages. There were three winners, each receiving identical olive crowns and a share in the cow sacrificed at the festival. Each winner had the right to leave a statuette of herself in Hera's shrine.

Hera's other great festival was her annual revival. Her worshipers bathed her image, renewing her youth and preparing her again for the seasonal cycle of vegetative maturation and death. Carrying the goddess's statue to the water to cleanse the winter from her marked how they, like the earth, would forever be reborn.

Unfortunately, the date for this ritual has been lost, although it would make symbolic sense if the renewal celebration were held in the spring. As goddess of women, Hera could be appropriately invoked today on International Women's Day, March 8.

In Rome, a goddess similar to Hera was the heavenly queen Juno, whose myth and figure were assimilated to Hera's during the Hellenistic period. She was celebrated on the feast we now call Valentine's Day, February 14—indeed, the very month derives its name from her, for she was Juno Februa. As such, she was queen of a feast called Lupercalia, celebrated the following day by priests who sacrificed goats and puppies, then whipped women with thongs made of goatskin (called februa), a ritual that ensured fertility. This may have originally been a full moon festival that, like many such events, was eventually assigned a solar date.

Also in Rome, the queenly Juno was invoked on the first day of the month named for her, June, under her title of Juno Moneta. We get our word "money" from this title, for her temple was the source of the city's coins. The word is, oddly, derived from the Latin word for "warning"—for the sacred geese kept at Juno's temple were reputed to have warned the city of an attempted Gallic invasion. Juno is also said to have told Rome's generals that they would be unable to financially support any war that was unethical, after which the city mint was moved to Juno's temple.

Finally, an important feast of Juno's was the Matronalia on March 1, in which the goddess was invoked as the primal mother of gods and humanity. Pregnant women especially prayed to her on that day for her protection in childbirth. In that role, she was called Juno Lucina (Juno the Light), the goddess who rules the first light that strikes the newborn's eyes.

Suggestions for Invoking Hera

If there is a goddess of feminism, it surely must be Hera. For she represents what happens to women's power in a world unwilling to acknowledge it. She's like that bitter joke: when a man promotes his own interests, it's because he knows what he wants, but when a woman does it, she's greedy and selfish. When a man gives orders, he's authoritative; when a woman does so, she's a carping ball-buster.

This isn't just a joke. It's real. Sociologist Dale Spender has shown that when women take up ten percent of the time in conversation with men, they're considered verbal; when they take up twenty percent (leaving only eighty percent to their male companion), they're judged as very talkative; and when they dare to take up one-third of the conversational time, men terminate the conversation and leave, feeling threatened and beleaguered.

It it any wonder that Hera instigated a palace revolt?

Look at what happened when she got in an argument with Zeus about their comparative reproductive powers. Zeus, claiming he didn't need Hera to have a child, gave birth to one himself—through his head. (Actually, he cheated; he swallowed Athena's mother first.) Hera did so too, by picking a flower and impregnating herself. Zeus was enraged. He threw the resulting son, Hephaestus, out of heaven, crippling him severely.

When a god gives birth by cheating, it's a miracle. When a goddess gives birth by herself, both mother and child should be punished.

No wonder Hera was in a bad mood!

Like Hera, women today can easily find themselves in a continual state of outrage. All it takes is consciousness and minimal contact with the society around them. How do you stay cheery in a world full of rape and battery, insult and endangerment? How do you smile when someone makes the hundredth appallingly anti-woman remark at work? How many times can you look away before it corrodes your soul?

But look what happens when you speak. Even today, women who command power are often demonized, just as Hera was. An earlier generation mocked Eleanor Roosevelt for being plain; today a brilliant first lady has been derided for being outspoken. Hera, hung from the sky, is an all-too-vivid image of women being pilloried for having power and inner authority—and showing it.

Strong women are misinterpreted, there is no doubt of it. But there is also another truth in this goddess's story: that not being heard tends to make one shrill. Thus Hera, fighting a rear-guard action against patriarchy for centuries, finally turns into a caricature of her strong and vibrant self. Thus many women, tired of trying to phrase complaints about gross injustice in restrained and acceptable language, finally resort to raging, whining, and weeping.

A ritual to Hera, therefore, must acknowledge the difficulties any woman has in maintaining her inner balance in a world where overhead there's a glass ceiling, not a dark-eyed sky queen. At the same time, such a ritual should offer a chance for women to come back to a natural inner authority. This is not a ritual to the wronged and infuriated Hera, raped into submission, unforgiving and angry. Rather, it evokes the dignity and grace of the three-phased woman's goddess, the original Hera, the cow-eyed sky queen who was beloved of all in the land.

To build a Hera altar, you'll need symbols for each of her three phases. Cuckoos and peacocks are relatively difficult to come by in most areas, so other emblems must substitute. For Hebe, the goddess's springtime form, a spray of flowers is an excellent emblem; for Teleia, the summer goddess, a piece of fruit or a peacock feather suffices. Her own chosen symbol of fall, the pomegranate, is usually available in grocery stores; if you cannot find a pomegranate, a piece of rock or weathered wood can stand in for this phase of the goddess as Theira, the crone. Display these objects on a background of blue, for the sky that was Hera's earliest abode. Place a candle in front of each of the objects symbolizing Hera's multiple phases.

This is a ritual that can be done by a woman alone, or with other women. Like several other goddesses in this book, Hera represents a special challenge to men who endeavor to invoke her. Men's experience in our culture is sufficiently different from women's that they may well find themselves baffled by women's anger, which often wells up at puzzling times. In addition, men do not generally find their lives falling into the virgin/mother/crone model, and so they may find no inner resonance to this ritual. For men to encounter Hera, it would be good for them to work with a woman willing to share her experience and her anger honestly; once these have been encountered and acknowledged, a man may learn a great deal about this goddess's significance.

To begin the ritual, stand before the altar and invoke the goddess using the Homeric Hymn to Hera, calling down the strength of the triple goddess into yourself. Repeat the prayer three times, in honor of Hera's three phases, identifying within yourself the energies related to each as you pray.

After lighting the candle in front of the Hebe image, call out the names of girls who seem to you to embody the power of the goddess at this stage. You may wish to name living people who are now older, or figures from art or literature, or even other goddesses. As you do so, name the qualities you associate with strength in the Hebe phase. (Jo March of *Little Women,* for instance, can stand for energy and will.) After you have finished naming, close your eyes and imagine the vitality and self-connectedness you experience when you think of those girls. Pull that energy into yourself. Then, with eyes still closed, move your body in ways that seem to express that energy. Let the movements emerge naturally, from your physical and spiritual center. (Don't peek; other women will have their own ways of experiencing this energy.)

At some point in this physical movement, you will begin to spontaneously repeat a motion. Perhaps, for instance, your inner girl loves to swing her arms about. When you find a motion that seems to you to express your Hebe energy, slowly stop moving and open your eyes. Remember that movement, and move on.

Repeat this process with the remaining phases of Hera, naming exemplars of the woman in her prime and as the crone, then feeling your own physical movements expressing those powers.

When you have completed this process, go back to the first phase again. Repeat, this time with your eyes open, the motion associated with Hera as the youthful Hebe. If you can articulate the meaning of the motion aloud, do so, although some motions are impossible to explain. Perform the action over and over, feeling the energy of the girl within you.

Then, find a way to make that motion as small as possible. If your girl wants to swing your arms widely, smashing her hands against each of her shoulders in turn, diminish it to just touching yourself briefly on one shoulder. Do this for each of your three chosen motions.

You have now found, from your inner resources, motions that express the best of your soul, in each of your Hera stages. By miniaturizing the motion, you have made it possible to use it in public to reconnect with your inner goddess. Next time you find your voice growing shrill as you fight to make yourself heard, you can touch your own shoulder, almost invisibly, and feel the springtime power of the articulate and self-confident girl well up within you. Making the gesture for Hera in her prime will remind you of the splendid power of fruitful summer, and you will remember again your own glorious talents. Make the gesture for the crone, and your wisdom will come back to you.

You may still be called shrill; you may still hit your head on the glass ceiling. But if you haven't lost yourself in the fight for your own space, you'll laugh off the names you're called, rub the bump on your head, and go on. As you close this ritual, repeat the Homeric Hymn again, once for each of the candles. As you blow them out, imagine their fire still sparking your soul to vibrant life.

~

Questions and Activities

1. Get a photograph of yourself as a child. As you look at the photograph, make a list of qualities you remember having then. Are there any of these qualities you've lost touch with today? How can you reclaim them?

2. Locate a photograph of your mother or grandmother as an old woman. As you look at the photograph, make a list of the qualities you associate with her. Which of these qualities are ones you share? Are there any that frighten or upset you, and why?

3. Collect several photographs of yourself. As you look at them, what words come to mind to describe yourself? Are there words that seem negative to you, and why?

4. Remember times when you have been discouraged from attaining something you wanted. What were your reactions then? What would you like to say to the discouraging person?

5. Are there goals you have set for yourself in life that you've not achieved? What reasons have you given yourself for this? What emotions do you experience when you think of these goals?

6. In relations with lovers and potential partners, how do you respond to rejection? What patterns of behavior do you see in these responses?

7. If you could be anything at all, what would you be? What's stopping you?

8. Make a list of women you admire for their strength. Collect pictures of them and make "holy cards" out of them by pasting them onto rectangles of paper and laminating them. Use them as bookmarks and in other ways to remind yourself of women's positive power.

9.   Make a list of powerful women whom you find unpleasant or frightening. Take each one in turn, and write a list of words you associate with that woman. Now ask yourself whether you would use those words of men in similar positions.

10. Make a list of symbols of positive power for you. These might be abstract, like a zigzag line; natural, like a rock; or human, like Xena. Find ways to surround yourself with these images—on jewelry, printed clothing, or photographs, for instance—in settings where you are frequently disempowered.

Amaterasu

Clarity

When I look up to the royal sky
I see her, a tranquil queen
behind a screen of clouds. The sun!

When I look up to the royal sky
I see her, a tranquil queen
behind a screen of clouds. The sun!

For thousands of ages may she shine.
For thousands of ages may we serve her.

May we serve her with reverence.
May we serve her with love.

∾

Myth and Meaning of Amaterasu

This invocation to the sun goddess comes from the Nihongi, one of the primary Japanese scriptures. Amaterasu ("great shining heaven") is the chief divinity of Shinto, the indigenous pre-Buddhist religion of Japan, and is the only goddess who leads the pantheon of a major religion today. Worshiped in simple tree-flanked shrines—for Shinto is a nature-honoring religion—Amaterasu is also seen in the simple circle on the Japanese flag, which represents the mirror that is central to her myth.

That myth involves a contest between Amaterasu and her brother, the storm god Susano-o. Shinto does not envision their disagreement as a conflict between good and evil, for in this religion there is no conception of evil—rather, Shinto judges action in terms of whether it is appropriate to its time and place. A harsh word spoken in anger to a vulnerable child is wrong, but the same word spoken to a threatening intruder is quite correct. Thus Susano-o represents wrongness and inappropriateness, while Amaterasu represents order and rectitude.

One day, the myth begins, Susano-o came to heaven to see Amaterasu. He had previously been disruptive, but now he claimed that he meant no harm. The sun goddess was wary, so Susano-o promised that he would undergo a ritual test to prove his good will. He would give birth, he said, and if his intentions were peaceful, all the children would be boys.

Susano-o asked Amaterasu for some of her jewels. She gave him five, which he cracked open to reveal five gods. Amaterasu was almost inclined to believe in the good will of her brother, when suddenly he grew wild with excitement at his creative feat and began to rampage through the world, destroying everything in his path. The final outrage came when Susano-o threw a horse's flayed corpse through the roof of the heavenly weaving hall, so startling one of Amaterasu's companions that she pricked herself and died.

This was too much for the sun goddess. Amaterasu, who had previously given her light so generously, shut herself up in her Sky-Rock-Cave. Without the sun, the world was blanketed with blackness. The eight million gods and goddesses, desperate for their queen's light, gathered to plead for her return. But to no avail: Amaterasu remained within the cave.

The shaman goddess Uzume finally solved the crisis. She overturned a washtub and, climbing on top, began dancing and singing and screaming bawdy remarks.

Soon the dance became a striptease. When she had shed her clothes, Uzume began dancing so wildly that the eight million gods and goddesses began to shout with merriment and delight.

Inside her cave, Amaterasu heard the noise. Baffled at how such a celebration could occur in her absence, she called out, asking what was going on. Someone answered that they had found a better goddess than the sun. Provoked and curious, Amaterasu opened the door of her cave—but just a crack.

The gods and goddesses had, with great foresight, installed a mirror directly outside of the cave. Amaterasu, who had never before seen her own beauty, was dazzled. While she stood there staring at her brilliant reflection, the other divinities grabbed the door and pulled it open. With a rope, they tied the cave's rock door open so that it could never be closed so tightly again. And thus the sun returned to warm the earth.

Symbols of Amaterasu

As her myth makes clear, the primary symbol of Amaterasu is the mirror. The original mirror, crafted by the smith goddess Ishikore-dome in the kami-ya (the time-before-time), is kept at the 13,600-acre Great Shrine at Ise, south of Nagoya, in the center of Japan. You can visit the shrine and see the building in which the mirror is kept, but you cannot see the mirror itself, for it rests in a series of boxes and brocade bags that have been added regularly over the more than 1500 years of the shrine's history. It is said that the mirror is eight-sided, but it's possible that eight—being the Shinto number for perfection—refers not to its shape but to the belief that the mirror is the most perfect one ever fashioned.

If we could see it, we would know that it is the very mirror that Amaterasu saw when she emerged from the cave because there would be a tiny nick on one side. This resulted from a god's excessive enthusiasm in pulling open the stone door of the Sky-Rock-Cave. Though we cannot see the original one, we can use other mirrors to connect with the goddess, for they all partake in some way of the solar essence. And because she is our great ancestor, they are magically connected to us as well, revealing the state of our souls; as the Japanese proverb says, "When the mirror is dim, the soul is not pure."

Aside from the mirror, Amaterasu's other two major symbols are the necklace and the sword. At the Great Shrine of Ise, a jewel from Amaterasu's necklace and a solar sword, together with the sacred mirror, are kept as the religion's most significant treasures. The necklace connects the sun goddess with the womanly craft of spinning, because round drop-spindles were once used as beads. The sword, conversely, reveals her martial aspect. As ancestral mother of the world's people, Amaterasu protects and defends us; some scholars believe her original worshipers were led by queens, who danced themselves into trances in order to divine what course of action was needed, and who also led soldiers into war when necessary. Thus Amaterasu's symbolism encompasses many aspects of the archetypal feminine.

Feasts of Amaterasu

In Japan, favored times for pilgrimage to the Great Shrine of Ise are mid-February and mid-June; September and April are also times when many visitors walk through the forested precincts of the shrine. On February 3, throughout Japan, the feast of Setsubun is celebrated to "close the door on winter." In this ritual, the family scatters roasted soybeans throughout the house while chanting, "In with good luck, out with demons." On March 3, the month-long Hinamatsuri (doll festival) is celebrated, in which girls display their doll collections and host ritual tea parties with them; putting them away before the end of February assures good luck for the year.

The major festival of Amaterasu, however, is not tied to an annual cycle; it is held every twenty years when the sacred mirror is ceremoniously carried to a newly built shrine, identical in all respects to the shrine that has preceded it. Thus Amaterasu's major ritual, like the myth of her return from the cave, emphasizes renewal.

As a solar goddess, Amaterasu can be invoked at any of the major turning points of the solar year: the equinoxes on March 21 and September 21, when the sun's light and its absence is perfectly balanced; and the solstices, June 21 and December 21, when the sun's light is respectively the greatest and the least of the year. As Amaterasu's myth is one of the sun's retreat and return, she is an especially appropriate goddess to invoke on winter solstice.

Suggestions for Invoking Amaterasu

Amaterasu, as the force of universal order, leads her followers to a life of balance and grace. Thus she is the goddess to invoke when you feel stressed or strained, when life seems out of control or disordered, or when you have lost faith and hope in a positive future. The goddess of "great shining heaven" is the one to call on when the sunshine seems to have diminished in, or disappeared from, your life.

Japanese tradition does not suggest that we simply blame others for the disorder we experience. Rather, the world can be seen as a mirror of our inner selves. When the mirror is dim, the soul must be examined. Thus if we find ourselves out of harmony with the world, it is necessary to seek inner reasons that contribute to this disharmony. Some afflictions are certainly the fault of others whose behavior we cannot control. But looking within, if done honestly and without evasion, allows us to distinguish our own responsibilities in creating our lives.

A simple Japanese ritual, easily incorporated into daily life, uses a mirror as a meditation device. This mirror could be a special one reserved for such meditations or could simply be the one above the bathroom sink. You need spend no more than five or ten minutes in this meditation. Looking into the mirror, put your hands together in a prayerful position and bow slightly—a traditional Japanese greeting. Clear your mind of distractions; repeating the goddess's name several times (eight would be appropriate) may help to calm racing thoughts.

Then, looking straight into the mirror, ask yourself about the state of your soul. Do not focus, in this meditation, on appearance—all too often the only thing we see when we gaze into the mirror today. Instead, look beyond appearance to determine whether there are points in your life where you are acting inappropriately. Looking into your own eyes is an especially powerful experience as you meditate in this way.

Especially look for points where you are acting out of control, where you feel an urgent need to act that you seem unable to put off or resist. Such actions are more often under the control of stormy Susano-o than of gracious Amaterasu. You may find some resistance to this meditation, because we all find it easier to believe ourselves victims of others than to perceive our own connections to the disorder of our lives. But if performed regularly, this simple ritual can help you align yourself with your most positive energies. After several moments of meditation, bow once again to close the ritual.

This ritual can be performed in a more formal way by preparing an altar with the symbols of Amaterasu upon it: a mirror, a jewel or necklace, and a sword (or knife to represent one). The mirror is the most important of these, for not only does it represent Amaterasu but, according to Shinto belief, it magically *is* the goddess. Following Japanese tradition, surround the mirror with fresh flowers. Lighted candles on the altar will reflect light from the mirror's surface. As always, preparation of the ritual space or altar is part of the ritual. In this case, polishing the mirror so that it shines like the sun will assist you in focusing on your own inner light.

Sitting before this altar, either alone or with companions, join your hands in prayer position and bow toward the altar. Then use the prayer from the Nihongi (page 70) to focus your mind on the goddess. Ask her, either aloud or in silence, for help in restoring balance and order to your life. Silently examine your life to determine where the light of the sun goddess is lacking, to find the areas where the storm god rages. It may help to imagine your life as filled with both sunlight and storm, and thus to acknowledge those areas that are most full of disturbance and pain. Then visualize the sun's generous light filling the disordered areas, driving the storms away with her brilliance and beauty.

If you have done this as part of a group ritual, you may wish to share, after this meditation, the insights that have emerged from your visualization. If you practice alone, take time to write down the information that has revealed itself to you. Finally, bow again toward the mirror as you close the ritual.

∾

Questions and Activities

1. Imagine your life as a house. What room in the house—in other words, what aspect of your life—seems messy and disordered? Has it been this way long? What have you done to bring order to it?

2. Examine your actual home. Which rooms are messy, which ones are clean? What feelings and activities do you associate with the different rooms? Does your house indicate areas in your life that are not in balance?

3. Make a list of words you associate with "order." What does this list tell you about yourself and your attitudes?

4. Examine your schedule. Are there areas of stress in terms of your use of time? Are there ways you can relieve this stress?

5. Describe your perfect home. Compare it to your real home. What is the difference? Can you make your home more graceful and comfortable by incorporating some ideas from your perfect home?

6. Describe your perfect day. Compare it to a real day in your life. What is the difference? How can you make your daily life more resemble your ideal?

7. Make a list of people who have annoyed you recently. Taking them one at a time, try to see the situation you encountered from their point of view. Are there things you are doing that make your life less easy with them?

8. Select someone who makes you feel agitated, to whom you respond with fear or anxiety. Make a list of their character traits. Imagine yourself acting out those traits. What keeps you from being like them? Are there unexpressed parts of yourself that they allow themselves to embody?

9. Do you have any self-destructive habits, habits that do not bring you closer to the life you desire? How can you begin to eliminate these habits?

10. When you dream, what villains appear? What qualities do these villains share? How can you begin to accept that their energy is part of you?

Hathor

Affection

Mistress of pleasure, ruler of joy,
Queen of the dance, mistress of music,
Ruler of ecstasy, queen of flirtation,
You, oh Hathor! Intoxication!
Intoxication! Oh Hathor! You!

1

I send up a prayer to my goddess Hathor.
I beg her to give me the one I desire.
When we are lovers, we will thank her.
Joyfully, we will thank her.
And my beloved will cry out to me:
Lover, lover, lover, in the whole vast world,
I am the one destined for you by the goddess.

2

Mistress of pleasure, ruler of joy,
Ruler of flowers, queen of the senses,

Queen of the dance, mistress of music,
Mistress of choirs, ruler of song,

Ruler of ecstasy, queen of flirtation,
Queen of the harp, lady of music,

You, oh Hathor! Intoxication!
Intoxication! Oh Hathor! You!

3

Praise to Hathor, praise the goddess!
Let me be the one who praises most,
for she has made me joyous in love.
Praise to Hathor, praise the Mistress!

A week ago I prayed to her, and look!
My lover came to me. Came and loved me.
Hathor heard me. Heard my plea.
She sent me love. She sent my lover.

At the door, my name was called.
At the door, there stood my lover.
Throughout the city, everyone breathed
the sweet wine fragrance of our love.

A week ago I prayed to Hathor, and
my lover came. It has been five days now.
What else can I do but pray again?
What else can I do but praise the goddess?

∿

Myth and Meaning of Hathor

More than three thousand years ago, when these invocations were created in Egypt, one goddess was the most beloved. And why not? Other goddesses brought wealth and fertility and power, but it was Hathor who brought the sweetest gift: love. From the moment when she received us into life—for she was one of the midwife goddesses—until the moment we encountered her at the sycamore tree in the west, where souls go after death, Hathor was intimately connected with our dearest pleasures and joys.

Is it any wonder that she was so beloved by the ordinary people who sang songs like these to her? Egyptian literature is studded with these gems of longing and joy, sensuousness and delight. Some of the world's most lovely poetry was written to this goddess during her long reign—almost three thousand years—in the hearts of her people.

She was called the lady of love, the golden one, queen of the dance. Dancing was one of her primary forms of worship. Egyptian art shows us that Hathor's people danced together in gender-segregated groups, expressing themselves with individual movements to the music rather than preordained steps. Women, Egyptian art suggests, danced more frequently than men, often clad in sheer robes or wearing only a little ribbon around the hips. These dances must have been exciting to watch, for paintings show women doing acrobatic back-bends and kicks and somersaults, as well as swaying to music we can almost hear, so vivid are the ancient paintings depicting Hathor's followers.

Accompanying the dancers were women playing musical instruments or clapping their hands in rhythm. Because of the joy it brought, music too was under Hathor's dominion. She was especially the goddess of percussion, her designated instrument being a kind of rattle called the sistrum. Often, in sculptures and paintings, her head decorated the base of the sistrum, topped by a crown of metal strips strung from wires between two poles. When her worshipers shook this rattle, a chiming rhythmic sound was created.

Hathor was one of the oldest Egyptian goddesses, far preceding the entry into the Nile valley of such foreign gods as the now-familiar Ra. In her original form, she appears to have been a goddess of the sun, for an ancient text shows her arguing with Ra over possession of the solar vehicle. She had returned from a sojourn in the south, only to find that Ra had replaced her with a sun god. Angry, she demanded the sun back, but Ra instead turned her into a snake and placed her on the crown of Egypt's pharaoh.

Another myth shows Hathor similarly angry, but this time at humankind. Disgusted with humanity for failing to worship the gods, Hathor began a worldwide massacre, killing people as fast as she could. Fearful that no one would be left alive after the goddess's rampage, Ra had vats of red ale brought and placed in Hathor's way. Mistaking them for blood, she drained the beer—and got very, very drunk. Unable to continue her attack on earth's people, she stumbled home to heaven to sleep it off.

These do not seem to be myths of a happy, loving goddess; in both stories, Hathor seems stern and angry. Neither of these myths explain why Hathor is the one invoked to bring love and affection into one's life. Perhaps there were other myths the Egyptians knew, but have since been lost, that explained how the wild-eyed, raging Hathor turned into the happy goddess of music and flirtation. Her connection with the gentle cat goddess Bast and with the raging lion goddess Sekhmet suggests that Hathor had a dual identity: as gentle protector and as fierce force of purification. If her myths show her in the latter form, her rituals tend to honor the former, for Hathor was invoked as a goddess of beginnings—including infatuation, which marks the beginning of love.

Symbols of Hathor

Hathor's primary symbol is the mirror. Egyptian mirrors were made of metal polished to a high shine; often the body or head of Hathor formed the handle, so that the user never forgot to honor the goddess in using her implement. In addition to small hand-held mirrors, massive ritual mirrors were fashioned for use in Hathor's festivals. Some of them were inscribed, all across the front, with symbols and depictions of the goddess and her myths.

The connection of goddess and mirror is often said to be because lovers make themselves attractive for each other by checking their appearance in the mirror; similarly, Hathor is said to rule cosmetics, used to make oneself more attractive to potential lovers. But there is another, deeper reason for the connection of this goddess and the mirror, and that is the ancient connection of Hathor with the sun, which is symbolized in many lands by the mirror. Mirrors bring the sun's light right down to us, making them magical implements allowing her worshipers to connect directly with the solar goddess.

Like the Greek Aphrodite, Hathor is addressed in invocations as "The Golden One," signifying both her solar identity and her connection with the golden light of love. Golden jewelry pleased her, as did the color yellow in robes and other clothing. Most pleasing of all was the golden glow of lovers holding each other's bodies and sharing delight.

Hathor also appears in two animal forms. As the winged cow of creation, it was Hathor who gave birth to the universe. She is often shown as a protective bovine, her head towering above that of the pharaoh whom she guards. As a cow, she provides sustenance for her worshipers; in this animal form she is also a symbol of maternal love.

Hathor also appears as a cat. The two Egyptian cat goddesses, Bast and Sekhmet, are connected with her through this image; they may have originally been separate goddesses who merged with the overwhelmingly powerful Hathor, or they may have been seen as aspects of her, the pleasant sun of winter and the scorching sun of summer, respectively. Rituals to Bast at her city of Bubastis are the same as Hathor's at Dendera, and the same story of drunkenness is told of both Hathor and Sekhmet. Hathor's cat identity, like the cow, connects her with maternal protectiveness, for the cat was a vital protector of the stored grain, keeping it safe from ravenous rodents.

Feasts of Hathor

The Egyptian ritual calender was an extremely complicated one, with dozens of festivals tied to specific dates, others depending on celestial or earthly events like the rising of the Nile, and yet others linked to political events such as coronations and setting the foundations of buildings. Of these festivals, one of the most important was Hathor's, celebrated on her birthday.

At her major temple in Dendera, Hathor was honored in an impressive and joyous ritual each September 17. It began before dawn, when the pharaoh danced before the goddess's image, singing to her that his heart was sincere and his soul was without darkness. Then the ritual emblem of the goddess, a huge mirror, was carried through her temple to the front steps, where it caught the first rays of the rising sun. That moment was a signal for revels to break out throughout the city. Bands of musicians marched about—there was literally dancing in the streets—and flagons were lifted in honor of the goddess's mythic drunkenness.

Drunkenness was also in order on the Feast of Inebriety, the ritual recalling how the goddess was turned away from destroying humankind. Beer was the drink of choice on August 7, for it was supposedly red ale the goddess mistook for human blood. More serious, but scarcely less festive, was the mid-May celebration in which a boat travelled from Dendera to Edfu, with ritual blessings of the fields along the route.

Suggestions for Invoking Hathor

The desire for love and affection did not die when Hathor ceased to be worshiped. It is without a doubt one of our primary human drives, one that can be as strong as hunger or thirst. We desire love's comfort the way we desire to be roofed against wild storms. We want to wrap ourselves in love like a cloak against the world's cold darkness.

There are many goddesses of love. Aphrodite is one, the Greeks' golden darling who brings such joyous trouble, the goddess of irresistible passion. Hera is one, the goddess of loving partnership and collaborative effort. Isis is one, the loyal goddess who does not rest until love is restored to wholeness. Oshun is one, the goddess of the love that heals both our souls and our bodies.

Although each goddess can be imagined to rule the entire spectrum of love, from flirtation through infatuation through secure comfort, their myths and rituals suggest a kind of division of labor among them. Aphrodite shows herself, through her myths, to be most interested in the kind of hunger that makes lovers forget everything but each other's touch, the obsessive desire to plunge deeper and deeper into the beloved's very soul. By contrast, Hera's is the province of committed love, the deep passion that comes with years together. Each goddess has her own speciality.

Hathor is thus the goddess of infatuation, that wonderful period when the lover's every action seems charming, when joy bubbles up from every encounter, when even sunshine seems giddy and effervescent. No matter what the lover's age, this is a youthful time, a time of hope and sheer delight. By extension, Hathor is the goddess of all beginnings—not for nothing did she stand beside the birthing bed, ready to receive the newborn. In all things, Hathor's province is happiness. When we invoke her at the beginning of any venture, we pray not just that it be successful or fulfilling, but that it be filled with joy and the juice of life.

The following suggestions can be adapted for any opening, whether it be a book launch or an art show, the beginning of a new career, or the start of a new love. The basic framework of a Hathor ritual is still so common (pleasant company, attractive settings, music and dance) that you could host a discreet one at your workplace without encountering objection. You may celebrate alone, but more energy is raised when there are friends and loved ones to help you rejoice. Men can as easily celebrate this ritual as women, or both in each other's company—for the purpose of this ritual is to spread joy, Hathor's favorite emotion.

Constructing an altar to Hathor should be a joyous dalliance with color and fabric and flowers and jewels. Any beautiful thing can represent Hathor, whether it be a statue or a piece of old embroidery or a branch of blossoms. A mirror should be part of the altar, to represent the goddess's solar identity and her connection with making oneself beautiful for love. Create the altar with attention to the ways the colors flow together, the graceful lines of the draperies, and the way the light strikes the objects you have chosen. Fragrance is vital to a Hathor altar, too, so find some especially delightful incense to burn as you invoke her. Or use scented candles, which will also provide lovely flickering light.

If you are holding an opening ritual in a public space where an altar is inappropriate, there's no problem: the whole setting can become your altar. Attend to every part of the arrangement as though you were creating a container to honor the goddess. Consider everything from the coat rack to the table setting. Don't do it in a frenzy of controlling behavior and neurotic self-doubt. Rather, let the beauty of Hathor's world reveal itself to you; dance through the preparations if you can, with music playing in the background.

You will need music for this ritual itself—joyous, full-bodied music, music that pounds in your veins like intoxicating love. Recorded music is good enough, but if possible provide live music, or at least some hand-held rattles so that participants can add to the music as they move. And don't forget a sparkling beverage—champagne, if appropriate, or sparkling apple juice or even fizzy water. Food should be sweet and sticky and luscious: fruit drenched in honey, candies, chocolate, cheesecake.

Depending on the occasion, the invocation to the goddess can be formal or informal, direct or disguised. At an art opening, for instance, you may choose to simply call down anonymous blessings on everyone who is assembled, and express your desire that the show is well-received. If you are invoking Hathor in order to draw love into your life, you may want to write a description of the sought-for love that you can lay, beribboned, on the altar as you invoke the golden one.

After invoking the goddess and telling her of your request, let the party begin! A ritual to Hathor needs to be loud and cheerful, full of movement and joyful noise. Let the champagne flow, let conversation bubble, let flirtations take flight, let jokes be told. Encourage dancing! Hand around the rattles and tambourines! If you have created the setting sufficiently well, the sensory pleasures of fragrance and taste and sound and sight will affect all participants, putting them in a pleasant and joyous mood.

Drunkenness and excess figure in Hathor's legend, but a contemporary celebration of her would be negated by excessive behavior. (See the Maenads for consideration of excess and ecstasy.) Thus it is important to hold a formal end to the ritual. Blow out the candles, turn off the music, thank the goddess for visiting with you, and send your participants (safely) on their way.

~

Questions and Activities

1. Begin with the sense of sight. What colors do you most enjoy? What shapes call out to you? What visual images make you feel flooded with happiness?

2. Next, proceed to sound. What sounds make you feel full of joy? These need not be sweet sounds; sometimes discordant sounds stimulate the senses more fully. Make a list of instruments, natural sounds, and music that pleases you.

3. Now, touch: make a list of things that feel good to you. What kinds of sensations give you pleasure?

4. Move on to smell: what fragrances make you feel giddy and joyous?

5. And finally, taste: what kinds of tastes fill you with pleasure? What specific foods and drinks have that effect on you?

6. Go through your memories to find as many settings as possible that seem joyous to you. What events occurred in those settings?

7. Think of yourself at the age of eight. What gave you pleasure then? Think of yourself at twelve, sixteen, and twenty. What gave you pleasure then? Is there any difference?

8. Consider your friends, lovers, associates. Who among them gives you pleasure, and why?

9. If you were given a month off and all the money in the world, with the only limitation that you cannot buy anything that will outlast the month, how would you make yourself happy?

10. If you had a month off and no money at all, what would you do to make yourself happy? How can you do that for yourself today?

Aphrodite

Passion

You already know her.
Do you need to ask her name?
Call her Love. Call her Joy.
Call her golden Aphrodite.

1

I sing of Aphrodite, the lover's goddess,
beautiful, gold-crowned, a blossom
riding the seafoam, resting on wind.
She comes ashore, and women
in gold bracelets meet her, bearing
silken garments for her lovely body,
copper rings for her shell ears,
chains of gold for her silver breasts.

They lead her from the seashore.
Do not look upon her! Your eyes
would dazzle from such beauty.
But you do not need to see her.
You already know her. It is she
who moves you in your dance.
She is the music of your life.
Do you need to ask her name?
Call her Love. Call her Joy.
Call her golden Aphrodite.

She is the moment when body
knits to body and the world flowers.
She enlivens everything: plants
in the meadow, the ocean's fish,
animals hidden in the forest,
birds tumbling on the wind.
She is our darling, she who under
the wheeling stars makes all
things blossom and bear fruit.
At her approach storms clear,
dark clouds dissolve to blue,
sweet earth and all the oceans
smile, and her light dances brilliant
through the flourishing world.

2

She came to Ida, flowing Ida, Ida of the streams,
with grey wolves behind her and bright lions
and thick bears and quick hungry panthers.
They moved like dancers around her.
She moved like a woman in love.
And when they saw this, they grew
hot and full of longing—even animals grow
hot and full of longing in her presence—
and two by two they left her, following
each other into the valleys to mate,
their bodies hot and full of longing.
And so, we too. And so, we too.

3

The golden one has left us, gone to her island,
gone to her temple there, gone to her shrine
with its incensed altar. She has left us behind
and closed the door. If we could see her now
how beautiful she would be! Imagine her there,
the Graces bathing her—those lovely handmaids—
and oiling her with fragrant sweetness, covering
every curve of her bountiful body with sacredness
and the green scent of olives, and dressing her
in filmy silken robes, and roping her neck
with golden chains, dropping gold from her ears,
ringing her fingers with gold. She is laughing.
How our darling loves to laugh! And now
look! she is leaving her temple again, coming
back to bring us more joyous trouble, laughing
and laughing, cutting a path right through the stars.

4

I will build you, goddess, an altar
high up on the mountain peak,
where everyone can see it, and each season
I will cover it with the richest offerings.
Think kindly of me therefore,
grant me a long and sunny life,
let me be happy among my loves,
and prosperous up to the ripe edge of age.

5

She has come back, piercing us all
with her sweetness, her power.
Birdsong swells, the antelope leaps
swift mountain streams, the west wind
wraps us in honeyed warmth.
She has returned, our golden one.
She moves laughing through our world
and we follow her. Through the forest,
through the fields, across the hills,
we follow her, all of us in love,
loving each other, in love with her.
When she returns, it is always summer.
Don't you hear the swallows and cicadas?
Don't you hear the nightingale?
Don't you hear the brooks running silver,
the rivers running darkly to the sea?
Don't you hear the whole world singing
her praises? Everything is singing, everyone
is in love, because our goddess has come home.

Myth and Meaning of Aphrodite

The Homeric Hymns to Aphrodite—source of the above passages—were not, as the name might indicate, written by Homer at all, but are assumed to be from the Homeric period in Greece, the eighth to the seventh century B.C.E. There are also Homeric Hymns to Demeter, Artemis, and other goddesses, each expressing the unique characteristics of that divinity. All are magnificent, but none surpasses the hymns addressing the goddess of sexuality, Aphrodite. Just as her statues were the most beautiful, so her hymns were the most voluptuous, the most gorgeous, the most redolent with sensuality and with passion.

Aphrodite is often called the goddess of love, but that is too ambiguous a word to define her. For there are many kinds of love, including those that Aphrodite does not rule. She is not the goddess of happy domesticity, although some who adore her can find that. Nor is she the goddess of partnership. Her domain is not that of loving parents or siblings, nor of friends who respect each other. No: Aphrodite rules physical attraction. It is too coarse to just call her the goddess of lust or even of sex, for physical passion can stir us when we look at splendid art or at nature's magnificence. Nor can we simply say that Aphrodite is the goddess of beauty, as we define it today—a checklist of visual attributes.

If Aphrodite is not these, who is she? She is served by handmaidens called the Graces, and sometimes she is called the chief Grace. And that is her secret: she is the goddess of gracefulness, of that which draws us to be closer, of whatever pulls us nearer to itself. She can be found in the fragrance of a summer rose as much as in the drooping eyelids of an attractive stranger. She is in the brilliant night sky, for which she is sometimes called Urania, as well as in the curving bodies of entwined lovers. She is a mythic symbol of all that binds us together—with each other, with our world, with the cosmos.

Her myths, as one would expect, emphasize her connection to love and sexuality. Born of sea foam impregnated by heaven, Aphrodite floated ashore on the islands near Greece, where she was greeted by the lovely maidens called the Graces, who dressed the goddess in attire worthy of her beauty and who became her constant companions. She married Hephaestus, the crippled god of smithcraft, but Aphrodite could not be contained in a single relationship and spread her favors liberally among divine and mortal males.

The most famous—perhaps notorious—of Aphrodite's affairs were those with Ares and with the beautiful young Adonis. She carried on scandalously and publicly with Ares, the god of war. All heaven knew of their assignations except the goddess's consort. When someone finally tattled to him, Hephaestus was humiliated. He retaliated as only a smith could do: he fashioned a mesh of gold in which he caught the lovers in flagrante and displayed them for all to see. Ares and Aphrodite were the laughingstock of heaven then, naked and damp, their limbs entangled in each other's and in the golden web that held them.

As for Adonis, it was said that Aphrodite fell in love with his youthful beauty and hid him in a chest that she gave for safekeeping to the underworld queen Persephone. But Persephone peeked inside to see what treasure she was guarding and, smitten, refused to give Adonis back to Aphrodite. Kingly Zeus, called in to arbitrate, ruled that Adonis would thereafter live one-third of each year by himself, one-third with Persephone, and the remaining one-third with Aphrodite. Each year, Adonis was killed while hunting a wild boar, and his spilled blood turned the river named for him red. Each year, then, the goddess mourned the loss of her beloved, and each year rejoiced when he was restored to her.

Given her centrality in human life, we should not be surprised that Aphrodite makes appearances in many other myths and epics. There is the story of the judgement of Paris: when the golden apple of discord, inscribed "To the Fairest," was tossed into an assembly of goddesses, Aphrodite was one of the claimants (the others being Hera and Athena) and, bribing the Trojan shepherd Paris with the love of the beautiful Helen, won the prize—and started the Trojan War. There is the story of Aeneas, the Trojan prince who founded Rome: son of Aphrodite, he followed her bidding in founding the imperial city, even though it meant abandoning the loving queen Dido of Africa. There is the story which, transmuted by George Bernard Shaw into the tale of Henry Higgins and the guttersnipe Eliza Doolittle, is perhaps the most famous of Aphrodite's myths today: how Pygmalion, a sculptor, insulted the goddess by falling in love with one of his own statues instead of mating with a living woman, and how she won him to her ways by enlivening the statue, who became Pygmalion's lover Galatea. In all her myths, Aphrodite is the force of attraction and connection, of passion and of the juiciest form of love. Such love can grow and become lasting, but that's not Aphrodite's concern. Broken hearts? Ruined lives? Troy in flames? Not her problem. Aphrodite doesn't care about the consequences, so long as there is passion. This goddess can be a troublemaker—but how dry our lives would be without her!

Symbols of Aphrodite

What does not represent Aphrodite? Anything that moves or grows, anything that blooms or flourishes, anything beautiful and shining—the symbols of Aphrodite are myriad.

Flowers are especially sacred to the goddess of love, as merchants even today recognize. And why not? Flowers are the sexual organs of plants. Thus Aphrodite is shown in art holding, wearing, stepping on, or surrounded by flowers. The lily, poppy, myrtle, narcissus, and crocus are among the flowers sacred to her. But no flower appears more consistently associated with Aphrodite than the rose. Fragrant, beautiful, and vivid, it still symbolizes passionate love today. The red rose—as courting lovers know—especially signifies Aphrodite, being the color of the heart's blood.

Fruit, too, is a symbol of Aphrodite's power, for she is the goddess who, drawing bees to flowering branches, creates the bountiful harvest. Among fruits, the pomegranate (shared with several other goddesses, including Hera and Persephone) and the apple (shared with Hera and the goddess of discord, Eris) are her special favorites. Trees that give forth fragrance, like myrrh and cinnamon, also are sacred to her.

As she is a sea-born goddess, water is naturally a symbol of Aphrodite, especially salt water; all the salty fluids of our bodies are similarly under her domain. Pearls, born in water, are a perfect emblem for Aphrodite. Similarly, waterbirds appear as the goddess's servants. Geese, ducks, and swans are some of her symbols; sometimes she rides on them, sometimes they are yoked like horses to a chariot that bears her. A few non-aquatic birds are also associated with her—especially the sparrow, who was thought by the Greeks to be especially sexually active.

Of all symbols of Aphrodite, however, the one most consistently associated with her is gold—not just yellow metal, but goldness as a quality of light. She is often called "the golden one," or simply, "the golden." In very ancient times, Aphrodite was connected with the sun and the dawn, whose golden light she embodies. Although we now connect love with the night, this goddess reminds us that we are drawn to each other in Aphroditian sunlight. And whenever we are filled with desire, our beloved seems glittering, radiant, all aglow. Golden rings and neckbands are beautiful—she is always described and depicted as wearing golden jewelry—but Aphrodite's real gold is found in the graceful movements of lovers toward each other.

Feasts of Aphrodite

What day is not suited to Aphrodite? Her feast is celebrated whenever lovers join in passion. However, there are times during the year when the ancients felt it was most fitting to acknowledge the power of this goddess.

In July, beginning on the twelfth of the month, the Greeks celebrated the major festival of Aphrodite. Called the Adonia, it focused on the young lost lover of the goddess, who was symbolized by quick-growing plants. Sown in little pot gardens, the Adonis gardens sprouted overnight, then died as quickly or were thrown into the sea. Women connected themselves with the life-and-death cycle of the goddess through this ritual.

A similar, though wilder, festival was imported from Anatolia (now Turkey) into the ancient Mediterranean. From March 15 to March 25, a feast honoring Attis (a form of Adonis) was celebrated in the ancient world. A pine tree, symbolizing the dying and resurrecting young partner of the goddess, was carried through the town, wrapped in linen and violets, then laid in a sepulcher. After a week of wild mourning, including self-mutilation by the most ecstatic worshipers, the priest opened the tomb to reveal: nothing. The god had been reborn. (Attentive readers will recall a later religious story based on this pattern.) The Hilaria followed, a day of public laughter and fun.

Aphroditian energies are strong in springtime, our foremothers knew. April 1 was, to the Romans, the Veneralia (yes, the word-base for *venereal* is hiding in there). Wearing wreaths of myrtle leaves on their heads, Roman women celebrated Venus, their version of Aphrodite, as "Goddess of Beauty, Mother of Love, Queen of Laughter, and Mistress of the Grapes." Another festival, called the Vinalia and held on August 19, celebrated the harvest; Venus shared this feast with Minerva, the Roman Athena.

Although not from the culture which gave birth to her, the Celtic feast of Beltane on May 1—with its tradition of joyous matings in the burgeoning forest—is an appropriate time to invoke this goddess. Conversely, Valentine's Day—the contemporary commercial feast of love—actually belongs to Juno, the queenly Roman goddess of partnership who resembles Hera (see page 59).

Suggestions for Invoking Aphrodite

Beautiful she may be, but Aphrodite is not an easy goddess. For she is amoral—not immoral necessarily, simply beyond consideration of whether any specific passion is appropriate or lasting. She can as easily bring pain as joy, as easily cause trouble as create harmony. She may be the chief of the Graces, but don't mistake that for a promise that all will be smooth in your life if you simply call on her.

Because of her power and the beauty of the prayers addressed to her, it is tempting to call on Aphrodite to solve any relationship problems. But that could be like using nuclear warheads for lawn care. Before invoking Aphrodite, spend some time clarifying your goals and desires. If you wish for a stable father for your children or a companionable partner, Aphrodite is not the one to call on. If you want security and commitment above all, she is definitely not a candidate for invocation.

Aphrodite—and the energy she represents—is neither selective nor calculating. Invoke her, asking for love in your life, and you may find yourself attracted to someone destructive or cruel. But that doesn't mean she hasn't answered your prayer. She enlivens life; feeling the energy of attraction flow through us can be most enjoyable even if we don't act on it. And you don't have to act on every attraction, just as a therapist doesn't have to act on an attraction to a client, or a parent to a child, or a pastor to a parishioner. Aphrodite will offer you the salty juice of love, but it is up to you to decide whether or not to drink it.

Thus it is important, before offering invocations or petitions to Aphrodite, to strengthen yourself so that you may deal responsibly with the energies you'll set loose. This is not a goddess to take lightly: never forget the Trojan War. Yet she is not necessarily destructive, so don't hesitate to invoke her when life seems dry or loveless. Just be prepared to deal with the rush of feeling and desire she provokes. Just be prepared to watch as your life is transformed like a burgeoning apple tree in spring.

A shrine or altar to Aphrodite cannot be constructed once and then left untended, because this goddess, above all others, represents life and life's forces. Thus she should be honored with fresh flowers and fruits, renewed regularly. These can be used to deck a shrine swathed with fine fabrics like silks and satins—all in bright, fresh colors. The creation of such an altar is an Aphroditian experience by itself, for you should open yourself to the textures, colors, and fragrances you employ. As goddess of the senses, Aphrodite is honored whenever you open to the beauties around you.

Your personal ritual to Aphrodite will depend on whether you invoke her privately, with friends, or with a lover. She for whom all acts of love and pleasure are her rituals is naturally pleased when lovers come together in her name; there is no action that is not part of her worship then, except those that hurt or that deny pleasure. Such a ritual cannot be scripted, for the spontaneity of joyous movement is the only way this goddess is appropriately honored. Aphrodite moves within you; listen to her promptings and act on them, moving with each other as you feel her passion within you.

You may also wish to create an Aphrodite ritual to invoke this goddess's power and draw it into your life. Whether alone or with friends, there is no way to call forth her power that is as effective as dancing, which should be the center of your ritual for this goddess. Begin the ritual by reading the invocation above (beginning on page 90), section by section, to the accompaniment of music; recorded music is fine, but drumming (or accompanying yourself with hand-held percussion instruments like the tambourine or rattle) will make the experience deeper and more memorable.

After reading each section aloud, dance the feelings that are stirred by the images within the hymn. Let the dance begin from within and move outward. There are no special steps to such a dance, which will be unique to each participant. Because Aphrodite is the breath of life that moves through us and unites us to each other, the dance is her best worship and most quickly draws her energy into those who practice it.

After you finish dancing, spend some time centering the energy within you. In many ancient statues of the love goddess, especially in her pre-Greek identity as Ishtar, the goddess is shown standing straight, her hands cupping her breasts. Although this is a posture suggestive of offering oneself to a lover, it is also one of self-containment, of directing one's energies within. Women can assume this posture, each hand cupped around a breast, while envisioning the goddess's energy within, available at any time. This posture is also one that can be readily imitated by men, who can cup their hands in front of their chests as though willing to receive the goddess's bounty. Conclude the ritual by taking one of the flowers from the altar and wearing it in honor of the blooming goddess energies within.

～

Questions and Activities

1. Remember the first time you felt the stirring of love. What did it feel like? What did you do? What was the result?

2. Remember the first time you felt sexual desire. (This may or may not be related to the occasion you remember in the first question.) What did you do? What was the result?

3. Remember the first time you had a sexual experience. (This may or may not be different than the earlier memories.) Was this a happy or unhappy occasion for you? Was there coercion or force involved? How did you feel during the experience? How did you feel after? How do you feel about it now?

4. Have you ever been forced or coerced into having a sexual relationship or experience? How did it make you feel then? How do you feel about it, and yourself, now?

5. Have you ever fantasized about lovemaking? If you have, what was the experience like? Did you feel any shame? If you did, who suggested to you that your desires are shameful?

6. As a young person, were you encouraged to believe yourself attractive and worthy of love? If not, what other messages were given to you, and by whom? Do you still believe them now? If so, why? How can you step past them?

7. What ways, other than sexual desire, does life's force speak in you? What draws you deeply and passionately toward itself? How do you respond?

8. How do you feel about other people's sexuality? What makes you feel excited; what makes you feel frightened? What does this tell you about yourself?

9. What images of powerful passion come readily to mind, from books, movies, television programs, or real life? The fact that these images come to mind suggests that they are significant to you. What do they tell you about your desires?

10. Take some time and write out an erotic fantasy starring yourself. If you feel safe doing so, share it with someone you love.

The Muses

Inspiration

Am I mad, or does the Muse call out to me?
Don't you hear her? Don't you hear her
in the rustling leaves, in the wind's soft voice,
in the water's laughter?

Am I mad, or does the Muse call out to me?
Don't you hear her? Don't you hear her
in the rustling leaves, in the wind's soft voice,
in the water's laughter? Don't you hear her?

If this is madness, let me go insane!
Let me go in search of her, calling out
to the bright sky: descend, singing goddess,
descend! Bring us your immortal music:

the sound of flutes playing like wind
over bending grass, the sound of strings
plucked like sudden sunshine, the clear bell
of your voice thrilling through the world.

∿

Myth and Meaning of the Muses

The Greek goddesses of art and inspiration are the most familiar ancient divinities today, for we still invoke them constantly. When we muse on something. When we are amused. When we go to museums. When we listen to music. We hear their name many times daily, although few recognize it as an echo of ancient goddess religion, growing dimmer and dimmer with each passing century.

Their memory still sounds within our language, even if we do not publicly invoke these goddesses as the great Roman poet Horace did in the song opposite. Their longevity is extraordinary, for the Muses were ancient even when Horace wrote almost two thousand years ago. They are so ancient that we do not know when their worship arose, for they were already worshiped when the Greeks came down from the north to the peninsula named for them. The new arrivals encountered impressive mountains, like Helicon in Boeotia, cloud-hung and occupied by resident goddesses. And there were freshwater springs like Castalia near Delphi; these, too, were already honored as connected to goddesses.

The Muses kept their residences, but they lost much of their power. The Greeks reinvented them as a swarm of siblings, all daughters of Memory—daughters, that is, of those who remembered the old ways. And, whereas the Muses had always been their own mistresses, the goddesses were now declared to be servants of the Greeks' own god of inspiration, Apollo. Now, instead of controlling access to inspiration, they merely served to inspire Apollo's lyrics—a role that the Muse has played historically ever since.

Their history as pre-Greek wilderness goddesses, each with her own spring or mountain, is doubtless the source of the confusion of names given the Muses by ancient authors. There are several listings offered; not even the number of Muses remains consistent. Most commonly, it was said that there were nine Muses: Clio or Kleio ("fame-giver"), ruler of history; Euterpe ("joy-giver"), the Muse of lyric poetry; "the festive" Thalia, Muse of comedy; the singing Melpomene, Thalia's opposite, Muse of tragedy; Terpsichore ("lover of dancing"), who ruled choral song as well as dance; Erato ("awakener of desire"), ruler of erotic poetry; Polyhymnia or Polymnia, the meditating one whose name means "many hymns" and who inspired them; Urania ("heavenly"), Muse of astronomy; and Calliope ("beautiful voiced"), ruler of epic poetry.

Sometimes, however, there were fewer than nine Muses. The three named by the Greek author Hesiod were obviously symbolic of the way an artist creates:

Melete ("practicing"), Mneme ("remembering"), and Aoide ("singing"). When there was only one Muse, she could be called by any of the names of the nine. To further confuse matters, the group as a whole had many names, usually derived from places sacred to one of them. Many of the names recall forest springs, beside which the Muses were said to dance: thus they are called Pieriades, Aganippides, Castalides, Heliconiades, and Maeonides, after sacred places of those names.

It may seem puzzling that the myths so rigorously enforce the connection of the Muses to wilderness areas, for to us art is a matter of civilization, an endeavor of the urban elite. But our foremothers had a different vision of art, an insight that is slowly being lost: that art is part of nature. Before she was an artifact of culture, the Muse was a natural force, a womanly presence that spoke in the woodlands, that sang in the bubbling springs, that danced in the ocean waves. And the artist who heard these songs and saw those dances brought back their beauty and mystery to the villages and towns, speaking nature to humanity. The inner landscape of inspiration and the outer landscape of nature was not separated by these wise ancients.

It was the role of the artist, then, not to create in the sense we often use it today—to make something new, something the world has not seen before. Rather, it was the artist's primary job to listen and to observe. Beside a dancing brook in a sunny forest, the artist would watch and wait until the power of that place made itself known. The poems and songs and other artworks that resulted from the inspiration of the Muses were, it was thought, easy to recognize. For the quality of art is special when the artist works to be a clear channel from the divine. To the original worshipers of the Muses, the divine lives in, and speaks through, nature's beauties. It is an insight that we can profitably muse on today.

Symbols of the Muses

As individual goddesses, each of the Muses had symbols sacred to them: Clio was depicted with an open scroll or a chest of books; Euterpe had a flute; Thalia wore the comic mask and wreaths of ivy; Melpomene, the mask of tragedy and vine leaves; Terpsichore and Erato were both symbolized by the lyre; Urania, a globe; and Calliope, a tablet and pencil. Some of these, like the masks of Thalia and Melpomene, have become stylized beyond general recognition of their ancient goddess reference; called simply "the masks of comedy and tragedy," they can be seen in theatrical waiting rooms around the globe.

As a group, the Muses were represented by the freshwater spring that bubbles, like inspiration, from a hidden source. Beside the spring was said to be a level grassy space, the dancing ground of the goddess. In such beautiful glades, to the merry sound of splashing water, these goddesses of inspiration were anciently invoked—as they can be today. Across the world from the Muses' homeland, the Chinese expressed a similar insight when they described the action of chi in running water as beneficial and positive to humanity. Thus a recirculating fountain, placed using principles of feng shui (Chinese art of placement), makes an excellent indoor location for invoking these goddesses.

Feasts of the Muses

In ancient times, the Muses were invoked every time a work of art was begun as well as each time it was presented. Before beginning a recitation, the poet would call out to the Muses to bring forth words as fluidly as the bubbling spring of Castalia. Often, at the close of a poem, a second invocation would thank the Muses for their presence at the creation or performance of a work.

There may have originally also been festivals dedicated to the ancient Muses, but these are not recorded, although their birthday is recorded as being on June 14. We also find, in Rome, a festival that honored goddesses very like the Muses. The Camenae, nymphs who lived in springs and were believed to foretell the future, were invoked on the Fontinalia, celebrated under the light of the full moon in October.

Suggestions for Invoking the Muses

How better to invoke the Muses than by performing the actions that please them?

Today, the arts have become a specialized form of expression, practiced only by a relatively small portion of the population. Yet we deny ourselves one of the greatest joys of human existence when we become spectators rather than doers. For the urge to create art is a deep-seated one, living in our hearts and souls, yearning to be fulfilled. Look at children: fearlessly, they paint big blue blotches on a piece of newspaper, admiring the color and shape without self-consciousness. Or they sing the same note, at a monotonous pitch, over and over, enjoying the sound that they can produce. Or they fling their arms overhead and whirl, whirl, whirl, for the sheer ecstasy of dancing.

Imagine what life would have been like in the days when the Muses were first invoked. People lived in small communities then, with each household producing most of its own necessities. Clothing, furnishings, decorative objects—all were produced by the people of the house. In doing so, they took pleasure in crafting each piece finely and decorating it well. Entertainment, too, was created spontaneously; there were dances and singing and recitations, sometimes for a special occasion, sometimes just because the rain wouldn't stop long enough for outdoor work. Each member of the household had an opportunity to serve the Muses. There were artists everywhere.

The arts were not a profession then. They were simply what people did. And this remained the case until relatively recently. Even a hundred years ago, Americans danced to the sounds of their neighbors' fiddles, wearing clothing they'd knit and embroidered themselves. But as recorded music, broadcast drama, and telecast dancing has become more the norm than the house concert or the county fair dance, average people create art less and less frequently than even a generation ago. And so the Muses are slowly being silenced, for they have fewer worshipers with each passing year.

To move into a creative relationship with the Muses, do just that: move. The Muses are not served by a contemplative order. To honor them, we must create.

First, however, we must listen to them.

The power of creation, the Muses tell us, comes to us through our senses. For it is not in a dreamy vision, dislocated from physical reality, that those goddesses appear. It is in the woodlands, on the mountaintop, by the bubbling spring. To begin to invoke the Muses, you do not have to travel to a mountaintop in the Himalayas. They are right near you: in your yard, in a park, down the street in a vacant field.

The Muses speak the clearest where nature remains the most untamed, but you can find them in a burst of crocus in the shadow of an office building. They speak in the language of the wind, and in the sound of water, and in the faint swishing of tree branches. Before you begin to create, you must find spaces where you can regularly encounter these wild goddesses. Spend some time exploring your neighborhood, or even your yard. They are there; you merely have to wait for them to show themselves.

Unfortunately for women in America today, it is not easy to find safe open spaces in which to encounter the Muses. Even if there is no immediate danger in a specific setting, the incidence of rape and murder in this nation makes it highly unlikely that a woman, alone in the woods, can relax long enough to attend to the quiet voices of the Muse. And it is not only urban dwellers, trying to hear the voice of the Muse in a forest preserve, who must contend with this limitation. Rural and even wilderness women can find themselves inhibited by knowledge of armed neighbors who might find a woman alone an appealing victim rather than a worshiper of the Muse.

Thus it is useful to find a partner or group willing to engage in this search with you. Make it understood before you start that your goal is to encounter the Muse, not to chat about work hassles or family challenges. Or get—even borrow—a dog, trained well enough to walk beside you and protective enough to scare away anyone who does not honor the goddess within women. Finally, you may be able to find well-maintained and guarded open lands, such as botanical gardens and arboretae, which provide a setting for semi-solitary contemplation while also protecting you while you loaf and invite your soul.

Once you have determined where and with whom to invoke the Muse, make several sojourns to her outdoor temple. While you are there, simply look around you silently. Don't pressure yourself to have brilliant insights or ideas for poems and stories and paintings. Just look, and listen. Listen to the birdsong and the wind's whisper. Look at the shapes of the plants, the changing colors of the sky. Breathe and enjoy the tangy taste of the land.

Such sojourns into the realm of the Muses should become a regular part of your life. Once you have had a few experiences with the sheer sensuous joy that the Muses can bring, you will be encouraged to continue. For there is a reason that the Muses are shown dancing in their green spaces. Even when the heart is burdened, the sensory stimulation of a beautiful natural setting will elevate the spirits.

Sojourning with the Muses, however, is just the first part of your attempt to invoke them into your life. The next part is through the creative process itself. And in order to do this most effectively, you must permit yourself to become an amateur—that is, as the word's Latin root points out, to be someone who does the art simply for the love of it. If you practice an art already, you may wish to attempt something that you know little about: painters can write poetry and poets paint, for instance. Or you may simply approach your art afresh, renewed with the experience of direct encounters with the Muses.

Once again, this part of the invocation could be done alone or with a group. The group with whom you've sojourned in the Muses' realm may be willing to join in group creation. Once again, however, you should commit yourself to the creative process, not to discussion of everyday matters or—worse yet—to critical analysis of your work. Criticism has its place, but not in this ritual.

While you may choose any art form in which to create your invocation, an especially effective way to proceed is to use freehand drawing. Find a fairly large piece of paper and a soft pencil (or pastel or crayon). Close your eyes and concentrate on the space you visited in the first part of this ritual. Try to capture again the feeling of the spot: the way the light fell, the subtle sounds, the fragrances and odors.

When you have called up the power of that place, open your eyes and begin drawing. Do not have a specific scene in mind as you draw. Do not criticize yourself as you do so. And do not rush. Draw very slowly. Draw one line, the line that seems most right to you at that moment. Then hold your pencil away from the paper while you look at what you have drawn. When you feel the call to add another line, do so.

A shape will begin to emerge from the lines you have placed on the page. This is a crucial point in this process, for you will probably feel a temptation to begin filling out the picture—drawing in a conventional way. But that pirate may really be a moose, or that tree a mountain. Let the drawing emerge, ever so slowly, from the page before you.

You can also try this with sculpting clay. Or you may want to attempt to write a poem this way, letting each line emerge slowly from the one before it. You may even wish to create a song in this fashion, or a dance. No matter what your medium, follow the same procedure: call up the space of the Muses, begin creating your artwork, and then proceed slowly, invoking and constantly reinvoking the sacred space of the goddesses.

When you have finished your artwork, you can offer it to the goddesses by destroying it; you can give it away; or you can keep it. Because the point of this invocation is to encounter the power of the artistic process, it is better to destroy or give away your art than to keep it. This emphasizes, to your deep mind, that the process of creation is more important than the resulting product. (Of course, there will be times when you find your own artwork so delightful that you cannot bear to part with it; that should, however, become the exception rather than the rule for these rituals.) Exchanging artworks as the ending point of a ritual to the Muses is an especially effective way to conclude your service to them. Repeat this ritual several times a year or more, and you will find yourself refreshed and more deeply in touch with your creative sources.

~

Questions and Activities

1. Close your eyes and picture a spot from your childhood that was very special to you. Recall it in as vivid detail as you can. What feelings do you remember having in that special place?

2. Remember what kinds of activities you enjoyed as a child. Were there types of art that especially called to you? Do you still practice them?

3. Get some fingerpaint or crayons. Spend some time playing, remembering what it was like to create as a child.

4. Take a stack of old magazines. Go through them quickly, looking for colorful pages. Tear them out. Then, tear shapes out of the pages. Lay the shapes onto a fresh piece of paper and arrange them to satisfy you. Paste them down, or just start over and make another.

5. Put on some music and sing, or at least hum, along to it. If you feel inhibited, ask yourself why. What inner messages do you give yourself about your singing abilities?

6. Remember a piece of art you started to create but didn't finish. Why didn't you finish it? Where is it now? What happened to make you stop?

7. Make a list of words you associate with the word "artist." Circle all the negative words. Do you see a pattern to your attitudes? What is it?

8. Make a list of artists you admire. What is it about them that draws you? In what ways do you want to be like them?

9. Think of an artist or performer you don't like. Make a list of words describing him or her. Look at that list and imagine those words being applied to you. How do you feel? Why do you feel these qualities are frightening?

10. If you could create only one work of art before you died, what would it be? What's stopping you from creating that artwork now?

Kuan-Yin

Mercy

Her mind is virtue, perfected.
Her body is wisdom, perfected.
Her face is bathed in holy light.
She is compassion itself.

1

Her mind is virtue, perfected.
Her body is wisdom, perfected.
Her face is bathed in holy light.
She is compassion itself.
Her orchid heart delights in mercy.

No matter what evils we face,
no matter what beasts or demons,
no matter what ill fortune or disease,
no matter even if we face death,
Kuan-Yin destroys them all
with her compassionate glance,
with her perfected soul.
She is infinitely blessed.
Let us bow to her in prayer.

2

If I were adrift upon the ocean
with demons and dragons all around,
I would think of sweet Kuan-Yin
and the hungry waters would subside.

If I were trapped within a furnace
as hot as hell's own blazes,
I would think of Kuan-Yin's power,
and the flames would turn to water.

If enemies pursued me, if I were thrown
from a high mountain peak, if knives
were raised against me, if I were imprisoned
or beset by beasts, I would call on her.

Her pity shields me from the lightning.
Her compassion is like a cloud around me,
which rains down sweetness and
puts out the fires of my sorrow.

Her very name is powerful
as thunder on the ocean.
Call it often, pray to her often,
for there is none like her in this world!

～

Myth and Meaning of Kuan-Yin

In religions centered on male divinity, we often find a magical girl or woman who stands in for ancient goddesses, satisfying the human desire for an image of divine femininity. In Buddhism, that figure is Kuan-Yin, to whom the traditional prayers above were addressed. She is not a goddess, for there are no such figures in Buddhism—although some call her a folk goddess, for she is honored among simple folk just as a goddess is. Nor is she a buddha, one who has attained perfect enlightenment. Rather, Kuan-Yin is a bodhisattva, someone who stands at the threshold of enlightenment; she is called a celestial bodhisattva, the highest rank of these semi-divine beings, for she stands as close as it is possible to heaven itself. In both China and Japan (where, as Kwannon, she is sometimes pictured as male), Kuan-Yin is by far the most popular—and powerful—of the bodhisattvas, honored for more than a thousand years in prayers and simple rituals.

The reason for Kuan-Yin's popularity is her great devotion to the people of this earth. She remains perpetually a bodhisattva, rather than progressing into utter illumination, because she made a vow not to attain enlightenment while a single person on earth suffered. "She who hears the suffering world" is one of the translations of her name, and she is said to answer all prayers directed to her.

Is it any wonder her people love her?

Kuan-Yin knows well the difficulties of life on earth, for she was born here, as a girl named Miao Shan. Her father, having no sons, based his plans for future prosperity on the girl's marriage prospects. Unfortunately for him, Miao Shan planned to become a Buddhist nun. And unfortunately for the girl, her father was not pleased. A nun in the family! It was absurd, embarrassing. He believed she would grow out of it.

While he waited, Miao Shan's father arranged for her to marry a man of the area, a man of great wealth, neither young nor handsome—not that youth or a pretty face would have altered Miao Shan's determination to remain a virginal nun. As the wedding day approached, Miao Shan asked no questions about her bridegroom. She did not bother to be fitted for a wedding dress. She showed no interest in what flowers should deck the house. She simply sat in prayer every day, for hours and hours and hours.

Her mother tried to argue in her favor, but her father would not listen. A marriage had been arranged; a marriage there would be. But all his anger and entreaties led to nothing, for the girl would not yield. So Miao Shan's father had her confined to a tower, where he hoped she'd come to her senses. But in the tower, where there was no one to talk to and only dry rice to eat, Miao Shan happily devoted herself to her prayers.

When he realized that he had been defeated, Miao Shan's father grew furious. In a passion of thwarted will, he ordered his soldiers to kill his daughter.

Like everyone in the household, these men loved and respected the girl. But they feared her father more. So they took Miao Shan from the tower and led her out into the forest. They were silent, ashamed of what they were about to do.

Miao Shan walked quietly behind the soldiers, her thin wrists tied with heavy rope. When the soldiers reached an open space in the trees and drew their swords, she took a deep breath, readying herself for her next life. The soldiers raised their swords, as one, into the air.

Suddenly a tiger bounded out of the woods. It was huge, bigger than any tiger ever seen. With a sweep of its long foreleg, the tiger knocked down the swords of the soldiers. It took Miao Shan in its mouth and carried her away. It ran through the forest until it reached a low mountain cave. There it dropped the girl on the rocky ground. Then the tiger disappeared.

Without warning, the cave dissolved. Miao Shan floated like a feather in the wind. She landed somewhere. It was a dark dismal place where ghosts drifted like smoke. Above them, she saw a huge man with flames darting out of his head and eyes. It was Yen Lo Wang, ruler of the dead. He held souls in bondage; as long as they were in his realm, they could not be reborn and work off the consequences of past misdeeds.

She challenged the god in a loud voice. The god scowled, flames springing like snakes from his head. The girl stood before him, shining like a saint. He opened his mouth to bellow. He raised his hand to curse. But when he saw Miao Shan begin to pray calmly, and the ghosts begin to drift toward her radiance, the god of death knew he had no power over the holy girl.

Miao Shan blessed the drifting ghosts. They drifted upward and disappeared. On earth, they slipped into the bodies of newborn babies, ready to live again.

Miao Shan found herself back in the cave on the earth's surface where she'd been carried by the divine tiger. As she always did, she began to pray. She felt light rising in her. The light grew clearer and clearer until the Buddha stepped from it, carrying a peach.

He handed it to the girl with instructions that she eat it, for it would keep her from being hungry or thirsty until she attained her goal. Then she was to depart immediately for the island of P'u T'o Shan. Her father, discovering that she had escaped from the soldiers, was hunting her down to make another attempt on her life. But in a year, she would reach perfect enlightenment and be beyond the reach of his swords.

And so Miao Shan followed the Buddha's instructions. And so she reached the place where she could have stepped right into the light, leaving behind the miseries of earthly life forever.

But right at that threshold, she stopped.

Of all who had reached this point, none had ever stopped. After many lives of prayer and practice, who would turn back from the great goal?

But Miao Shan remembered all those who still suffered, those who could not find their way to the light because of the difficulties of their lives. And so the girl made a vow: to remain on earth until every living thing was holy.

And thus was the girl transfigured—but not into buddhahood. She became the compassionate Kuan-Yin, who sat on her paradise island P'u T'o Shan answering every prayer addressed to her. The mere utterance of her name in prayer was said to assure salvation from physical and spiritual harm. Even better was the observance of Kuan-Yin's own testimony of peace and mercy; her most devout worshipers ate no flesh and lived entirely without doing violence to other beings.

Symbols of Kuan-Yin

It is easy to find an image of Kuan-Yin, even in the United States. In cities where there is a Chinatown or even a single Chinese gift shop, simple white porcelain statues of Kuan-Yin are readily available and extraordinarily inexpensive. Larger, often multi-colored, statues are also available for a greater investment, as are scroll paintings with her image. Catalogues bring her image to those outside such resources.

These statues show her dressed in flowing garments, making symbolic gestures of generosity and the banishment of fear and hardship. Often she is attended by the dragon-girl Lung Nu and the male child Shan Ts'ai. She may hold willows or jewels; sometimes she bears a kind of vase, in which are stored the waters of compassion, known as the "sweet dew." Sometimes she wears a necklace, usually colored gold to indicate her celestial nature. She may be standing on an open lotus blossom, or carrying one in her hand. On her face is always an expression that combines serenity and concern and kindliness.

As with many Buddhist figures, the lotus or waterlily flower often symbolizes Kuan-Yin. Beautiful and fragrant, it floats upon the water like the soul should float upon the divine essence. It is also an emblem of purity and grace arising from the unlikely mud of ordinary reality. Both the blue lotus, signifying rebirth in the Pure Land, and the white lotus, signifying a pure soul, are among her emblems. Although not unique to Kuan-Yin, the lotus is a powerful image of her spiritual significance.

The lotus is one of many emblems of Kuan-Yin, some of which are listed in a Chinese sutra as being the following: the wish-fulfilling gem, a rope to bind harm, a jeweled bowl containing healing water, the long-life vase, a brush for banishing hardship, a solar disc to bring light, a lunar disc to counteract poison, a willow branch for sweeping away sickness, a jade bracelet for piety, the mirror of wisdom. She has many weapons: a sword for subduing evil spirits, a thunderbolt for killing demons, an axe to kill oppressors, a dragon-headed tablet for killing wild beasts, a dagger for her enemies, a bow for high flight, an arrow for friendship. In some depictions of the goddess, she is shown with forty-two hands, each holding one of these objects or making a gesture (mudra) with special power.

Of the many emblems of Kuan-Yin, perhaps none is as meaningful as water. She is said to live on a magical island surrounded by the ocean; many legends show her taking special interest in rescuing sailors and fisherfolk. And when she wishes to offer us her compassion, it takes the form of a shower of unearthly water. Thus her shrines were often situated near running water, or with an especially lovely view over a nearby lake or sea.

Feasts of Kuan-Yin

Until recent years, when under communist rule China has become much less religious than the great land has traditionally been, Kuan-Yin was honored at lovely shrines in the countryside. Usually situated near water and surrounded by a grove of trees, these simple park-like shrines were the settings for equally simple rituals. Dropping in on Kuan-Yin for a few moments, local residents would pour out their pleas to her: for a good harvest, for a happy marriage, for strong and healthy children. And, once she had granted their requests, they returned for a short and simple prayer of thanks.

The more devout might make the pilgrimage to Kuan-Yin's holy island, off the coast of Chekiang, where her actual footprint can be seen in the rock. (A very deep footprint indeed, it is said to have been created when the girl arrived on the island by making an impossible leap from the nearby island of Lo Chia Shan.) There she lived in the Ch'ao-Yin Cave, where she is sometimes said to have shown herself to visitors even long after her removal from this sphere of existence. Other miracles have been attested at that site, such as the miraculous appearance of lotus flowers in the sand of the cave floor. In Japan, too, pilgrimages to Kwannon's temples are popular ways to honor the bodhisattva; a special song is sung at each of the thirty-three temples containing Kwannon statues.

There were traditionally several major festivals to Kuan-Yin, each celebrated on the nineteenth day of a lunar month—the second, sixth, and ninth. The first was her birthday; this did not celebrate her birth in human form, but rather her first appearance as a beam of light from the very eye of god. The next, now conventionally celebrated on July 12, marks the occasion of her vow to remain on this side of enlightenment in order to help humanity. Seven days of meditation on Kuan-Yin's role as the hearer of cries from the weeping world followed, and the goddess was invoked with the prayer *Namu ta-tzu ta-pei Kuan Shih Yin P'u-Sa* (give praise to the great, compassionate, and merciful bodhisattva Kuan-Yin). Readings from the great works about her—parts of the *Lotus Sutra,* or the *Dharani of Great Compassion*—also help focus the mind on her special greatness. The final feast honors the moment when she was assumed to bodhisattvahood.

Suggestions for Invoking Kuan-Yin

Of all the ways of honoring Kuan-Yin, the most deeply rooted is through chanting. And of all the chants praising Kuan-Yin, the most significant is the *Dharani of Great Compassion,* called in Chinese the *Ta Pei Chou.* So powerful is it that, if correctly uttered, it is said to cause one's very consciousness to be permeated by divine light. When Kuan-Yin herself spoke this sutra before the Buddha, the entire earth trembled.

What are these magical words? The sutra begins like this: *Namo ratna-trayaya namah arya avalokitesvaraya bodhisattvaya mahasattvaya mahakarunikaya om sabalavati sudhanatasya tha srimahapatasami sarvaatodhusuphem asiyum . . .*

And on and on it goes, in rolling syllables that, alas, cannot be translated, not even by the devout who recite it. The words once had significance in Sanskrit, but changed into Chinese they no longer make sense. The sutra is more like glossolalia—speaking in tongues—than like a learned treatise or even an impassioned prayer.

But it is unnecessary to understand the words of a chant in order for it to have a powerful effect on consciousness. Indeed, sometimes understanding the words gets in the way of prayer. For example, the use of Latin for Catholic chants continued for more than a thousand years after the language fell from use, and many people living today can still attest to the mind-altering and hypnotic effect of hearing magnificent Gregorian chants without the mind being bothered by meaning.

You do not have to know the entire *Dharani of Great Compassion* to call on Kuan-Yin. The simple chant *Namo Kuan Shi Yin P'u-Sa* (essentially a greeting to the goddess), or the even shorter *Kuan-Yin P'u-Sa,* is held to be effective, especially if spoken aloud while walking meditatively. Merely uttering her name also is said to suffice to draw her aid to you.

This kind of invocation, accepted as a form of yogic concentration in China, is similar to that once employed in Christianity, which for many centuries encouraged the simple pronunciation of the names of god (or saints) as a means to sanctity. Both the recitation of Kuan-Yin's sutra and the repetition of her name are variations on a type of worship that has somewhat fallen out of favor in mainstream religions, but which is often used by those on the goddess path.

The use of sound to initiate or to deepen the state of worship—whether that is called meditation, prayer, or ecstasy—is widespread. From the drums used by Mongolian shamans to the voices lifted in holiday carols in Episcopal churches, sound is integral to many religions. In goddess religion today, it is most often employed in two ways: in toning, a kind of wordless chanting that is used to raise power; and in the chanting of repetitive songs.

Toning is quite simple. Breathing naturally and deeply, the worshiper begins to voice the breath—not forcing a sound, but keeping the vocal cords in a relaxed state. Eventually a tone will emerge. Breathe more sound into the tone, holding it as long as possible. At times tones will subtly shift to a different note; do not try to either avoid or encourage this natural process.

Because all human vocal cords are similar, many people toning together will sound relatively harmonious. A large group easily creates a swelling sonority that is not only very pleasing to the ear but assists in creating a reverent and even ecstatic mood. Tones will alter and change a number of times during any session, but there is rarely an unpleasant sound. After some moments of toning—perhaps ten, perhaps a bit more—let the breath slowly resume being unvoiced, and fall back into the silence from which the sound was born.

Women's spirituality circles generally use toning to "raise power" at the beginning of a ritual. Participants usually do experience a heightened sense of connection, both with each other and with impersonal or divine forces. Having toned together, a group is more connected and therefore more readily moved into other forms of worship.

In addition to toning, those on the goddess path frequently chant songs to the goddess. Typically, these have simple words and monotonous melodies. If they sound rather dull to the listener, with their limited range of notes and sometimes unpoetic words, that is because they are being compared to liturgical music of the kind well-trained choirs sing in today's churches. But these goddess chants are not designed to be listened to; they are designed to be sung, repetitiously, in order to create an altered state of mind.

The best chants are those that can be learned quickly and that do not take great skill to sing. Thus some very lovely melodies may be too complicated to make good chants, while some rather dull ones are perfect for chanting. Once the chant starts, keep it up for some time. Twenty, fifty, even a hundred repetitions of the same phrase may be necessary to produce the desired effect.

You do not need a group for toning or chanting. Set up an altar, light a candle, and spend ten minutes creating a joyful noise for the goddess. Chanting and toning can create a meditative state more readily for many people than just silence, in which the sound of the mind grows ever louder. This simple form of worship can easily be incorporated into daily practice.

Less frequently used in contemporary goddess religion, but a highly effective form of worship, is the repetition of the goddess's name aloud. To Kuan-Yin's followers, this is the most effective single way to attract the attention of the goddess; some recite her name hundreds of times each day. (You can use any goddess's name; invoke the one whose energy you wish to see active in your life.) Although just saying it over and over in a regular tone of voice can create a surprisingly deep mood of worship, drawing out its syllables into a chant is even more effective. As the Kuan-Yin rituals suggest, moving—even simply walking—while chanting the goddess's name is an especially powerful ritual. Simple as it sounds, its effects are extraordinary. Many worshipers have expressed a strong sense of active presence, as though the goddess had come to the sound of her name. Others find transformative thoughts and ideas come suddenly to mind during such chant-meditations. Worship need not be complicated to be effective. Kuan-Yin's worship shows us how simple it can be to follow the goddess path.

～

Questions and Activities

1. When you were a child, what were your spiritual aspirations? What spiritual moments do you remember? Are there common themes among them?

2. How often, today, do you take time for spiritual endeavors? What form do they take? Do you find yourself hungry for more time for spiritual practice?

3. What stops you from engaging in more spiritual practices? What takes up the time you might otherwise spend that way?

4. To make more time for spiritual practices, what will you need to change in your life?

5. What spiritual practices have you found to be effective in creating a sense of the divine for you? What spiritual practices have been ineffective?

6. Can you discuss your spiritual yearnings with your friends? Your family? What encouragement or discouragement do they give you?

7. What religious ideas—from any religion—hold the most power for you?

8. How comfortable are you with the religious tradition in which you were brought up? What have been its positive benefits? Its negative?

9. In what areas of your life do you feel a need for divine help?

10. Do you feel inhibited in any way from praying for divine aid? If so, why? If not, how do you prefer to pray?

Artemis

Protection

Let me sing of the maiden of contradictions,
goddess of the wild chase
and the busy spindle.

1

Let me sing of the maiden of contradictions, goddess of the
wild chase and the busy spindle. An archer, a hunter, she races
through the mountain shadows and the windy hills, drawing
her bow and loosing her arrows of sadness. The mountains
tremble, and the forest resounds with the agony of animals.
Earth and sea both shudder as the strong-hearted one delights
in her hunt. And then, when she has had enough, she leaves
the forest. Hanging up her bow and quiver, she robes herself
in splendor and goes forth to lead her maidens in dance,
smiling as they sing of her mother Leto, of how she bore
such a wondrous daughter.

2

Maiden goddess, holy one,
    protector of hills and forest,
    protector of mothers in labor,
    protector of the buds of infancy,
triple goddess, I invoke you:

bless the trees around my home,
    the ones that shade me,
    the ones that screen the wind,
    the ones that perfume the air.
May they protect me as you do.

How will I thank you?
    When I eat flesh, I will thank you.
    When I eat fruit, I will thank you.
    When I drink clear water, I will thank you.
Your trees will never lack for offerings

as long as I live and breathe,
    maiden goddess
    triple one
    my protector
as long as I live and breathe.

∼

Myth and Meaning of Artemis

The wild maiden Artemis was worshiped throughout the ancient world for untold centuries, as these two invocations show; one is from the Homeric Hymn to Artemis, while the other was written nearly a thousand years later by the Roman poet Horace. One of the most beloved of Greek goddesses, Artemis was honored in art and song, in invocation and in ritual, for generation after generation.

Artemis was born, it was said, to Leto—mistress of kingly Zeus in Greek times, but originally a pre-Greek mother goddess whose name is thought to mean "Our Lady" and who had no known consort. As the myth was told by the Greeks, a curse was placed on Leto that she could not give birth anywhere that the sun shone. To make matters worse, the expectant mother was pursued by a snaky monster who kept her from pausing long enough to bear her children in caves or other darkened spaces. Leto would have wandered the world, miserable and perpetually in labor, had her sister Asteria not come to her aid by transforming herself into an island. That magical place, Ortygia, floated on pillars under the ocean's water, just out of reach of the sun's rays and therefore exempt from the curse.

The beleaguered Leto was thus able to give birth to Artemis, who immediately became her mother's midwife and safely delivered her twin brother Apollo. The magical island, renamed Delos ("brilliant"), was then declared sacred and taboo; no person was ever again allowed to be born or to die on the island. After giving birth to Artemis, Leto disappears from her daughter's myth, except for a single incident: angered by the queen Niobe, who bragged that her many offspring were better than Leto's few, Leto called on her archer daughter for vengeance. Artemis used her arrows to destroy her mother's rival, killing all her children, and Niobe was turned into a block of stone from which a weeping fountain endlessly poured.

This was not the only case in myth where Artemis employed her arrows—or other handy weapons—for revenge against those guilty of moral or ethical violations. She killed the serpent Python, as well as the giant Tityus, both tormenters of her mother. She executed the spying Achteon, a hunter who ogled her at her bath, by changing him to a stag and setting his own dogs upon him. When Teuthras murdered one of her sacred pigs, she gave him leprosy so that he would die slowly and miserably.

Dozens of others are named in Greek myth as victims of the archer goddess. So why was she so popular among the Greeks? Because she was not seen as needlessly cruel, but rather as sustaining life, especially the life of the wilderness where she made her home. Artemis was a sort of cosmic game warden, keeping the wilderness safe from predatory hunters who might kill for sport rather than for need; such hunters could expect to meet a fearful fate at Artemis's hands. She also hunted down those who attempted to kill pregnant animals and thus interfere with nature's replenishment. She herself hunted, it is true, but only as a way of culling from her wild herds those animals not vital enough to reproduce strong offspring.

She was, similarly, the goddess who protected women. As heaven's midwife, she kept pregnant and laboring women healthy and safe. As goddess of the woodland nymphs, she kept their virginity safe as well as protecting them from peeping hunters. And as goddess of girlhood, she was the guardian of young women, who danced before her wearing yellow robes in one of the most famous of her rituals. Although virginal herself—she never had children—she is thus appropriately pictured as a mother bear, fiercely defending those she loves.

Artemis had little to do with men. In her myths, men who encounter her usually meet a harsh fate, often a hideously painful death. Although she is called the twin sister of Apollo, in fact they never spent time together; in late legends she is connected to the moon while he is associated with the sun, so they did not even accompany each other on their sky journeys. Artemis is, of all Greek goddesses, the one most closely associated with women. Her myths suggest that men can only encounter her by paying close attention to her boundaries and limits, and by similarly respecting women's needs for privacy and seclusion.

Symbols of Artemis

The moon is usually considered the preeminent symbol of Artemis, although her connection with earth's changeful satellite came late in her historical worship. Despite its being a late addition to her symbology, it is a vital and stirring one. The moon, moving from slender crescent through round fullness and back to invisibility, has in many cultures been seen as a natural image of our own lives' progress from youth through vigor and into old age. As goddess of nature's cycles, Artemis is appropriately symbolized by the many-phased moon.

Some depictions of Artemis make a visual pun by combining the lunar crescent with the archer's bow, showing the goddess bending the moon into a sickle shape and aiming an arrow through it. The bow, arrow, and quiver are among Artemis's most important symbols. Many beautiful Greek and Roman sculptures show her wearing only a brief garment (called a chiton, it was like a minidress tied at the waist), often with one youthful breast bare. Over one shoulder the goddess has tossed a quiver filled with arrows; she carries her bow strongly, though casually. As her myths show, these arrows were especially used to dispatch those who broke the sacred rules of the goddess: that animals should not be killed wantonly or indiscriminately, and that women's bodies should be respected.

Animals, too, are often associated with Artemis as her symbols or familiars. Although she was the one who protected all animals, two are especially important to her: the bear and the dog. The bear, known as one of the world's fiercest mothers, seems an especially apt symbol for this protective goddess. She seems to have been especially charged with protecting girls before they reached menarche. In her honor, at the city of Brauronia, a ritual was held for prepubescent girls each year. Dressed in yellow robes, they danced in a lumbering way before the statue of the goddess, apparently imitating Artemis as the bear mother and therefore bringing her power within themselves.

Dogs, too, were depicted as her sacred animals. As she hunted with her band of merry nymphs through the wild forest, Artemis was accompanied by packs of hounds. They served not only to assist with the hunt, running down deer and other animals, but to protect the women as well. In return, Artemis took care of them. The herb Artemisia—the common silver-leaved dusty miller is one—is named for the goddess, and is commonly called wormwood because she was reputed to use it to relieve her hounds of intestinal parasites. Sometimes, as in the story of Achteon, the hounds act as doubles of Artemis's main weapon, the arrow, killing those guilty of sacrilege or insult to the goddess.

Feasts of Artemis

In Athens, in April, one of the great festivals of Artemis was celebrated. Called the Mounichion, it featured a procession of celebrants bearing amphiphontes—cakes decked with a circle of lighted candles. The festival's date was determined by the goddess herself, as it was celebrated on the night of springtime's first full moon. Another, at the full moon in August, invoked Artemis for protection against the storms that might destroy the harvest. At the Agrotera a month later, goats were sacrificed to Artemis as huntress, and a great moonlit feast was held.

Artemis was traditionally honored in rituals on the nights of the full moon. There is some indication in ancient literature that one of the reasons for the popularity of this goddess is that her rituals were rather ecstatic affairs, taking place in the moonlit woodlands, involving lots of dancing and leading in some cases to sexual explorations.

Anyone who has ever been in the wilderness when the moon is full has witnessed the effect of Artemis's beaming light on animal life. (Bartenders and entertainment workers in cities claim to notice the same effect.) As the moon rises above the horizon, shedding her light on the forests she rules, the animals make wildly excited noises. Wolves and coyotes howl, owls call out, ravens scream. Throughout the bright-lit night, animals hunt and sing and run. Daylight patterns do not hold during these monthly revels. Humans are animals too, so why should we believe that these lunar effects are not felt within our bodies as well? Artemisian revels on nights of the full moon may well have had the same exploratory and somewhat raucous energy that animal activity under the full moon's face still does.

A goddess similar to Artemis was Bendis, a spear-bearing Thracian divinity who was honored on May 24 with an all-night torch race. Similarly, the Roman goddess Diana was associated by ancient people with Artemis; she was honored on August 15 in the Nemoralia, when torch-bearing women brought their leashed dogs to the grove of the goddess for blessing, then returned to the city to wash their hair ritually while praying for ease in childbirth. Originally an August full moon festival, the Nemoralia became fixed at a solar date that later was converted to a Christian feast of Mary.

Suggestions for Invoking Artemis

In her myths, we see Artemis as a protector goddess, one who defends women and (especially) girls, as well as any pregnant or laboring animal. By extension, too, she is guardian of the forests and wild spaces of the world. Thus Artemis is appropriately invoked when protection is sought for self or for the earth. Such a ritual could be seen as drawing up the Artemisian force from within as well as drawing it from a transcendent goddess energy.

A question that needs to be addressed with Artemis, as with no other goddess, is the role of men in rituals of women's spirituality. For Artemis is mythically depicted as occupying woman-only space; no men are permitted to join her wood-land band, nor to observe the nymphs at the hunt or at play. Following this sacred trail, women who worship only with other women often call themselves Dianic, after the Roman woodland goddess assimilated to powerful Artemis. Dianics argue that women are sufficiently wounded by society that woman-only spaces are neces-sary for emotional and spiritual healing. In addition, some find that men are gen-erally more adjusted to hierarchic structures and thus do not function well in the organized anarchy of women's circles, claiming more space and time than they should. Finally, some Dianic circles are lesbian and find no compelling reason for men's presence.

Goddess-honoring groups that admit men to rituals usually do not define them-selves as women's spirituality groups; rather, they are inclined to call themselves pagan or neopagan, or say that they practice an earth religion. Those for whom incorporating men into goddess rituals is important will argue that change does not come by excluding those most in need of it. By giving up the power of an exclusive male godhead and honoring a feminine divinity, individual men can thus be encouraged to become aware of—and correct—other relationships in their lives.

In honoring Artemis, the question of who should be involved in her rituals is especially significant, for she is preeminently the goddess of women. There is a great opportunity for healing and growth when men approach this goddess, but her fierceness will demand much from them. She will challenge them to determine where and how they have participated in the wounding of women and of the earth. Honestly facing her challenge can be significant and moving for male worshipers.

In most cases, however, rituals to Artemis will be based on the Dianic model: women, celebrating together, calling on the bear mother to protect them. There are several historical Artemis rituals on which contemporary celebrations could be based. The Amazons—those women warriors—were said to worship Artemis by holding circle dances in her honor, celebrated by shield-bearing women who clashed their weapons together like cymbals. At Brauronia, yellow-robed girls imi-tated bears in an apparent women's initiation rite. And there were, too, those woodland dances under the full moon, about which we have no specific historical ritual information.

Such a ritual would most effectively be held out-of-doors, under a full moon if at all possible. Groves of trees that grow naturally in a rough circle are especially delightful spaces for such rituals. If held indoors, some attempt to bring nature inside should be made. But because Artemis abhors injury to any creature, avoid cutting down tree branches or similar decorating strategies. Rely instead on light, air, scent, and living creatures. A picture window that faces the full moon, open doors, massed potted plants, some companionable dogs—these are more to the goddess's liking than darkness and dead air and dying boughs.

Tambourines, bells, cymbals, and other sharp-toned hand-held percussion instruments are easier to handle than swords and shields, so prepare yourself or your group with such implements. Gather in a circle, invoking the goddess with one or both of the above prayers. Then, clanging the instruments, dance around the circle. Call out the goddess's name, drawing out the syllables so that it makes a sort of chant, ending in a long hiss. As you do so, imagine yourself as the protective goddess; draw on the Amazon energy within you. Make gestures as though striking an enemy, drawing a bow and shooting, or protecting yourself with a shield.

If anyone in the circle has suffered an injury against her womanly spirit—especially rape or violence—the group can circle around her and, turning their backs to her, form a protective shield as she calls out for Artemis to give her the strength to fight back against her violator. Those invoking Artemis alone can similarly envision her wrapping her strong arms protectively around her daughter or warding off attackers with her sharp arrows.

For young girls coming into their womanhood, an Artemisian celebration is an excellent rite of passage. Echoing the girls of Brauronia, these celebrants should wear yellow garments (tee shirts are fine!). Their dance will be different from that of the full-grown Amazons. Lumbering about and throwing their shoulders forward as they walk, they embody and invoke the great bear mother. Their silent prayers should be to her as their guide and protector.

After dancing into the energy of the goddess, center again in silence and envision the world as a young woman being pursued by an attacker bent on violence. For that is, indeed, the situation of wild spaces today. No matter how vast and magnificent they may seem, ecological systems are fragile, easy to destroy. Imagine the goddess reaching into her quiver, drawing an arrow, and placing it carefully in her bow. Imagine her drawing back on the taut bowstring and aiming.

Then stop to examine what part of your life Artemis might target in this way. For while it is easy to blame corporations for the degradation of the rainforest, there would be no profit in such exploitation if we were not such willing customers. Notice what parts of your life most damage the wild spaces where Artemis lives, and make a solemn pledge to the goddess that you will correct your deficiencies. Imagine her slowly releasing her grip on the bowstring, staring into your eyes as she does so, and letting you go to correct your deficiencies. Articulate that promise verbally to the group, calling on them to witness your intention to make the world a safer place for the goddess of wilderness. Then, when the ritual is over, keep your pledge—for Artemis is not a goddess you wish to find angry at you.

Questions and Activities

1. Using crayons, color an image of yourself in childhood. If you had a pet name at that time, sign your artwork with that name. What energies do you remember from that period of your life? What were your hobbies? What did you like to do?

2. What were the circumstances of childhood's ending for you? What experiences were significant as you moved from child to young adult? What was gained—and what was lost?

3. Draw a crayon picture of the house where you spent your childhood. What positive and negative memories are associated with it?

4. Make a list of your childhood friends and/or your siblings. What qualities do you remember for each of them?

5. Make a list of your childhood teachers. What do you remember of school and your performance there? What messages about your own performance did your teachers give you?

6. Write a "table of contents" for the book of your childhood. Give each year, or each important experience, a title. What does your book show about this period of your life?

7. Examine your relationships with children today. When and where do you spend time with them? What feelings are evoked by spending time with children? If you do not spend time with children, what does this mean for you?

8. If you have borne a child or children, what do you remember about the birth? In what way did you experience it as a spiritual event? Were there circumstances that kept you from attaining that awareness?

9. If you have not borne a child, what are your feelings about how people speak to you about that fact? Do you feel pressure, shame, support? What do you wish people would offer you?

10. If you were a child again right now, what would you most want? What is stopping you from giving it to yourself?

Demeter & Persephone

Initiation

I am one of those who serve the goddess.
Here is my proof:
I have eaten from her drum.
I have carried her sacred objects.
I have prayed in her secret chamber.

1

When grief strikes a mother,
there is no end to it.
The earth parches, its
glittering waters gone.
Everything is barren. Cattle starve
for lack of grain. Nothing grows.
Even the gods are destitute,
even the altar flames blow out.
Such is a mother's grief, bitter
and endless, for her lost child.

2

I am one of those who serve the goddess.
Here is my proof:
I have eaten from her drum.
I have drunk water, mixed with
barley meal and pennyroyal.
I have carried her sacred objects.
I have prayed in her secret chamber.

~

Myth and Meaning of Demeter & Persephone

Once the flowerlike Persephone, earth's loveliest daughter, disappeared—stolen away by the king of the underworld. Unable to find her precious child, the great goddess Demeter searched, weeping, through the fields, crying for the daughter who was so dear as to seem her very self, her childhood, her gentle youth.

She searched everywhere, asking all the gods, all the nymphs, all the powers of air and sky. But no one had seen where Persephone had gone. Demeter fretfully clutched her blue-green cloak, then thoughtlessly shredded it into tiny pieces, scattering them as cornflowers in the grass. But flowers and grasses soon faded, for Demeter was the source of all growth. As she mourned, the goddess withdrew her energy from the plants, which began to wilt and shrivel. So, it was said, Chloe ("green one"), the happy earth, changed for the first time into the yellow-gold, autumnal Demeter.

The goddess wandered through the dying earth until she came to a town near Athens. There she took a job as nursemaid to the queen of Eleusis, Metanira, whose son Triptolemos she decided to make immortal by smoking him like a log in the fireplace. The queen discovered her at this project, and the disguised goddess—explaining herself and her magical powers—was revealed. Demeter stayed on in Eleusis, often sitting sadly by a well as she wept for the loss of her beloved daughter.

One day the queen's daughter Baubo saw the sad goddess at the well and tried to comfort her. Demeter refused all her consoling words and so, to make the goddess smile, Baubo exposed her vulva salaciously. Surprised, Demeter chuckled, the first laughter the starving earth had heard from its goddess in many months.

Shortly afterward, Persephone was restored to her mother, though not forever. Hades, lord of the underworld, had kidnapped the fair girl, stealing her from the meadow where she had been picking narcissus with her maidens. No one had been able to find her, because Hades's realm was hidden even from the sun. Finally, the magician Hecate expressed suspicions, and Zeus—supporting his brother-god's desire for the girl but fearful of what would happen to the gods if humanity died from starvation—found a way to satisfy both Hades and Demeter. Persephone could return to Demeter, he said, but only if she had not eaten any of the foods of the underworld. Just before returning the maiden, Hades pressed six pomegranate seeds into Persephone's mouth so that, when asked, the girl had to confess to swallowing those tiny blood-red seeds. Thereafter, Persephone stayed half the year with her mother and the other half ruling with Hades as queen of the underworld.

This Greek story is one of the most famous and most beautiful of all the ancient myths. We hear the power of its sadness in the first invocation, from the Homeric Hymn to Demeter. And we hear as well the great power it held over those initiated into Demeter's secret rites, the Eleusinian Mysteries. These ritual mysteries are reverently enacted by people on the goddess path today, who use as a pledge to each other the second invocation, words that the third-century scholar Clement of Alexandria ascribed to participants in the rites of the mother goddess Cybele.

Greeks and foreigners alike were initiated into the mysteries for more than a thousand years. Sworn to secrecy about what they witnessed, these initiates kept that promise. Not a single word was ever written by someone who had worshiped in the sacred precincts of the mother and her daughter. We know the dates of the events, and the preliminary parts of the ritual, performed in public view. But of the initiation itself, held by torchlight in the goddess's temple, we know nothing. This is nothing short of astonishing, for at least a million people underwent the initiation ceremony. How sacred it must have been for the secrecy to have been so profound over so many centuries!

Symbols of Demeter & Persephone

Demeter and Persephone are often described as a dyad, an inseparable couple. Nonetheless, they have quite different symbols associated with them. For Demeter, grain is the most important symbol, for she is goddess of the plants that feed us. Because of her connection with growth, Demeter was always worshiped in fireless sacrifices, demanding all offerings in their natural state. Honeycombs, unspun wool, unpressed grapes, and uncooked grain were laid on her altars. Not for her the offerings of wine, mead, cakes, and cloth, for Demeter was the principle of natural, rather than artificial, production.

Only one animal is associated with Demeter, and that is the pig. Pigs were sacrificed to her, and barley cakes in the shape of pigs. Pigs were washed in the ocean as part of the initiation process; they symbolized the goddess on coins from Eleusis. Today we are inclined to view the pig in a negative way, as an emblem of excess and filth. (That, despite discrimination on the basis of species, Miss Piggy has become a film star is a testimony to her personal drive and indubitable charm.) To the ancients, the pig was a gifted creature, almost miraculously fecund, able to sustain itself on an extraordinarily varied diet. It was able to digest evil itself, so it was an excellent choice for sacrifice; anything impure within us could be channeled into the pig and, when the animal was sacrificed, would be eliminated. Then, when sacrificed and cooked, the pig made a succulent meal—transforming all that was negative into positive energy.

As for Persephone, one symbol is most deeply associated with her: the pomegranate. That many-seeded plant, a few bites of which separated Persephone from her mother for half the year, is an image of the ovum, clustered in their sacs within a woman's body. Opening the seedpod of the pomegranate, Persephone permitted herself to become a fertile woman. Thus the pomegranate reminds us that, to become a woman herself, Persephone has to separate from her mother, no matter how difficult that break may be on both sides.

Feasts of Demeter & Persephone

The greatest festival of the ancient world was the celebration of Demeter and Persephone at Eleusis. There, annual mysteries brought the initiate into a gracious and grateful relationship to the goddess. At the three-day event, the *mystai* (initiates) imitated the searching Demeter and rejoiced as, once again, she was reunited with her daughter. In their mimicry, they were at first Demeter Eryines ("angry"), furious and sad at the loss of Persephone; then they acted the happy role of Demeter Louisa ("kindly one"), the mother transformed by reunion.

The festival began on February 26, when the Lesser Mysteries were held. At this point, those who would receive initiation six months later began their purification. Held at Agrae, these rites required that the candidate be rubbed with ashes and plunged into the sea. The group then attired themselves in new clothes and marched together by candlelight, begging for the blessing of the goddesses.

The full festival of Eleusis was held at the autumnal equinox, approximately September 21. A series of rituals was held over the seven days dedicated to the event, each day having a special name: the Day of Assembly; Initiates to the Sea; Now Come the Pig Victims; Purification; Torch Day; Holy Night; and the Pourings of Plenty. The names of the days indicate what occurred on them. The initiates assembled with those who would conduct the initiations, in a great gathering in the famous Agora of Athens. The next day, they marched to the sea near Athens, where they, and the pigs who would be sacrificed to help purify them, were cleansed ritually in the ocean. On the third day, sacrifices on behalf of the city and the initiates were held, then another day of preparatory instruction was held before the final acts of the initiatory drama.

That drama took several days. First, the initiates walked to Eleusis, bearing torches and singing as they marched. Together with priestesses and priests, dignitaries and sponsors, the parade of the torch-bearing initiates must have been huge and impressive. At a special bridge called the Kephisos, participants recalled Baubo's outrageous behavior by hurling insults and degrading comments at the most important citizens in the parade, causing raucous laughter like that which had erupted from Demeter's throat.

The most secret part of the ritual was the Holy Night. We know little of what occurred once the initiates were taken into the temple and the secrets of the religion were revealed to them—secrets that have never been revealed outside that hall. Fasting, exhausted from the long march to Eleusis, the initiates were in a receptive state to receive the transformation they were offered. Finally, the last day involved ritual pourings of water onto the fields, probably to magically encourage rain to fall and germinate the winter seeds.

In addition to the mysteries, several other festivals to Demeter and Persephone occur in the Greek calendar. A minor festival, held on the full moon in June, noted the time when Persephone was abducted. Called the Skiraphoria, it entailed a procession, a ritual plowing, the sacrifice of piglets, and the ritual eating of garlic. On the October full moon, the Strenia was celebrated, an all-women's rite that involved dancing in the moon's light on the seashore. At approximately the same time, the Thesmophoria called for the goddess, under the name of Demeter Thesmophorus, to help the crops to grow; suckling pigs were sacrificed by being tossed into chasms in the earth, and the remains of last year's offerings were brought up (fully composted, one imagines) to mix with seeds for the planting. Finally, on the dark of the moon in January, the Haloa festival was a great feast prepared by men and eaten by women, at which pomegranates were barred from the table.

In Rome, where Demeter was associated with the grain goddess Ceres, her festival was called the Ceralia. Celebrated each spring, during the week of April 13, the festival's high point was a torchlight dance through the fields, with farmers leaping as high as they hoped their grain would grow.

Suggestions for Invoking Demeter & Persephone

Of all the great rituals of the ancient world, none was so fervently celebrated as the Eleusinian Mysteries. Nor is there any that holds such magic for those following the goddess path today. A ritual held for a thousand years, with a million initiates, about which we know virtually nothing—who today would not wish for the power to travel back to those days, to wash in the sea with the other initiates, to travel by torchlight the path of the goddess herself, to see the great secret of the inner chamber?

But what would be the good of just seeing the secrets? Initiation into the Eleusinian Mysteries was a process, one that began when the worshiper became aware of the goddess's power, proceeded through months or years of instruction, and continued long after the Holy Night. The moment of initiation was just that: a moment, more dramatic than others that preceded or followed it, but a moment nonetheless. The moment of revelation was a station on the journey to the goddess; it was not the journey itself.

And, although it is easy to focus on the mysterious secrets revealed in the inner chamber, that was never the real point of initiation. The real secret was the transformation of the hearts of the initiates. Something happened to them when they entered that secret chamber. When they emerged, they were different. Centuries of initiates attested to that. They knew they had gained some inner wisdom that could not be gained in any other way.

But just seeing what they saw would not create the same dramatic and life-changing effect for us today. We do not hear the myths of the goddess as children, we do not work her dark soil each day, we do not sacrifice to her each year, we do not honor her in citywide rituals. Seeing the symbols of the goddess in a torch-lit temple would be an exotic rite, not something rooted in every moment of our lives.

There has been a great deal of speculation about what the initiates might have experienced on the Holy Night, speculation that ranges from an altered state induced by drugs to delusions caused by simple circus tricks. What seems most convincing, in light of the myth that authorizes the Mysteries, is that the worshipers experienced some deep connection between themselves and the goddess. One commonly expressed belief is that the initiates, after great preparation, were shown a simple stalk of grain. The truth about life and death then flooded the initiate's consciousness so that she or he was forever changed.

That is the point of initiation: to move an individual to a newer, higher state of consciousness by the manipulation of sensory images. A successful ritual, it could be said, is much like a dream—full of deep meaning cloaked in vivid symbols. Verbal explanation is not the point of initiation, for initiation is not instruction. It is direct experience, and it changes lives.

Much has been written about the lack, in our culture, of acknowledged initiation rituals. Most cultures have some formal way to mark the movement between girlhood and womanhood, for instance, or between boyhood and manhood. On the spiritual plane, such sacraments as baptism and confirmation serve to locate the individual's progress along the pathway of life.

But for those who follow the goddess path, what initiation is appropriate? This is a question that should be considered seriously. There are many groups and individuals who will offer to provide initiatory services for you—often for a surprisingly high fee. And, if you put sufficient emotional and spiritual intensity into the process, you may indeed find yourself transformed.

But no one can truly initiate you. Ultimately, you must initiate yourself. You must hold yourself open for change and awareness. To the open heart, any experience can be an initiation. To the unprepared or critical or close-minded, no initiation is possible, no matter how big the cashier's check.

Thus, if you seek initiation as part of your progress along the goddess path, you may want to create your own initiatory ritual rather than accepting another's. If you do, the great Mysteries of Eleusis can serve as a template for designing it. Those Mysteries break down into several parts: preparation; assembly; movement toward the goal; a darkening or testing; the revelation; thanksgiving; and petition. Using this model, you can create your own initiation rite, one suited to your own beliefs about the goddess.

Preparation is extremely important, for initiation favors the prepared mind. Recall that, in addition to study and increased awareness, the Eleusinian initiates ritually expressed their intention to move into greater connection with the goddess many months before it happened. They did so bathing in the sea (washing off the old life) and donning new clothes (taking on a new identity). This is typical of a preparatory ritual, one sending a message to the deepest parts of the self that change is imminent. To begin to move toward initiation, you should make some changes in your life, ones that symbolize to your deepest self your intention to become more focused on the goddess path.

The first act of the initiation proper is the assembly. To be effective, an initiation should involve some break with the outer world, the world of ordinary reality. If you are going through a group initiation, consider staying overnight together; or, if you are initiating yourself solo, go away from your familiar places for the rite. Select appropriate activities that prepare for the complex changes to follow. Readings, creative work, dance: all these are more appropriate to create the initiatory mood than a night of television and junk food.

Next comes purification and sacrifice. To move into a new spiritual dimension, it is necessary to give up bad habits; that seems almost ridiculously obvious. But beyond purification is the additional need for sacrifice—giving up something that is not necessarily bad. Those piglets who were washed in the sea and then killed were not, of themselves, negative beings. But the great tradition of initiation requires that we give up something valuable to move closer to something even more valuable. Most of us find it easier to pledge to purify ourselves than to truly make a sacrifice. Consider carefully what you wish to purify and what to sacrifice, and create symbolic representations of them to burn or otherwise destroy at this point in your initiation.

Initiation must be earned. It is important to tell the deep self that this journey to the goddess is a difficult one. A seventeen-mile hike and a bath in frigid water, such as the Eleusinian initiates endured, is more than most today could handle. But you must create some relatively arduous journey for those seeking closeness to the goddess. And this journey must be physical, not merely mental. This prepares the body-mind to receive the information given through the initiatory process. Walking is of course the best possible image of the journey, but more stationary activities such as yoga or dance could suffice as well.

After the journey, some additional physical test must be endured. It is thought that the initiates might have been kept up all night so that, when they witnessed the actual initiation, they were dizzy from sleep deprivation. Again, the point of this is not to be arbitrarily difficult. Initiation is not a series of hoops to jump through. Parts of the self resist change, and must be awakened to the self's desire for such change. Thus some additional physical stress must be applied at this point. Fasting is a traditional and effective mechanism for attaining a receptive inner state; so is the holding of difficult physical poses, as in meditative practices that require sitting upright for many hours. Deliberate infliction of physical pain, used in many cultures to move to the next initiatory state, may be too fraught with negative connotations for most women and thus should probably be avoided.

It should be obvious, as we discuss initiation in this fashion, that it is extremely difficult to truly initiate oneself. How can you both orchestrate such an event and engage in it? While possible, it is clearly very difficult. The vision quest, used by many native American peoples to mark the boundary between childhood and adulthood, is a form of self-initiation. Great physical testing—nights in the open air, lack of food, continued meditation—prepared the mind and soul for the message that came, mystically, when the tests had been endured.

Like the power animal that reveals itself to the vision quester, revelation comes after the initiate has been tested and has endured. It is, rather ironically, not especially important what the revelation is, because whatever is shown to the initiate will be seen with new eyes, understood with a new heart. Handing a stick of wood to a thoroughly ready initiate can result in a deep and massive shift of consciousness, for the initiate will suddenly see the deepest meaning in that object. The revelation should symbolically convey the great truths that the initiate desires to incorporate into her essence. But that symbol need not be a complicated one; indeed, the plainer, the better.

After this moment of revelation, the initiate will need time to recover, to incorporate and ground the revelation. This is time for meditation and for silent worship. When sufficient time has passed, a final set of ritual motions are in order: ones that acknowledge thankfully the revelation that has been received, and prayers of petition for the betterment of the world. With these final acts, the drama of initiation closes, leaving the transformed person ready to re-embark on daily life.

This pattern of preparation, testing, revelation, and recovery is an ancient one, one that can be traced in many other cultures than the Greek. Using this model, you can design an initiation ceremony that expresses your desire to attain greater connection with the goddess. Initiation is by no means a necessary part of the goddess path. An initiation ceremony does not make you better than someone who has not undergone such a ritual. But it can be a deeply meaningful experience. The great Mysteries of Eleusis will never be celebrated as they were, but the transformation of minds and hearts continues even today.

∾

Questions and Activities

1. Explore your earlier religious experiences. In what ways did you experience an initiation rite? How did it change you?

2. Initiation rituals are used in many non-religious contexts. What other initiation rituals (such as graduation) have you experienced? How did you feel? Did it change you?

3. Some important transformations in our lives pass without ceremony. What are some of these for you? What ceremony would have seemed appropriate?

4. Make a list of images that express the goddess for you. If possible, draw or otherwise create artwork from one of them. Explore, in words, why this image expresses feminine divinity for you.

5. Examine your history with groups of women. Have you experienced being scapegoated or outcast in any way? How does this affect your ability to interact with women in a spiritual setting?

6. Examine your relations with your mother. What are you still withholding from her, or lying about to her? What effect does your relationship to your mother, past or present, have on your relationship with other women?

7. If you have a daughter or daughters, explore your relationship with them. Do you hold them back when they are ready to move on, or have you supported their movement? If there are difficulties between you, how can you begin to resolve them?

8. What mother-surrogates have you brought into your life? What aspects of mothering do they represent for you? Have you let them know how important they are to you?

9. What daughter-surrogates have you brought into your life? How have you assisted them in being strong and vital within your relationship?

10. What aspects of your own mother do you find in your image of the goddess?

Inanna

Inner Strength

Is there a god who can conquer me?
The gods are sparrows, I am a hawk
The gods trudge along like oxen
I am a splendid wild cow!

1

Before she descended,
she took all her ornaments
of power, the seven
symbols of her queenship:
she put on her head
the desert crown,
put tiny lapis beads
around her neck
and longer lapis beads,
dark and sleek,
fell to her breast
where two perfect
oval jewels made
a bewitching breastplate;
took in her hand
the measuring rod
and the measuring line,
put on her wrist
the golden ring.
Shadowing her eyes
with seductive kohl,
drawing over her shoulders
the robe of heaven,
the goddess Inanna
began her journey, began
her descent into hell.

2

Heaven is mine, the earth is mine
I am a warrior am I

Is there a god who can conquer me?
The gods are sparrows, I am a hawk

The gods trudge along like oxen
I am a splendid wild cow!

~

Myth and Meaning of Inanna

From the ancient lands of the eastern Mediterranean comes one of the most glorious of all goddess myths. Captured in prayers and invocations like those opposite, the story of the descent of the goddess Inanna to the underworld has deep resonance and meaning for women today, more than 3000 years since it was composed.

Inanna, the goddess who dared to explore the realm of death, was the primary goddess of ancient Sumeria, in the area we now call Iraq. Goddess of heaven and earth, of sovereignty and fertility, she was the mother of human culture, one who brought civilization to this world.

Here is how it happened, according to the ancient myths of the Sumerians: across the immeasurable distances of the sweet-water abyss lived Enki, god of wisdom, and with him were the Tablets of Destiny and other magic civilizing implements. These were his treasures, which he kept away from humankind. But Inanna, crafty queen of heaven, took pity on the miserable primitives of earth and fitted her boat to travel to her father's hall. There she was grandly welcomed with a banquet of food and wine. Wise he may have been, but Enki loved his daughter beyond wisdom, so much that he took cup after cup from her at the table and then, drunk, promised her anything she desired. Instantly Inanna asked for the Tablets of Destiny and a hundred other objects of culture.

What could a fond father do but grant the request?

Inanna immediately loaded the objects onto the boat of heaven and set sail for her city, Erech. Awakening the next day from his stupor, Enki remembered what he had done—and regretted it. But he was incapacitated by a hangover as massive as the previous evening's pleasure, and he could not pursue his daughter until he recovered. By then, Inanna had gained the safety of her kingdom, and even the seven tricks Enki played on her did not regain his treasures.

This myth shows Inanna in typical form—wily and wise and willful, brave almost to foolhardiness, devoted to her human children. She is casually powerful, queenly but far from remote. She is also adventurous, as the central myth told of Inanna reveals.

It started long ago, when the lovely queen of heaven had two suitors, the farmer Enkidu and the shepherd Dumuzi. Both brought her gifts; both wooed her with flattery. Her brother urged the farmer's suit, but the soft woolens that Dumuzi brought tipped the scales of Inanna's heart. And so Dumuzi became the goddess's favorite consort.

It was not long before Dumuzi grew arrogant, assuming that his position came from his own worth, rather than the goddess's desire. He grew restless as a mere consort and began to imagine himself as king in his own right.

Dumuzi's opportunity came when Inanna decided on a bold adventure: to visit the land of the dead, where her sister goddess Erishkigel ruled. No one had ever done this before, but Inanna was unafraid. She knew, however, the danger of her quest. And so she arranged with her prime minister, Ninshuba, that if she did not return within three days and three nights, he would stage mourning ceremonies and would appeal to the highest deities to rescue her. And then Inanna began her descent.

At the first of the seven gates of the underworld, the goddess was stopped by the gatekeeper, Neti, who demanded one of her symbols of sovereignty, the magical ornaments with which she had hoped to protect herself. So it was at each gate. Piece by piece, Inanna gave up her jewelry and clothing until she stood splendid and naked before Erishkigel, the black-haired goddess of death, who turned her eyes of stone on the goddess from the upper world.

At that Inanna lost all life and hung for three days and three nights, a corpse in the realm of death. When Inanna failed to return to her sky kingdom, Ninshuba did as instructed. Enki, the goddess's father, came to her aid. Fashioning two strange creatures, Kurgurra and Kalaturra, from the dirt beneath his fingernails, he sent them into the wilderness of the afterlife with food and water to revive the lifeless Inanna.

But no one can leave the underworld unless a substitute is found to hang forever naked in the land of doom. And so demons followed the goddess as she ascended to her kingdom. One after another, the demons grabbed those they met. Each in turn Inanna freed, remembering good deeds they had performed for her. But when Inanna reached her holy city, Erech, she found that her paramour Dumuzi had set himself up as ruler in her stead. Angered at his presumption, the goddess commanded that he be taken as her substitute to Erishkigel's kingdom. Luckily for Dumuzi, his loving sister Gestinanna followed him to the underworld and won from Erishkigel her brother's life for half each year—the half of the year when the desert plants flower, for Dumuzi was the god of vegetation.

In some versions of the tale it was Inanna herself, not Gestinanna, who freed Dumuzi. But Gestinanna's name incorporates that of the other goddess, and Inanna herself was sometimes said to be Dumuzi's mother, while Ninsun claimed that role in other versions. All these apparent contradictions cease to be problematical, however, if one extends the "three persons in one god" concept to this trinity of Sumerian divinities. Then we see that the mother, the lover, and the sister were all aspects of a single grand figure: the queen of heaven, who ruled all life beneath her.

Symbols of Inanna

In one of the great myths of Inanna, the goddess plants a garden, in the center of which she places a huluppu, a sacred tree. In a waking dream, as she awaits her lover, she sees a threatening snake coiled around the tree, from which her hero Gilgamesh (a kind of Sumerian Hercules) frees her. As this myth arose in the same area as the familiar story of the Garden of Eden, it is highly likely that the serpent-and-tree motif preceded Adam and Eve—and that the garden was originally the domain of the goddess, not of the sky god. Thus living plants, especially boughs of trees, stand as symbols for Inanna.

Seven different symbols, called the seven me, are described as representing Inanna's sovereign power: the Shugurra, the desert crown; measuring instruments; two necklaces, one long and one short; a magical breastplate; a golden ring or bracelet; and the robe of heaven. Seven was a magical number in ancient Sumeria; Inanna had seven cities and seven temples. The exact objects may not have been the source of power, but rather their number. Thus the number seven is considered sacred to Inanna.

Finally, a symbol often associated with Inanna is the star. As queen of heaven, she appears in both the morning and the evening star, which comfort her children and remind them of her love. In the morning, Inanna brings light to all our mundane tasks (remember that her symbols of power include measuring instruments), while in the evening she brings us the soft prospects of love. In her stellar aspect, then, she is both a guide and a protector.

Feasts of Inanna

Because she was Sumer's primary goddess, the entire annual ritual cycle of that ancient city was dedicated to her. On the first day of each year, the goddess was invoked with thanksgiving for bringing new life to the earth. Throughout the year, plants and other offerings were bestowed on the goddess, in recognition of her assistance in making the crops productive. Finally, in the autumn, when the next year's seeds were to be planted, the most important of the year's rituals was celebrated. Preparing a luxurious bed and covering it with fragrant plants, the people urged their goddess to descend to earth and mate with her consort, Dumuzi. This would insure that vitality would be seeded again within the earth and that the next year's harvest would be plentiful. It is not known whether priestesses took the part of the goddess in a living reenactment of this ritual, although that suggestion is often made. Thus a ritual to Inanna could be staged at any time and find resonance with her ancient ways of worship.

Suggestions for Invoking Inanna

Every woman will feel, at some time in her life, as though life has become a living hell, as though she has fallen into the grasp of Erishkigel, the ruthless naked queen who tears everything from us. There are periods when it seems as though we're being stripped of everything that makes life bearable. Your mother dies, then you lose your job, then your child crashes your only car, then your refrigerator self-destructs, then your partner falls in love with someone else.

Doesn't it seem as though when one major problem confronts you, another six are just waiting, like Erishkigel's demons, to pounce on you?

Inanna's descent is a vivid metaphor for the experience of being stripped to our essence by life. Every life offers such an underworld descent—with luck, only one, although some find themselves experiencing this drastic reshuffling of the deck of life more frequently. We're not referring, here, to those minor periods of chaos that occur regularly, when centripetal force seems to strike all household appliances and every minor object that can fail, does. Such periods are annoying, but they don't tear us down to bedrock. They don't hang us naked on a hook in the center of hell.

No, Inanna's descent is more than dysfunctional computers and lost address books. It's an existential crisis, a complete breakdown in the structures that have held our lives together. It asks us to discover what we are, once everything we thought we were is gone. Divorce, death, bankruptcy, cancer, AIDS and other illnesses, fire and flood—these crises test our inner strength, leading us to greater self-knowledge in the process.

If we are lucky, if we are blessed, we survive. Like Inanna, we give up the outer symbols of our strength and emerge again, our inner strength intact.

The invocation of Inanna need not wait for such crucial times. An autumn ritual of conscious stripping back to basics, for instance, can be spiritually effective because it is in keeping with the year's cycle. But in times of enormous pain, Inanna's story takes on vital and important meaning. To celebrate her descent and her return at such points can be an illuminating and greatly nurturing experience.

To invoke and enact Inanna's return, begin by asking others to join you. Pain and emotional suffering are isolating enough; you don't need to endure more separation. You will need at least two other people, to enact the roles of Erishkigel and Enki. Others can, if they wish, serve as hell's demons or as saving messengers.

Determine what objects will symbolize your losses. A photograph of yourself, beaming in the unconscious exuberance of good health, can sufficiently represent its loss. Try to focus on yourself, not on others; thus if you have been divorced or widowed, a ring is a more appropriate symbol than a picture of the lost partner, for what you have lost is not only a person but a part of your identity. Select items that have symbolic resonance and express the best features of what you have lost. Sometimes selecting such symbols can be difficult, if for instance a terminated relationship was difficult. But a whisky bottle to symbolize a deceased alcoholic parent doesn't indicate your inner loss; look for something expressing the most positive part of the connection. If the ritual is to focus on a single loss, find several symbols that represent aspects of it: a bike map for limited mobility, a newspaper calender for cultural activities you'll miss. If the ritual focuses on a number of losses, use one symbol for each.

Finish this part of the preparation by selecting a shawl or other loose covering to wear; you will take it off during the ritual to represent succumbing to Inanna's final nakedness.

Prepare the setting for the ritual by shrouding the furniture, as much as possible, in dark coverings. Create an altar by draping dark cloth over a table, putting only a representation of Inanna's star in the center (the star card from a tarot deck is appropriate). Finally, lower the lights so that the room is as dark as comfortably possible.

Begin by reading the first invocation. Then pick up the symbols of power you have selected. One by one, explain their significance to those who have gathered. As you do so, place each on yourself in some way: in a pocket, around a wrist, near your heart. In this way, prepare yourself for the descent. These actions reflect your actual life situation, for you did surround yourself—empower yourself—with those relationships, objects, and positions you are now foregoing.

The person representing Erishkigel (or one of her minions) will then ask you, one at a time, for your symbolic objects. Give each one to the dark goddess, who places them in turn on the altar. Do this slowly, but in silence, experiencing fully the pain of separation and loss. When all the objects have been taken, give up the outer covering—whatever final protection you have imagined might see you through this crisis. Imagine yourself naked, stripped of everything that seemed to protect you.

A period of silence, representing the three days when Inanna hung in the death queen's palace, gives everyone at the ritual a chance to reflect on the vicissitudes of their own lives and to experience the loneliness and isolation that major changes entail. Do not rush through this break and onto the next act, for surviving when one feels that survival is impossible is part of this goddess's gift, so it is important to feel as though the silence will never end.

But then the saving creatures arrive, dispatched by Enki (if there are only a few participants, Enki himself can assist with Inanna's revival). These saviors can be representatives of the group, or everyone at once. Making gestures to free her, they break the hold of the silence and darkness, permitting Inanna to return to the upper world. The person enacting the goddess can then pantomime the long walk up from hell by traversing the room several times. (This ritual can be done on a stairway, with an altar at the top and bottom to represent Inanna's and Erishkigel's worlds respectively; the climb is literal, then, as well as symbolic.)

After the return journey, however, the sacred objects of power are left behind. And part of Inanna remains as well, for the goddess never completely returns, as the myth, with great wisdom, tells us. Her alter-ego, Gestinanna, descends to spend half of every year in darkness. Once we have experienced being totally stripped to our essence, we never become exactly the person we were before our descent. Some part of us remains naked of all but our inner power.

No one can give you power; you must seek it within yourself. Thus the last part of the ritual is reinforcement of your awareness of this power. Pick up the symbol of Inanna's star from the altar; if it is a piece of jewelry, put it on, otherwise hold it tightly. This is what you are left with, when everything else is gone: this symbol of inner strength and courage. It is, you will find, all you really need.

It is a new Inanna—a new you—who emerges from the underworld journey. Stripped once to the essential self, no one can ever again believe so strongly in anything beyond it. Thus, though her initiation is a painful one, the gift Inanna gives us is magnificent. As the ritual ends, bring the lights up in the room and read the second invocation above, in which Inanna expresses her inner power. And believe that, because you have survived the descent, you can survive as well the ascent to renewed life.

∾

Questions and Activities

1. What experiences have you had that resemble a descent to the underworld? What were you forced to give up?

2. When you feel grief, what does it feel like? How do you recognize it?

3. Make a list of what you have lost and can never recover. How do you feel about these experiences of loss? How did you cope?

4. Among your friends and loved ones, there are people who have undergone or are undergoing periods of loss. How do you feel when you are with them? How do you support them? What fears do you have when you think of them?

5. Write down the following words: pain, loss, grief, sorrow, sadness. How would you express the differences among them?

6. If you were to make a gesture for each of the words above, what would that gesture look like? Where is sorrow, for instance, experienced in your body?

7. Unexpressed pain and grief sometimes cause physical symptoms and pain. Are there any such pains you believe might result from loss and grief?

8. Anger is often a part of the grieving process. Are there people you find yourself angry at, who in some way represent a loss you have experienced?

9. It is common to speak of descent experiences in terms of learning. In considering what you have lost, can you express what you have learned from the loss?

10. What strengths have you found in yourself that assist you in enduring life's inevitable pains and losses?

Isis

Restorative Love

Cease your tears now, for I have come to help you.
I looked down and saw the sorrows of your life.
All things will soon change for you, as under my watchful light
your life is restored, renewed.

1

Because of Isis, there is a heaven.
Because of Isis, there is an earth.

Because of Isis, winds blow on the desert.
Because of Isis, the sweet sun shines.

Because of Isis, the river floods in spring.
Because of Isis, plants bear fruit.

Because of Isis, we live and grow strong.
Because of Isis, we have breath to give thanks.

2

I have come, my child, in answer to your prayer.
I am Nature, mother of all, mistress of elements,
daughter of time. I control the realms of spirit,
I am sovereign of death, I am queen of the immortals.
I am all gods and goddesses at once.

By a gesture I command the shining vault of sky, the gentle
breezes of the sea, even the dark silence of the underworld.
I am worshiped everywhere. Each nation has its own name
for me, seeing only one of my aspects, knowing only one of my
myths, worshiping me with only one of my possible rites.
In ancient Phrygia I am Pessinunica, mother of gods;
in Athens, where men are birthed from the soil itself, I am
Artemis; on the island of Cyprus I am golden Aphrodite.
The Cretan archers call me Dyctinna, the trilingual Sicilians
Proserpine, and the Eleusinians the ageless Mother of Grain.

Some call me Juno, others Bellona of the Battles, others Hecate
or Rhanumbia. But there are those who know me best,
those upon whose lands the sun shines first, and they call me
by my truest name: lady Isis, queen of the sky. Cease your tears
now, for I have come to help you. I looked down and saw the
sorrows of your life. So dry your tears now. All things will
soon change for you, as under my watchful light your life
is restored, renewed.

~

Myth and Meaning of Isis

One of the great myths of the ancient world is that of winged Isis, daughter of sky and earth, who lost her love to death but restored him once again to life. It is a story that suggests the powerfully restorative force of love. It was deeply secret, told only in the sacred silences of the desert temples. It would have been lost to us today had it not been revealed by an outsider—Plutarch, a Roman author—who did not consider himself bound by Egypt's religious tradition.

Isis was worshiped for thousands of years. Almost a millennium separates the first invocation, a prayer to Isis deciphered from hieroglyphics, from the much later statement by the goddess to her follower, the great African poet Apuleius. During those many years, the goddess's followers took great comfort in the myth that tells of how death is followed by resurrection at Isis's hands.

Isis, it was said, was born in the Nile swamps, on the first day between the first years of creation. From the beginning, Isis turned a kind eye on the people of earth, teaching women to grind corn, spin flax, and weave cloth. The goddess lived with her brother, Osiris, god of Nile waters and of the vegetation that springs up when the river floods.

Alas for Isis, her beloved was killed by their evil brother, Set. The mourning goddess cut off her hair and tore her robes to shreds, wailing in grief. Then she set forth to locate her brother's body. Eventually Isis arrived in Phoenicia, where Queen Astarte, pitying but not recognizing the pathetic goddess, hired her as nursemaid to the infant prince. Isis took good care of the child, placing him like a log in the palace fire, where the terrified mother found him smoldering. She grabbed the child from the fire, thus undoing the magic of immortality that Isis had been working on the child.

When the goddess's identity was revealed, she explained her sorrowful search. Then Astarte had her own revelation: that the fragrant tamarisk tree in the center of her palace contained the body of lost Osiris. Isis carried the tree-sheltered corpse back to Egypt for burial. But evil Set was not to be thwarted; he found the body, stole it, and dismembered it.

Isis's search began anew. This time her goal was not a single corpse, but fourteen pieces to be found and reassembled. The goddess found the arms and legs and head and torso of her beloved, but she could not find his penis. Full of assurance in her magical abilities, Isis substituted a piece of shaped gold. Then Isis invented the rites of embalming, for which the Egyptians are still famous, and applied them with magical words to the body of Osiris. The god rose, as alive as the corn after spring floods in Egypt. Isis magically conceived a child through the golden phallus of the revived Osiris: the hawk-headed god Horus.

Another tale was told of the magician Isis. Determined to have power over all the gods, she fashioned a snake and sent it to bite Ra, highest of gods. Sick and growing weaker from the serpent's attack, he called for Isis to apply her renowned curative powers to the wound. But the goddess claimed to be powerless to purge the poison unless she knew the god's secret name, his name of power, his very essence. Ra demurred and hesitated, growing ever weaker. Finally, in desperation, he was forced to whisper the word to her. Isis cured him, but Ra had paid the price of giving her eternal power over him.

When she was born in Egypt, Isis's name was Au Set (Auzit, Eset), which means "exceeding queen" or simply "spirit." But the colonizing Greeks altered its pronunciation to yield the now-familiar Isis, a name used through the generations as her worship spread from the delta of the Nile to the banks of the Rhine. Isis took on the identities of lesser goddesses until she was revered as the universal goddess, the total femininity of whom other goddesses represented only isolated aspects.

She became the Lady of Ten Thousand Names. She grew into Isis Panthea ("Isis the All-Goddess"). She was the moon and the mother of the sun; she was mourning wife and tender sister; she was the culture-bringer and health-giver. She was the "throne" and the "Goddess Fifteen." But she was everlastingly, to her fervent devotees, the blessed goddess who was herself all things and who promised, according to the great Apuleius: "You shall live in blessing, you shall live glorious in my protection; and when you have fulfilled your allotted span of life and descend to the underworld, there too you shall see me, as you see me now, shining . . . And if you show yourself obedient to my divinity . . . you will know that I alone have permitted you to extend your life beyond the time allocated you by your destiny." Isis, who overcame death to bring her lover back to life, could as readily hold off death for her faithful followers, for the all-powerful Isis alone could boast, "I will overcome Fate."

Symbols of Isis

In Egyptian artwork, Isis is easy to locate, for she wears enormous outspread wings falling from her arms so that it looks as though she could simply flap her arms to fly. Often she kneels, opening her wings protectively. These wings, which make her look quite angelic, indicate her celestial nature. For unlike many other goddesses, Isis was not connected with the earth so much as with the sky. In this winged form, she was associated with waterbirds, who migrate over water as well as rest on it. Her most sacred bird was the wild goose, whose craning neck was used as the form for the prows of boats dedicated to Isis as queen of the sea.

In her hands, the winged Isis carries an oval shape that ends in a cross—the symbol called the ankh. It is the hieroglyph meaning "life," and is thought also to represent a mirror such as are used in some of Isis's rituals. Isis, as mother of life's mysteries, is appropriately symbolized by this letter.

Feasts of Isis

The greatest festival of ancient Egypt was the Mysteries of Isis and Osiris, celebrated for a month each fall. In preparation for the Mysteries, the festival of Lamentations was held on October 3, when a priestess with the goddess's hieroglyph tattooed on her arm enacted the part of the mourning Isis. Then, from November 12–14, the Mysteries began with three days devoted to Isis's loss and quest. Each day marked a specific part of the goddess's quest for her lover: on November 12, she sought for him; on November 13, she grieved his loss; and on November 14, she found his body. Specific rituals reinforced the associations of each day.

Two midsummer festivals also celebrated Isis. Her birthday, on July 17, was called the Night of the Cradle; her mother Nut, the sky goddess, was also acknowledged on this day because "the mother gives birth to the daughter, and the daughter gives birth to the mother." The next day was also an Isian feast. Because Osiris was connected with the annual rising of the Nile River, celebrated as New Year's Day, Isis was worshiped as well. The Egyptian version of New Year's Eve was the Night of the Drop, when the grieving Isis was imagined to swell the Nile with her tears. As the Osiris festival was July 19, the evening of July 18 was the goddess's festival.

Finally, a fall festival celebrated the motherhood of Isis, who was fertile enough to be able to conceive through an artificial phallus. Woman's sexuality and fertility were the center of the feast called Opening the Bosom of Women, celebrated with appropriate orgiastic behavior on October 16. These feasts were part of religious and civic ritual for many thousands of years, from the third millennium B.C.E. to the first of the Common Era.

March 3 was celebrated as Isidis Navigatum, the Blessing of the Fleets—the feast when Isis, as ruler of the seas, opened the Mediterranean to navigation. A statue of the goddess was carried to the water, where flower-wreathed women offered her mirrors so that she could see her beauty. Priests poured milk on the sands from a pitcher shaped like Isis's breast, then sprinkled the statue with precious perfumes. As the final part of the ritual, a crewless boat, whose prow was shaped like a water-bird, was filled with spices and sent out to sea as an offering to the goddess.

A similar feast was held in Rome, where Isis was one of the most popular of the imported goddesses. She was invoked at the Sellisternia on May 31 under the title Stella Maris, star of the sea. This title was later bestowed on another imported female figure, the virgin Mary, mother of the savior Jesus; she took on several of Isis's most important titles, including Queen of Heaven. On the Sellisternia, cakes were offered to statues of the goddess, and she was invoked to keep travelers safe, especially those traveling by sea.

Suggestions for Invoking Isis

Grief, the search, and restoration: the pattern of Isis's myth is the same one that any healing must take. Whether what is lost is health, wealth, or love, first we must grieve the loss; then we must search for wholeness; and finally, after what seem to be insurmountable obstacles, we find ourselves made whole again.

For although the story shows the goddess searching for and re-membering her lover Osiris, it is in reality always ourselves whom we must make whole.

But we cannot do this until we grieve our loss. The ritual of Isis shows great wisdom in devoting as much time to the goddess's grieving as to her celebration of renewal. Grief is as intense as love; it is a kind of passion. But today we fear grief. We are cut off from death, which typically takes place in hospitals—although hospice workers are struggling to bring death back to the home where, until recently, it was mostly likely to occur. And we are similarly cut off from grief. Those experiencing it often feel that others fear witnessing their pain. And so they muffle it—thereby distancing themselves from true healing.

It is not only death, of course, that gives rise to grief. We also grieve other losses: a home lost to fire, a job terminated, a precious ring that disappears in a hotel room. And some of the most poignant times are when we must grieve the loss of a dream: an interrupted friendship, a cancelled marriage, the project that never comes to fruition. Miscarriage of a child is the quintessential such loss, for something that dies before it is truly born is especially difficult to properly mourn.

After her period of grief, the goddess enters the next phase of her cycle: the quest. Similarly, those who have experienced a loss enter a period of confusion and searching. There is a hole in one's life, once filled by what was lost. Like the goddess, the bereaved wanders, trying out this and that to ease the pain. And there will be a moment when it seems as though the quest has ended—when Isis finds the body of Osiris in the tamarisk tree. But then we will be forced to begin again, just as Isis had to do to find the dismembered Osiris. The quest of the goddess seems endless, but only through perseverance does she come at last to complete healing, the last stage of her process in the ancient Mysteries.

It is important to realize that the revived Osiris is not the same as the Osiris who died the first time, for he is as much changed as the goddess is. We cannot ever exactly replace what we have lost; there is no perfect replica of the lost love, the lost job, the lost memento. Even if we think we have found it, life will force us to accept that loss again, just as Isis is forced to lose Osiris twice in order to finally regain him. Similarly, when we too-quickly find a new lover to replace one who has left us, we're likely to lose again—to find ourselves back on the trail to wholeness, having suffered yet again.

True healing comes from accepting that whatever comes to replace what we have lost will be something new, surprising, and ultimately, the myth tells us, something better—for Isis is able to conceive a miraculous child with the revived Osiris. Through her quest for her beloved, Isis is able to create a new life. And we, too, by enacting the goddess's tragedy of loss and searching, can ultimately create a new life for ourselves.

In honor of Isis, it is appropriate to reenact her search in the same way that the ancient Egyptians did in their great Mysteries. Although such a ritual could be part of an annual cycle—marking the passage of the fall harvest time and the annual descent into darkness—it could also be used by those who are enduring a period of grief and loss. It is important to realize that this ritual will not hasten the end of the process of grieving; in fact, it may seem to make it worse, just as some medicines seem to make a condition worse before bringing about improvement. If you have been thwarting your natural need to mourn, for instance, such a ritual may take down such boundaries; grieving may be more extreme afterward. But no one can grieve forever; after grief has been exhausted (and no matter how deep that well, it will finally be emptied), the process toward healing will continue unimpeded.

Beginning the ritual by creating an altar to Isis will focus your energies on the problems to be confronted and the quest to be endured. Feathers and even entire wings of birds can symbolize the goddess, as can her ankh expressed in metal or embroidery or any other material. A rough image of the beloved Osiris can be created from a number of materials, but for this ritual it should be made of edibles: vegetables or bread are good, although other food can also be used. Arrange the objects in the form of a figure on an altar draped with dark material that recalls the starry sky that is Isis's abode and creates a somber mood for the ritual space.

The ritual should begin in darkness, with only enough light to read the first invocation above. If there is someone for whom the ritual is especially being done, let that person take the role of Isis; otherwise, each person in turn will act the part of the goddess. Begin by describing the past and acknowledging what has been lost. Paint as vivid a picture as possible. While you are doing so, pass around or focus your eyes on the image of Osiris. Try to imagine all the good things being described as contained in that symbolic representation.

Then begin to mourn the loss. In many lands, it was acknowledged that grief is sometimes so painful that it cannot be readily expressed; therefore designated mourners were chosen, usually women who wailed piteously and loudly, acting out the grief that others felt. In the same spirit, you can designate one or two of your group to act as mourners; they should, as expressively as possible, cry out the pain that loss engenders.

After this period of mourning, the goddess enters her time of searching. Binding the eyes of the one acting as Isis with a scarf, the mourners then dismember the image of Osiris, hiding the pieces around the room. In keeping with the myth, one of the pieces should be completely destroyed by being quietly eaten by those assembled. After her eyes are unbound, it is Isis's job to find the pieces of Osiris. As she finds each piece, she should return it to the altar, until the entire body of the beloved god is reassembled.

Then, in the final act of her healing, the goddess takes into herself the body of the god. In myth, this is done through intercourse; in this ritual, it done by eating. If the entire group is acknowledging loss, then all should eat; if the ritual is intended for one bereaved member, she alone should eat the body of the god. This communion between the goddess and her lost love represents the deepest form of healing, when we are able to understand that what we have lost lives on for as long as we do, absorbed within us, part of the very texture of our lives. Reflecting on this insight, read the second invocation on page 160 as the ritual concludes.

∽

Questions and Activities

1. Take a piece of paper and cover it completely with a dark color. As you do so, pay attention to your feelings. What ideas and emotions are connected with darkness for you?

2. What dark times have you experienced? How did you cope with them?

3. When you are feeling depressed or anxious, how does this feel physically to you? Explain it in terms of bodily sensations.

4. When you feel depression or anxiety looming, what do you do?

5. Are there activities or habits you have adopted in order to blot out the pain of losses you've experienced? Are there better habits you might adopt?

6. Make a list of the ten most important things in your life. Imagine how you would survive if you lost any of them.

7. What do you fear losing most? What does that fear feel like?

8. Make a list of people (fictional characters are acceptable) who have survived apparently impossible losses. What characteristics do they share?

9. What ideas or values have helped you survive dark times? Ask this question of others in your circle as well.

10. Imagine a dark cave, at the far end of which is a treasure. What does that treasure look like? Draw, paint, or write about how valuable that treasure is.

Brigid

Survival

Brigid, gold-red woman,
Brigid, flame and honeycomb,
Brigid, sun of womanhood,
Brigid, lead me home.

1

Every day, every night
that I praise the goddess,
I know I will be safe:
I shall not be chased,
I shall not be caught,
I shall not be harmed.
Fire, sun and moon
cannot burn me. Not
lake nor stream nor sea
can drown me. Fairy
arrow cannot pierce me.
I am safe, safe, safe,
singing Her praises.

2

Brigid, gold-red woman,
Brigid, flame and honeycomb,
Brigid, sun of womanhood,
Brigid, lead me home.

You are a branch in blossom.
You are a sheltering dome.
You are my bright precious freedom.
Brigid, lead me home.

∼

Myth and Meaning of Brigid

These Christian prayers address a figure who, although called a saint, is a goddess in thin disguise. Probably the clearest example of the survival of an ancient goddess into modern times is Brigid (pronounced "breed"), the great triple goddess of the Celtic Irish who was "converted" to Christianity along with her people. Although few myths are left from her earlier identity, we have many legends of the saint called Bridget. She was said to have been the daughter of a Druid (a pagan priest) and to have been baptized by St. Patrick himself. So deeply was Bridget moved by her conversion that shortly afterward she vowed to become a nun. But before she could do so, she was threatened with marriage by her unconverted father. This encouraged Bridget to perform her first miracle—a rather strange one, in which she made her eyes pop out of her head so that she was too mutilated to attract a husband. Then, putting her eyes back in their places, she wandered across Ireland with a band of nuns until she found a place to build her convent: Kildare or Kildara, the holy place of the oak, a tree sacred to the Druids. She tricked the land's original owner into donating it to the church, saying she wanted only enough land for her cloak to cover and then magically expanded her garment so that it covered miles and miles of countryside.

The disguised goddess shines right through her saintly wrapping. The Christian Bridget was given the power to appoint bishops for her area—a strange role for an abbess, made stranger by her requirement that these bishops also be practicing goldsmiths. We should not be surprised to find that the ancient Brigid was goddess of smithcraft. The Christian saint was also invoked both as a muse and as a healer, continuing the traditions of the goddess as ruler of poetry and inspiration.

Some aspects of the early goddess did not translate so readily. The Irish said that the goddess Brigid brought to humanity a number of useful things, including whistling, which she invented one night when she wanted to call her friends. And when her beloved son was killed, Brigid invented keening, the mournful song of the bereaved Irishwoman; this story draws her close to the great mother goddesses of the eastern Mediterranean and, like them, Brigid was identified with the earth herself and with the soil's fertility.

There are many charming legends of the saint who bears the goddess's name. We have no way of knowing how closely they are connected to the myths of the original goddess, but it's probable that at least the images are similar to those myths of Celtic Brigid. In one such story, Saint Bridget came in from the rain, soaked to the skin. Finding no peg on which to hang her cloak to dry, she hung it on a sunbeam, which became stiff and hard until it was no longer needed. In another, she magically restored sight to a blind companion who, on seeing the magnificent world around her, asked to be made blind again so that her soul would not be tempted from prayer by the beauties of nature. This latter story recalls the connection of the goddess Brigid to wells that were said to cure eye diseases.

Symbols of Brigid

Brigid's primary symbol is fire, for her very name means "bright arrow" or simply the "bright one." Almost into modern times, the ancient worship of the fire goddess Brigid was practiced at her sacred shrine in Kildare, where nineteen virgins tended the undying fire and where, on the twentieth day of each cycle, the fire was miraculously tended by Brigid herself. There, into the eighteenth century, the ancient song was sung to her: "Brigid, excellent woman, sudden flame, may the bright fiery sun take us to the lasting kingdom." But for more than ten centuries, the Bridget invoked was a saint rather than a goddess, and her attendants were nuns rather than priestesses. After the Christianization of Ireland in the fifth century, the shrine at Kildare became a convent where the ancient rites nonetheless continued undisturbed. Six hundred years later, the ever-burning fire was doused by Henry de Londres, archbishop of Dublin, who saw the clearly pagan meaning of the flame. For many centuries, the fire remained doused, but in 1993 the sisters of Saint Bridget, called the Brigandines, re-lit the sacred fire of Kildare and now keep it continually blazing as a symbol of healing and peace.

Water, too, is a symbol of the goddess. At Kildare, more than thirty sacred wells once gushed forth; the largest well is still in use as a healing shrine. Throughout Ireland, sacred wells are still acknowledged as sites of power, dedicated to the goddess-saint. Because of their source deep within the earth, they are thought to contain the energy of the night sun; in addition, the way water catches and traps the sun's fire shows the identity between the two. Bridget wells are like the earth's eyes, looking at the sunlight. When sunbeams sparkle in the water, the well is considered especially effective as a remedy for human eye disorders.

Finally, the eye itself is a symbol for the goddess. The shape of Brigid's straw ritual crosses resembles what is called, in other cultures, the *ojo de dios* or "eye of god." Brigid's myths are replete with references to eyes (including that improbable and rather macabre one about how she avoided marriage). And the wells that capture the sunlight like bright eyes are another variant of this ocular imagery.

Feasts of Brigid

Candlemas Day, plant beans in the clay,
Put candles and candlesticks all away.

That was the song that villagers in Wales sang to each other on February 2, the day on which winter's back was said to be broken, the day on which the goddess emerged from the underworld where she had spent her winter. (See the Cailleach for more information on her transformation.) This, the primary feast of Brigid, was called Imbolc by the Celts and was converted to Christianity as Candlemas Day. (It may be significant that this Celtic feast of the arts is also the birthday of two great Irish writers, James Joyce and James Stevens, as well as of that muse of modernity, Gertrude Stein.) One of the four feasts of the traditional Celtic ceremonial cycle, it was said to be the time when the goddess was seen, in the form of a snake, departing the hill or cave in which she had spent the winter. As she emerged, so did springtime, for which the day is sometimes called Spring's Awakening; it was also the time at which lambs were born, from which the alternative name Feast of Milk derives.

One of the popular rituals in Ireland on this feast was the procession of the "Biddy Boys," young men cross-dressed to represent the goddess. Begging pennies and treats, they asked for "something for Poor Biddy," and were rewarded by householders hoping for good luck in the next growing season. Similarly, women left out cakes for wandering Brigid and corn for her cow, so that she would remember the generous farmer and bless her fields. Alternatively, loaves of bread and ears of corn could be shared with neighbors to invoke the goddess's good will.

Another Imbolc ritual involved plaiting straw crosses from the previous year's harvest and hanging them on the front of the house. These crosses have a lozenge-shaped center and three or four rayed arms. Because Brigid was a fire goddess, her crosses protected the home from flames during the following year. Annually, the previous Brigid cross was removed and hung in the rafters—an odd gesture, for a collection of old straw ornaments in the attic seems to encourage, rather than prevent, house fires.

American folklore transformed this feast, and its emergent goddess, in a peculiar and unexpected way. Each year on February 2, the nation waits eagerly for the underworld divinity to emerge with reassurance that winter is almost over. But the goddess now appears as a rodent—specifically, in her current incarnation, as a male groundhog. Groundhog Day shows the goddess in her prophetic mode, announcing whether she will continue the reign of winter or permit spring to arrive. While it is not established how this festival is connected with the Celtic Imbolc, it appears that Brigid, goddess of survival against all odds, has become a media celebrity far from her native home, in such deep disguise that only the very alert will notice her.

Suggestions for Invoking Brigid

There is perhaps no goddess more appropriate to invoke when survival—whether physical, emotional, financial, or spiritual—is an issue. For while many goddesses have survived the destruction of their culture by cloaking themselves in new names and new legends, we know of none who have lived so long in disguise as Brigid. It is 1600 years since her worship was suppressed in her homeland, yet her wells are still visited and her name kept alive by devotees who still honor her feminine essence, even when they no longer define her as a goddess.

It is appropriate that this goddess should survive by changing herself, for in her ancient form she ruled three kinds of transformation: the transmutation of ideas into art; the forging of metal into useful objects; and the transformational energies of healing. It is similarly appropriate that we acknowledge that, for survival to occur, transformation will be necessary. Whenever we are so directly challenged by life that our very life seems at stake, we are also offered the opportunity for great change and growth.

Thus Brigid's image can be called on, and her wisdom heeded, whenever we feel threatened and overwhelmed. On the physical level, she is invoked as a healing goddess, even at the point where death seems close. She tells us that whatever happens, we will be transformed; surviving physically means we are changed deeply through the experience, while moving through the doorway of death is a transformation that will forever remain mysterious to those left behind.

When we face other life crises, we can feel as though our very life is threatened. And we often act in the reverse of Brigid's wisdom. When we face the possible end of a relationship, when our bills are higher than the tiny resources we have, when we are emotionally drained by negative working conditions—it is all too easy to cling to what we have known previously, to hope for restoration of the order we have been comfortable with. But Brigid tells us otherwise. She urges us to submit to what seems like defeat in order to continue with our life's task. This is a challenging message, one not easy to receive. Yet this goddess is firm: transformation is the only way to survive.

Invocations to Brigid are naturally most appropriate to her special feast of Imbolc, when the very world is transforming itself from winter to spring. In contemporary women's religion, this is the day for inner transformation: the day on which you dedicate yourself to the goddess path; the day on which you assume a new name; the day on which you pledge to make specific changes in your life. It could be thought of as a kind of goddess-specific New Year's Eve, a time for resolutions and rituals that move the inner self toward a greater clarity of vision.

Individual rituals to Brigid are called for when the soul is in wintry conditions and wishes to move onward to a better, warmer time. She is good to invoke after a separation or divorce, when a period of grief is ending, when there has been a financial or professional loss. She is a goddess of recovery, of moving forward like a bright arrow. It will do no good to hurry her, however, for her transformations come when she deems appropriate. Like the groundhog emerging on the goddess's feast, she will not respond to attempts to hurry her process—she may, rather, retreat until we have endured more pain. When the season is ripe for change, however, Brigid is the goddess of choice.

An altar to Brigid should be constructed using her major symbols. Shallow dishes of water that reflect the light of shining candles will symbolize the goddess. If you have a Brigid cross, or can create one, use that as part of the altar decoration, or use an ojo de dios. Arrows, should you happen to have access to some, are also appropriate decorations.

You may wish to prepare for this celebration by making some significant change in your appearance. Monks and nuns take on habits or carve tonsures in their hair when they pledge themselves to god, not only to show the outer world their intention, but to convey it as well to their receptive subconscious. Wearing new clothes, changing your hair color, getting a tattoo: all these are similar ways of announcing your willingness, to both inner and outer worlds, to undergo the process of change.

After reciting the invocation above, begin the ritual by dedicating a handful of coins for each celebrant. Change is often symbolized in dreams by the small coins we call by that name, and so a ritual to Brigid can make use of that unconscious pun. Sprinkle some of the water over the coins while invoking the power of the goddess. Then, holding the coins in your hand, pray for the change you hope to bring into your life. Acknowledge to yourself and to the goddess that change does not come without a price, and pledge that you are willing to pay that price.

Then, if you are celebrating with a group, give some of the coins to each person in the circle, while accepting their coins from them. If you are celebrating alone, take the coins with you the next time you leave the house, and find someone to give them to. Don't spend them, give them away—to homeless people, children, charities, coworkers in need of a candy bar. You wish to symbolically affirm that you are willing to give up whatever you need to in order to move out of the stagnant time you have experienced. And the goddess will hold you to it. You may need to give up cherished ideas of yourself or others, possessions to which you have been clinging, outworn friendships or loves. But letting go will free your emotional and psychic space for new ideas, new relationships. As you give away the change charged with Brigid's fiery energy, imagine seeing yourself free and vibrant, no longer burdened by your cares.

Close the ritual by reciting again the invocation to Brigid and blowing out the candles. When you leave the circle, you will enter a new world, one in which the goddess's arrows of transformation are already flying.

∾

Questions and Activities

1. Think back to the most recent difficult period you endured. What, ultimately, did you learn from the difficulties?

2. Think of a mistake you made recently. What were the consequences, and what did you learn from them?

3. When you made mistakes in your childhood, how were they dealt with? Were you punished, and if so, how? Are there ways you act now that are based on those experiences?

4. What is the worst mistake you can imagine making right now, and what do you fear would happen if you made it?

5. What is the worst mistake you have ever made? How did you manage to recover from that mistake?

6. When you have been criticized, how do you feel? How do you respond?

7. Consider the ways your mother and father criticized you. Were there specific things you were always "in trouble for"? How has your life been altered by those criticisms?

8. How critical are you of other people? How do you express that criticism?

9. When something happens that is beyond your control, do you feel it is a judgement on you? Where did you get this idea?

10. When you have suffered a loss, do you feel blamed or judged by the world in any way? If so, how can you release this feeling?

Saule & Saules Meita

Family Healing

Goddess-mother Saule
reached her hand above the river.
Her shawl, her gilt shawl,
slipping from her shoulders.

1

Saule wears silken garments,
with a silver crown,
with a silver crown,
made of gilded leaves.

Saule crosses the lake,
brilliant as tinsel,
a crown of gold on her head,
polished slippers on her feet.

Goddess-mother Saule
reached her hand above the river.
Her shawl, her gilt shawl,
slipping from her shoulders.

2

Saules Meita wears
a dress made of dew.
Saules Meita has golden
hair under a thick veil
of fog. And over the veil
is a wreath, made all
of leaves shaped like jewels.

∼

Myth and Meaning of Saule & Saules Meita

The sun goddess Saule and her star daughter, Saules Meita, are central to the mythology of Lithuania and Latvia, east of Poland on the shores of the Baltic Sea. Tender folksongs like those above, called dainas, attest to the love the Baltic peoples had for their goddesses; a million dainas have been recorded and can be found in the folkloric archives in Vilnius, capital of Lithuania. The last European regions to become Christianized, the Baltic states held to their goddess traditions into the late Middle Ages. Even afterward, everyday life was filled with small rituals—like greeting the sun as she rose each morning—that connected the Baltic people to their ancient ways.

The story of Saule and her daughter is one of sorrow and pain, as well as fierce love and deep connection. It began at the dawn of time, when Saule married the moon-man Meness. At first the marriage was happy, as they rose together and traveled the skies each day in their chariots. Their first child was the earth; after that, countless children became the stars of heaven. Among these, Saule's favorite was her daughter, Saules Meita, sometimes called Valkyrine or Austrine, the star of morning.

For eons and eons, life was happy for the sun goddess and her family. But slowly, things grew strained. The moon became moody and withdrawn. He often refused to mount the sky in his chariot in the morning, claiming he was not feeling well. But Saule, a responsible mother to her world, never missed a day of work. Each morning, she bade a tender farewell to her family, kissed her husband sweetly, and took her brown horses into the air. She had many tasks to do as she traveled: nipping too-tall trees with her silver shears so the forests would not block the sun; blowing clouds away from Lithuania so that they darkened other skies; finding lost items for her human children.

When the day ended, Saule bathed her weary steeds in the Nemunas River and hitched them to the apple tree at the end of the earth. She sat there for awhile, drawing to herself the souls of people who had died that day. Then she went to her sky palace and checked on her family. Always the happiest moment of her day was seeing the smiling face of her lovely daughter.

But one day, Saule found her palace ominously quiet. Meness was nowhere to be found, and neither was Saules Meita. The sun goddess, growing ever more anxious, searched and searched. Finally, she found the girl sitting dejectedly by a stream at the end of heaven. Saules Meita dangled one hand listlessly in the cold water of a fountain, and tears streamed from her lovely eyes. At first she refused to tell her mother what was bothering her, claiming only that she had lost a ring in the water. But finally Saule learned the bitter truth: that in her mother's absence, Saules Meita had been raped by her father.

Furious beyond words, Saule left her daughter and went to seek her husband. Without listening to his excuses, the sun goddess took a sword and slashed the moon's face—leaving marks we can still see today. Then she banished him forever from her presence. Although they once traveled side by side through the daytime sky, they have never been seen that way since. When he must be near the sun, Meness hides his face in shame, causing the moon's dark phase. Only when he is across the sky from his former wife does he dare show his entire visage.

After that tragedy, Saule lived as a single mother, raising her star children by herself. She remained as reliable as she had always been, lighting the sky for her earthly children. Life was happy again, for her daughter was once again safe.

As for Saules Meita, she lived a normal girlish life again: getting in trouble for running off to Germany when she was supposed to sweep the sky in Lithuania, objecting to being forced to do so many household chores, arguing with her star sisters. Later, she was courted by the twin sons of god, who rescued her from drowning in the sea and found her ring when she dropped it again in the fountain. The dainas suggest that Saules Meita will grow up to become the sun herself, when her mother Saule finally retires from the job.

Other myths from other lands deal with the question of incest, but none is as powerful in its depiction of a mother's pain in witnessing her daughter's anguish, nor are any so stern in the immediate punishment of the guilty father. This is an especially significant story, then, for women who have suffered from the wounding experience of incest in the family. Mothers, even if they were themselves unable to be as strong as Saule was, can embrace her image; daughters can find in the sun goddess the image of a healing maternal force in nature. Women for whom the experience of incest has not been part of their life's path can also draw strength from the bond between mother and daughter, for it is rare that any woman feels sufficiently mothered in our culture. Thus the myth of Saule and Saules Meita is one holding forth the promise of healing from family wounding and violence and indifference.

Symbols of Saule & Saules Meita

The preeminent symbol for the feminine in Baltic culture is that golden jewel, amber. Even in the United States, Lithuanian and Latvian women treasure their magnificent amber jewelry and wear it with pride on special occasions. Few remember the old tales, the ones that tell how the first amber was formed from the tears of Saule as she wept over her daughter's rape. But they recognize that amber represents the strength and the power of the Baltic feminine.

Most of the amber in the world—and, arguably, all the best amber—comes from a relatively small area along the Baltic coast. There, vast pine forests sank beneath the ocean in some long-forgotten cataclysm. Like coal, amber is formed by the pressure of the earth against an organic substance—in this case, the resinous sap of those ancient trees. Sometimes tiny leaves and insects that happened to be trapped in the resin when the forests were drowned are visible, captured forever in the honey-toned jewel.

How apt this process is as a symbol for memory! Memory traps fragments of the past in its sticky resin. And how appropriate, too, that amber should be the symbol of the sun goddess and her daughter. For recovery from family violence and from incest requires, first, the recovery of memory. In our bodies, as in amber, all our memories lie captive. Polishing amber lets us see all the impurities—the wings of a fly, a shred of bark, a bumblebee's leg—trapped within. Similarly, to become our most shining selves, we must first acknowledge all the damage we have experienced. Saule's amber tears are a beautiful metaphor for family healing, and gifts of amber jewelry are especially appropriate for women who have embarked on that process.

But just as Saule's myth is not limited to the story of the moon's assault on her daughter, so her symbology reaches beyond amber. Silver and red were her special colors: red forest berries were her dried tears; the tree in which she slept flowered red each morning as she rose; she was a red apple setting in the west. Or she was a silver apple falling from a tree; she sailed a silver sea, scattering silver gifts; she sowed the earth with silver; and she lived in a silver-gated castle over the hills at the world's end. On summer solstice, she danced on the hilltops wearing silver shoes. In her honor, Lithuanian women embroidered their bodices in red and wore red ribbons on their headdresses; the amber of her tears is even today mounted in silver, to connect two of Saule's most important symbols.

Saules Meita's most important symbol is the ring she lost when she was raped, and again when she was courted by the sons of god. This ring is described in the dainas as golden, so rings made of gold and set with amber are appropriate recollections of the sun's daughter. An alternative image, often encountered in the dainas, is the garland of flowers or leaves that the sun's daughter wears around her neck. Ring and garland are variations of the same archetypal symbol: the circle that signifies the virginal purity of the soul.

Feasts of Saule & Saules Meita

The primary festivals of the sun goddess are the two solstices, those days in which we experience the extremes of light and darkness. The celebrations, in Baltic tradition, were quite different, as befits a land quite far north, where summer would be filled with pearlescent sunshine and winter would be drearily dark. Summer solstice, celebrated on the feast of Ligo, was a bright neighborly feast of song and celebration; winter solstice, Kaleda, was a feast of change and renewal.

Ligo, which is held on June 24, is named from a word that means "to sway" or "to swing," apparently a reference to Saule's motion as she moves through the months. On Ligo, it was said that the sun goddess rose crowned with a braid of red blossoms to dance on the silver hills wearing silver shoes. On this festal day, Saule changed colors in the sky, hopping and jumping about like a lamb. Beneath her, people sought out streams that flowed toward sunrise in which to bathe themselves; water catching the sunrise sunbeams was thought to bring health and beauty. Women donned braided bridal wreaths—even married women who, on this day of the year, could be free in dress and behavior. Everyone walked through the fields, singing and calling down Saule's blessings on the crops, while the sun goddess sang along with them from the sky.

Finally, celebrants gathered around bonfires to sing the night away. Many of the Ligo songs are teasing jests that allowed the accumulated tensions of village life a ritual outlet. But everything ended on a note of harmony and hope when the farewell daina was sung, asking the goddess to bless the places of celebration and to make the harvest plentiful.

On the opposite feast, Kaleda, it was believed that the sun was worn out, and a new sun had to be fashioned. (This belief reinforces the idea that Saules Meita replaced her mother at the end of the latter's reign.) Kalvis, the heavenly smith, remade the sun, using a magic hammer and capturing the liquid light in a golden cup. A day after the solstice, the reborn sun rode into the sky, urging on her horses with silken whips as she rode an iron-wheeled chariot over the hilltops of dawn.

Suggestions for Invoking Saule & Saules Meita

Any woman whose history includes family violence or incest is deeply wounded—not only by the actions themselves, but by the inaction of other family members. Most wounding is the frequency with which mothers fail to defend their daughters from abuse. They may be honestly unaware of their daughter's danger. They may blind themselves to it in order to maintain a marriage or other relationship. They may be too frightened themselves to stop the abuse. Or they may even actively collude with the abuser.

Both mother and daughter are hurt by these actions and inactions that destroy the basis of the mother-daughter bond. For mothers and daughters are deeply connected by their womanhood; they experience the same biological processes as each other, so the mother sees reflected in the daughter her own earlier years, and the daughter sees her future written upon the face of her mother. Part of the experience of closeness in such relationships, however, comes from the daughter's trust that her mother will care for her and protect her as she grows and develops. The shattering of that trust is a great loss for the daughter, who has difficulty knowing when and how to trust thereafter. It is also damaging to the mother, whose sense of failure can erode her self-respect.

Incest and family violence are woefully common. Statistics vary wildly, but there is no question that millions of women in the United States today experienced a shattering of the trust between mother and daughter during their childhood. In most cases, the person responsible for the assault was close to the family—often, as in the myth of Saule, the father or father figure of the household. Thus the ancient myth of Saule and Saules Meita has unfortunately wide resonance today.

Saule, like many mothers, leaves her daughter in the company of someone she trusts. But like few mothers today, she immediately realizes the wrongness of the situation when she returns. And she acts immediately and powerfully when she learns the truth: she chooses her daughter over her husband. How many women wish they had the strength to act so strongly! How many women wish their mothers had had such strength!

Thus the myth suggests that rituals of healing from family violence and incest are appropriately dedicated to this pair of goddesses. And what better time to experience a rebirth from darkness than at the winter solstice, the year's darkest day? From the depths of an unforgiving winter of the soul, the woman seeks to be reborn into new growth and ultimately a new harvest.

Should it be necessary and possible, celebrate this ritual with the women of your family of origin. That may not, however, be possible. Healing takes place in its own time; it may not be yet appropriate to join with family members in this venture. It is possible, therefore, to create this healing space alone, or with friends who substitute for family.

An altar to Saule and her daughter can be built using red and silver and amber as the ritual colors: a red tablecloth with silver candlesticks holding amber candles, for instance. The women who wish to be healed could wear amber jewelry to connect them with the power of the feminine; silver jewelry and red garments are also appropriate. Headdresses of red ribbon can capture the ethnic flavor of the Baltic region.

Begin by invoking Saule and her daughter with the dainas above. Then, if you are creating this ritual with others, select two women who can play the parts of Saule and Saules Meita, as well as one who will serve as narrator. (It is unnecessary to cast anyone as Meness, for each person in the room will imagine the violent or violating person who played that role for them.) If you are working alone, you have the choice of playing both parts in this drama, or of selecting only one. In either case, it can be profoundly moving for women to play the part opposite from the one they have played in real life; to enact the part of the righteously angry mother, when one has never been so protected, can greatly empower a violated woman, while becoming the injured daughter will release intense emotion for the mother of such a woman.

Tell the story. Feel free to imagine details that the short tale above does not include: how many rooms were in the palace of heaven where Saule searched, how many trees lined the pathway to the fountain where Saules Meita wept. Tell the story as slowly and with as much care as you can.

As you tell the story, the chosen actors will pantomime each episode. (If you are working alone, tell the story as you act out your selected part or parts.) Do not rush through the action; let each character experience her inner reactions as she experiences the story and connects it with her own personal story.

Acting out stories may sound childish, but there is great power in embodying such goddess energy. For a mother who failed to protect her child to use her previously helpless arms to slash at the envisioned violator is an enormously moving experience for both actor and witnesses. Similarly, for the woman who lived as an unprotected daughter to feel herself held, and then see the upraised arm of her protector, or to enact that powerful rejection of violation herself—these moments can help heal the deep wound of incest and violence. The healing must go on outside the ritual, just as it doubtless began there. But if a ritual is the message from the conscious to the unconscious, just as a dream is the message from the unconscious to the conscious, then such a ritual will let the deep parts of the self begin, again, to trust that there can at last be protection from abuse—even, or especially, if one provides it oneself.

∾

Questions and Activities

1. If you believe you have experienced wounding from your family, whether incest or family violence of another sort, what support have you sought to deal with the pain?

2. Have you read books or seen movies that describe the kind of family relationship you experienced? What did they tell you about yourself?

3. How do you define forgiveness? Where did you learn that definition?

4. If you have not experienced family violence, how do you react when you encounter someone who speaks of such problems? Are you able to understand their anger and pain?

5. What does comfort feel like? How do you experience it in your body?

6. Who, today, offers you comfort and support?

7. Whom, today, do you comfort and support?

8. What ways do you offer yourself comfort when things are difficult?

9. Interview your friends. What ways do they have of comforting and supporting themselves? Are any of their ideas adaptable to your life?

10. For a week, give yourself something comforting every day. How do you feel when you treat yourself so well?

Oshun

Healing Love

Hey! She has a light step, don't she?
Hey! She dances down richness!
Call Oshun. She always say:
Live, my children, live without fear.

1

Oshun is brass and parrot
feathers in a velvet skin.
Oshun is white cowrie
shells on black buttocks.
Her eyes sparkle in the forest,
like the sun on the river.
She is the wisdom of the forest.
She is the wisdom of the river.
Where doctors fail,
she cures with fresh water.
Where medicine fails,
she cures with fresh water.
She feeds the barren woman
with honey, and her dry body
swells up like a juicy coconut.
Oh, how sweet, how sweet
is the touch of a child's hand.

2

Hey! She has a light step, don't she?
Hey! She has some fine clothes!
Hey! She dances down richness!
Look at those bracelets shake!
Her bracelets like water!
Water, like the bracelets of Oshun.
Dance when she shake those bracelets,
dance and call Oshun. She can do
what the doctor can't. She can heal
with just cold water. Call Oshun.
All her answers are wise ones.
Call Oshun. She always say:
Live, my children, live without fear.

Myth and Meaning of Oshun

When African peoples were forcibly brought from their ancient homelands to the New World, they were allowed to bring little with them. Family heirlooms, favorite clothing, prized ritual objects—these were left behind when men, women, and children were crowded onto treacherous ships on the Middle Passage.

But these newly enslaved people managed to bring something secure in their hearts and their minds and their souls: their goddesses and gods. If the ritual objects were left behind, the rituals themselves were carried, engraved on the memories of these unwilling travelers. If the sacred tools were not with them, the myths and songs were there. And so, when the boats were unloaded many weeks later in the Caribbean and the Americas, Africans set about making their divinities happy in their new homeland.

But there were already religions native to the lands where the water goddess Oshun and her friends arrived—religions of the Taino and the Cuna and other Native Americans, who had their own panoply of symbols and their own pantheons of divinities. In addition, the Christianity of the slaveholders demanded that the old gods be left behind and that only one divine story be told.

From this collision of cultures, new religions emerged, among them Santeria in Cuba, Voudoun in Haiti, Macumba in Brazil, Candomble in Bahia. The old African gods survived, merging with Catholic saints and indigenous divinities in what is called a syncretic religion. New rituals were celebrated, new symbols were employed, and sometimes new names were granted the goddesses.

Oshun was one of the goddesses who traversed the Middle Passage with her suffering children. Originally the Yoruba goddess of the river that bears her name, she is the primary divinity of Oshogbo, an African orisha religion. She is not only goddess of the river, she is the river itself.

A myth was told to describe how the goddess became a river. It happened this way: flirtatious Oshun desired the god Chango, who was already mated to the goddess Oba. So Oshun, never one to be discouraged where love was concerned, concocted a plan to steal Chango for herself.

One day, Oshun pulled a nasty trick on Oba. Claiming that Chango preferred her cooking, Oshun shared her secret: that she cut off parts of her ears and put them in the dishes. It was really only mushrooms that Oba saw floating in the soup, but they looked enough like parts of ears for the goddess to be convinced. The next time Oba cooked for Chango, she cut off a whole ear and mixed it with the food. This, alas, made the dish revoltingly foul-tasting, and Chango was even more revolted to see his mangled mate. When Oshun arrived to gloat, Oba attacked her. The two goddesses turned into rivers, and where their waters meet, there is always turbulence.

To these rivers came the ancestors of the Yoruba people. Among them was a princess who, not long after settling into her new home, took a bath in Oshun's waters and drowned. But soon after the funeral she reappeared, attired in gorgeous garments Oshun had given her. In commemoration of this event, Oshun's chief festival, called Ibo-Osun, is still held in Nigeria.

On this side of the Atlantic, Oshun gained new names and titles but kept her original flirtatious nature and her connection with living waters. She also kept her popularity—not a surprising public reaction to a goddess of love and healing. She is Oxum in Brazil, where she rules the ocean; in Haiti, she is the coquettish Erzulie-Freda-Dahomey; and in Cuba, she became Ochun, or "Our Lady of La Caridad," patron of the island itself. Various rituals emerged to honor her, ranging from candles lit in Christian churches to possession by her spirit in midnight dances.

The essence of Oshun's power rests in her power to heal through love. As we have seen, other love goddess have other specialities. Oshun's is the deep healing that love brings. As the traditional prayers above show, she was believed to be able to heal physical illness as well as the emotional dryness that comes from lack of love. Bathed in her waters, we emerge not merely physically refreshed but alive and full of the juice of love. Is it any wonder that she was held closely to the hearts of those who suffered so much as they carried her to her new homelands?

Symbols of Oshun

Water is preeminently the symbol of Oshun. In Voudoun, when she "rides" or possesses a dancer, the woman will make swimming motions, jangling her arm bracelets as she does so, while others welcome Oshun's appearance with shouts. Altars to her may hold shallow dishes of water; her festivals often are connected with bathing in rivers, lakes, or seas.

But Oshun is also the playful goddess who loves, above all else, beautiful jewelry and mirrors—the latter so that she may better admire her beauty. In Haiti, the Voudoun dancers whom she mounts often stop to admire themselves in a mirror, or to pantomime doing so. She is offered jewels and yellow copper to get her good will. In Brazilian Macumba, Oshun shows her sensuous nature by wearing jewels, holding a mirror, and wafting a fan. Altars to her hold copper bracelets and fans, as well as dishes filled with Omuluku (onions, beans, and salt).

Because she is a love goddess, some syncretic religions make the heart an emblem of Oshun. Haitian Voudoun paintings show her as the Mater Dolorosa—the Catholic Virgin Mary who points to her pierced heart, through which several swords have cut. In this guise, her colors are blue and pink, which are also colors symbolic of the Virgin.

Feasts of Oshun

In Nigeria, at Oshun's feast of Ibo-Oshun, a dinner of yams begins the evening. Then women dance for the goddess, hoping to be chosen as one of her favorites. Those who are selected are granted new names, which include that of the goddess: Osun Leye, "gift of Oshun," or Osun Tola, "treasure of Oshun." Once selected in this way, a woman serves her community as advisor, particularly assisting with family problems and illnesses. Oshun is especially consulted by those who wish to have children, for she encourages this womanly activity.

In Haitian Voudoun, Oshun (called Erzulie or Ezili) is honored especially on Tuesdays and Thursdays. Feasts of the Catholic Virgin Mary are also special to her, for she has been syncretized into that figure. Oshun as Erzulie is especially honored on riverbanks and seashores, where she is offered perfumes and other toiletries as well as fancy, expensive foods.

Suggestions for Invoking Oshun

Like the Hindu goddess Kali, Oshun is invoked throughout the Americas; thus it is possible to see a traditional ritual to her performed by those who still follow her ways. But you are unlikely to find the local Santeria group advertising itself in the yellow pages or Voudoun ceremonies mentioned in the newspaper calender. When the goddess visits, you may well not be present, unless you come from her people or have been specially invited.

The people who worship Oshun did not come to this hemisphere by choice; their religions have endured centuries of oppression and persecution, and even today there is substantial discrimination against some of their practices. Spirituality is not connected with social status, political power, or economic standing—but religion is. And most practitioners of Oshun's religions have had little status, power, or money as they fought to better themselves in a land far from their goddess's original home.

The United States prefers to consider itself a classless society, and those who occupy the upper rungs of the invisible class system usually take care to be unaware of their privileged position; those on less elevated rungs are inclined to only look upward, and not be aware of those struggling beneath them. Thus when such spiritual seekers find themselves excluded from religious services they find intriguing (those of Native American people as well as those of the African diaspora), they can become confused and angry.

Why not share the spiritual wealth of Oshun and her companions? Such is the question that eager seekers put to those who have no special desire to share in such a way. But there is no spiritual law that requires all rituals be made available to anyone interested. Thus to begin to honor a divinity who is not yours by heritage means encountering challenges that seem, at first, to be less than spiritual: questions of wealth and class, of privilege and the sorry weight of history. Yet to truly honor a divinity is like truly loving another human being. You have to deal with the whole person; you can't just pick and choose what you want to love.

The powerful goddesses of the African diaspora offer a special opportunity for those on the goddess path, whether of African or other heritage. For where do we need the healing love that Oshun holds out to her followers, if not between and among people of different races and cultural backgrounds?

It is especially difficult to talk about questions like these today, when the label of political correctness is readily thrown at anyone who broaches them. Yet the United States grows steadily more socially segregated with each decade. Fear of others grows up on all sides. Differences among people—racial, of course, but also cultural and economic and religious—are the cause of seemingly unending wars around the globe. Would not some of Oshun's water of love help move humanity forward to a more peaceful future?

There is no ritual, no program, no policy that is guaranteed to make that happen, but there are rituals we enact every day that make it difficult. When we eat lunch only with our own kind. When we invite only our own kind to our house. When we shop only in certain neighborhoods. When we hire only certain kinds of people. When we read only books by certain kinds of authors. These are the rituals that reinforce the divisions under which we suffer.

And just as we support separation with these tiny rituals, we begin the process of healing with tiny actions. We read a book by someone not like ourselves. We go to a concert by a musician who opens our ears to a new sound. We make a special effort to talk to someone from a group we fear. We invite someone to our home for the first time, someone whose parents our parents might not have been comfortable entertaining.

And, for those on the goddess path, we study goddesses of our own culture to become familiar with our heritage; but we also study goddesses from cultures other than our own. We learn the beliefs of our ancestors, and we also honor the rituals and beliefs of others. We try to see the goddess in every woman, and every man, we meet.

A simple ritual can help remind us that, despite our many differences, we are all members of the same species. Once each day, sit down in a quiet place with a glass of water. Do not drink it immediately; just hold the glass while you look into the water. As you do so, name as many of the great rivers of the world as you can. The Congo. The Amazon. The Nile. The Mississippi. The Thames. The Rio Grande. The Danube. The Boyne. The Peace.

As you name them, imagine the people along their shores. Watch the rivers pass farms and towns and cities. Imagine yourself high above the earth, watching the waters of each river flow into another river, and then finally out to the ocean. Watch the clouds as they are driven forth from the ocean onto the continents. Watch the rain flow, pouring finally into those rivers again.

As in so many cultures, you cannot drink until you have offered libation: a drop or two of water offered to the spirits that surround us. Offer a libation, then drink the glass of water. Imagine as you do that there is a drop in the glass from each river in the world. The Wabash. The Ohio. The Ganges. The Seine. The Yukon. The Yellow River. The Rhine. The Volga.

The Oshun.

Thus are we joined. In the water of this communion, acknowledge and embrace that joining.

∾

Questions and Activities

1. What do you know about the culture and religion of your ancestral homeland?

2. What events, festivals, or other cultural expressions were practiced by your family? Do you practice them yourself now? If not, why not?

3. What memories do you have of special foods from your heritage? Can you recreate the recipes?

4. What cultures or goddess figures draw your attention? What do you know about their special kind of spirituality?

5. Are there cultures with which you feel uneasy or uncomfortable? What about them makes you uneasy?

6. Think about your friends and acquaintances. Are they all the same kind of people? What similarities do they have?

7. What comments do you remember from your childhood about people of other cultures, classes, or races? Do you still believe these comments to be true?

8. If you find someone of another race, class, or culture unlikeable, how do you evaluate this? Do you blame them, or do you consider what your own expectations and prejudices are?

9. What benefits have accrued to you because of the race, class, or culture that you were born into? What has been difficult for you because of your upbringing?

10. Who is the friend you think of as most unlike yourself? Why do you like that person? What special benefits does knowing this person bring to you?

Kali

Freedom

What has Kali to do with me?
Everything.
Think hard upon the wild-haired goddess,
and all becomes clear.

1

In the world's great market
sits a mother, flying a kite.
A hundred thousand kites
fly in the air above her.
She has covered her kite-string
with fine powdered glass.
It cuts the string of another kite.
Then, as that kite soars
upwards into free infinity,
the mother laughs.
How she laughs! How she
claps her charmed hands!

2

What has Kali to do with me?
Everything. Her lotus feet
are the end of every pilgrimage.
When I meditate upon her
I float like a lily on an ocean of bliss.
I think of fire consuming fuel:
that is Kali. Devotion to her
is the root of all happiness.
Salvation is her companion.
Think hard upon the wild-haired
goddess, and all becomes clear.

3

How I love that dark beauty,
seducing the world
with her black hair,
how I love her!

How I love my black darling
who lives in the heart of the world,
in the heart of our hearts,
in the heart of the gods,
how I love her!

Because she is black,
I love black.
Because she dances,
I love dancing.
Because she is beautiful
and black with dancing
hair, I cannot help
myself, I adore her!

∾

Myth and Meaning of Kali

When you first encounter her, blue-skinned and garlanded with human skulls, Kali seems a terrifying goddess, not an appealing one. Yet look at the prayers to her! The great eighteenth-century Indian poet Ramprasad wrote innumerable paeans to Kali, depicting her as a mother, as the first invocation does; in her fiercer form, as in the second invocation; and as a lover, as the third invocation shows. Beautiful as they are, these famous prayers merely hint at the great love and devotion of Hindu people to this great and powerful goddess.

How does one love Kali? Black Mother Time, she is called. Her tongue juts out of her black face; her hands hold weapons; her necklace and earrings are strung with dismembered bodies and guillotined heads. Uncompromisingly alone, she is the mother of death, who swims in her womb like a babe; she is the force of time leading ever onward to destruction. And then, when she has destroyed everything, Kali will be the timeless sleep from which new ages will awaken.

In several Hindu traditions, Kali is the most important goddess of our age, which is named for her: the kali-yuga, the time of Kali. In such times it is vital to understand this goddess in order to survive, to endure, to finally reach peace.

She was born at a time like this one, when the masculine force had become predominant and threatened the universe with total destruction. Even the great gods had no power against the asuras, the demons who kept the world captive.

Finally one, the demon Mahisasura, appropriated divine power itself and threatened the gods. Helpless against him, they scattered in fear.

But the great goddess Parvati, daughter of the Himalaya mountains, came to their rescue. Under her guidance, the gods joined forces and breathed all their power forth together. It roared from them like streams of fire, and the great warrior goddess Durga was thus born.

But even Durga had difficulty conquering the ravaging demons. Mahisasura took on the form of a buffalo and attacked the goddess, over and over. She killed him, over and over. And he kept reforming himself into the huge and powerful buffalo.

Finally Durga knitted her brow in consternation over the enduring battle—and from the space between her eyes sprang yet another goddess, black Kali, already armed with a trident and ready to strike, even more powerful than great Durga. Between the two, the goddesses conquered the demons and restored the balance of the universe.

Another version of the story tells how Durga conquered the buffalo demon single-handedly, then transformed herself into a woman of surpassing beauty who retired to the Himalayas to meditate. Followed by a few of the remaining demons to her hermitage, she turned on them in fury. Her face grew black with anger, and from her brow sprang Kali, bearing a noose and a sword, holding a skull. With a terrible laughing roar, she ate up the demon army and all their weapons. More and more demons came to reinforce their fallen comrades, and she sang out her magical Om, drinking blood to keep up her strength, until she had cleared the world of evil.

Thus, fierce as she is, Kali is essentially a protective goddess, one who makes the world safer for her human children. Kali is a form of shakti (female energy). Worship of this feminine force goes back untold generations in India, to the prehistoric cities of Mohenjo-Daro and Harrupa, where magnificent goddess statues have been found. After the arrival of the Indo-Europeans, whose language became Sanskrit on the Indian subcontinent, the earlier goddesses did not disappear, but became part of the complex of deities in Hinduism. The feminine force was balanced with a male one, the shakti with shiva.

It is an indication of how powerful a female force Kali is that she is paired, in Hindu myth, with the god who bears the name of masculine force itself: Shiva, the Lord of the Dance. Once, their myth tells us, Kali challenged Shiva to a dance competition. At first it was merely an entertainment, but they would not stop dancing. They grew wilder and wilder, more competitive and acrobatic, until it seemed the world would shake itself to pieces—and so it will, for beneath all appearances that dance continues.

Another time, it is said, Kali fought and killed two demons and celebrated her victory by draining their bodies of blood. Then, drunk with slaughter, she began to dance. Thrilling to the feel of lifeless flesh beneath her naked feet, Kali danced more and more wildly—until she realized that Shiva himself was underneath her and that she was dancing him to death. The god's tactic slowed Kali's wildness, but only for the moment, and eventually she will resume the dance that ends the world.

Kali is still one of India's most popular goddesses: her picture hangs in many homes, her name is familiar in Calcutta (Anglicized from Kali-Ghatt, or "steps of Kali," her temple city). Served at one time by murderers called thuggee (from which derives the English word thug), the goddess of cemeteries was thought to thrive on blood; most often, however, goat rather than human blood was sacrificed to her, and it is still poured out in some parts of India today.

Blood, severed heads, the dance that will end the world—how does one love a goddess like this? Yet, as Ramprasad's lyrics show, meditation on Kali offers a route to freedom. As long as we are unconscious of the presence of death, we are unconscious to life itself. As long as we refuse to look our own mortality in the eye, we cannot truly live. Thus devotion to Kali wakens the worshiper from an oblivious trance into vivid consciousness. She is not an easy goddess to love, but she rewards with precious freedom those who dare!

Symbols of Kali

In Indian art, Kali is instantly recognizable because of her facial expression: she juts her tongue out and widens her eyes. Often that tongue is colored an impossibly bright red; other times it extends an undue length. In yoga, what Kali is doing would be called the lion pose, which is said to bring great power from the center of the body and out through the tongue. This seems an appropriate gesture, then, for this powerful goddess to make. (Another goddess who is depicted with this expression is snake-haired Medusa, who may be distantly related to Kali.)

Weapons of all sorts are also Kali's symbols. She is often depicted bearing a three-pronged spear or trident; she carries knives and swords; she brandishes a spear. Rather than being symbols of war, in Kali's case they indicate her role as banisher of evil. A connected symbol is the dismembered body. Although this is on the surface the least pleasant of Kali's symbols, its mystical significance may be related to shamanic traditions that say that we must be dismembered in order to be reborn in a new, more enlightened form. Like the sharp weapon she carries, Kali's necklace of skulls and her waistband of severed heads may have a more complex and spiritual meaning than first appears. Letting go of our head—our thinking center—is an especially appropriate symbol for this goddess, who cannot be understood logically.

Finally, two colors are consistently connected with this goddess. Her worshipers wear red, as bright as possible; she is also often painted with red skin or red garments. Red is, obviously, the color of blood, which Kali sheds so casually; it is also the color of transformation, over which Kali presides. Black, too, is a color connected with her; many paintings show her with black skin, the only Hindu divinity so depicted. The meaning of this was described in one scripture thus: "All colors disappear in black, and all names and differences disappear in her." This darkness connects her to night and to death; the affirmation of blackness as powerful and beautiful, as our third invocation shows, indicates as well a spiritual understanding of the importance of what is apparently negative to the universe's cycle.

Feasts of Kali

Throughout India, but especially in her sacred city of Calcutta, Kali is still honored with rituals throughout the year. The Hindu calender is not the same as the Gregorian one used in the west, so the dates of the festivals may change from year to year. The most important festival, Kali Puja, is celebrated in the fall, during the month of Kartik (mid-October through mid-November). Sacrifices are made of sugar cane and goat meat, while young girls clad in festive attire are honored as embodiments of the goddess herself.

A midwinter festival, the Ratanti Puja, is celebrated on the evening of the new moon during the month of Magh (mid-January to mid-February). Again, goat sacrifices are part of the event; sugar cane is also offered to the goddess. During the next month, Falgun (mid-February to mid-March), a festival honors Sri Ramakrishna, one of the most famous saints of Kali. Pilgrimages to the monastery where he lived and worship in his room are part of the ritual at that time.

Suggestions for Invoking Kali

There she stands, her neck roped with severed heads, brandishing a sword in one of her four arms, her red tongue jutting out of her blue face, looking straight at you.

How do you come to love this goddess?

There are other choices, ones who offer a more serene or pleasant appearance. Why, just a few pages back—there she is, abundant Gaia! Why not turn back to her embrace? Or joyous Hathor! Almost any goddess seems less fearsome than Kali.

Yet the mystics of India tell us that, until we can love Kali, we are never truly free. The sword she carries cuts through the illusions of our life, which bind us like heavy cords to our habits and our everyday concerns. Thus the journey to Kali, however difficult, is an important one for those on the goddess path.

For most of the goddesses in this book, rituals must be created or recreated. The Panathenea is reenacted in Tennessee at the replica of Athena's temple, but even the most careful restaging is not the same as a ritual continuously celebrated for gener-ations; women's circles may gather under the full moon and invoke Artemis, but the thread of worship was cut many centuries ago and what exists now is a respin-ning. Not so for Kali. Hindu temples in the United States and other countries cel-ebrate Kali rituals regularly. Many are magnificently theatrical and lavishly beauti-ful, none more so than the annual adoration of the goddess.

Non-Hindu worshipers are welcome at many such events. So to honor Kali, nothing is more appropriate than to attend a ritual celebrated by her devout fol-lowers. Hindu congregations are listed in telephone books among other churches, in cities large enough to support a temple facility. In smaller towns, rituals are likely to be held in private homes; expressing interest to Indian friends and acquaintances may result in a welcome invitation.

Call ahead and discuss your interest with your host or with members of the con-gregation to assure that your presence will not detract from the ceremony. Ask what preparations you should make, what offerings you should bring, and how you should conduct yourself. Listen carefully to the information you are given, and follow it with just as much care. If the host or ritual leader seems hesitant to include you, withdraw your request and hope that the goddess may smile on you at a later date.

If you are invited to attend, prepare by reading as much as you can about the goddess, the festival, and Hinduism in general. While you need not be a scholar to offer Kali honor, such research will both prepare you for your experience and show respect for the goddess and her followers. When you do attend the ceremony, remember that you are a guest; the ritual is not being conducted for your benefit, so remain unobtrusive and reverent in behavior. Watch others around you and act as they do. If you make a mistake, don't draw attention to it or to yourself; just continue to follow as best you can.

Many who attend such ceremonies find it a very moving experience. For those brought up in religions that have no acknowledged goddesses, seeing the figure of a divine woman reverenced can be almost overwhelmingly moving. But the point of Kali's worship is not to entrance yourself with emotional experience. It is to understand the fleeting quality of such experience, no matter how beautiful and moving it may be.

In solitary meditation, you can concentrate on the image of Kali as a yantra, a visual meditation tool. Images of her are readily available in art museums and

Indian stores; you may wish to create your own, or even to use a skull or other symbol to represent her. Focusing your eyes on the image, breathe slowly and naturally. Observe the thoughts that come to you as you concentrate on the goddess. Notice your emotional response to her image. And as you do, imagine those thoughts, that response, as they might appear from a hundred years hence. Then a thousand years. How significant does your life, your death, appear from that vantage point? You are no more, and no less, important than anyone who has ever lived before. Try moving forward five thousand years—as far distant in the future as the beginnings of Kali's worship are in the past.

Now look at the concerns that have preoccupied you in the past few weeks. How trivial does that worry about money seem! How little does a new possession mean, in the scale of thousands of years!

This meditation can give you a sense of proportion and perspective about your own life. It can make you more tolerant of others, for you will begin to see that we are all equal in the goddess's eyes. With the long view of time, you can see that the petty conflict at work is just that, a petty conflict. You can see how unimportant are fads and fashions, needs and desires.

What remains, from such a vast distance, is the pattern of life. Like a vast ocean, it swells and subsides: birth, life, death, birth, life, death. And the energies of human beings appear, too, for good and ill: war and pain, truth and love. From the starry distances of Kali's time, we can see ourselves in the truest way, in terms of what life energies we support, which ones we thwart.

And this is the freedom Kali offers us: to be slave no more to the things of this world that demand so much of our time and attention, but rather to be true to what is lasting in the great sweep of time. Love, connection, generosity, beauty—these last. However fleeting they are in the momentary present, they echo all the other loves and beauties of all time, swelling into a great chorus of magnificence.

And that is Kali's gift: freedom from the tyranny of concern for the present, and all the joy that goes with such freedom.

Questions and Activities

1. If your house were to be covered with the ash of a volcano, and uncovered 15,000 years later, what would archaeologists think was most important to you? Look around your house as though you have never seen it before. What is most prominent; what do you have the most of? What does this tell you about yourself?

2. If you were to simplify your life by eliminating one activity from this week, what would it be? Why?

3. Have you made preparations for your inevitable death? Have you made a will? If not, why not?

4. How do you wish to be buried? How do you want your funeral service to be? Have you made these wishes known to your friends and family?

5. When you think about the world after your death, what images come to mind? What emotions do you feel?

6. If you could live for a thousand years, what would you do with your time?

7. Have there been times in your life when you felt threatened by death? How did it feel to you?

8. Is there anything you could imagine dying for? What? Why?

9. Is there anything you could imagine killing for? What? Why?

10. Draw a picture that represents what you believe the face of death to be, or purchase or draw a picture of Kali. Meditate on it, imagining yourself dying, looking into her face. Pay attention to any changes in your attitudes as you do this meditation.

The Cailleach

Power

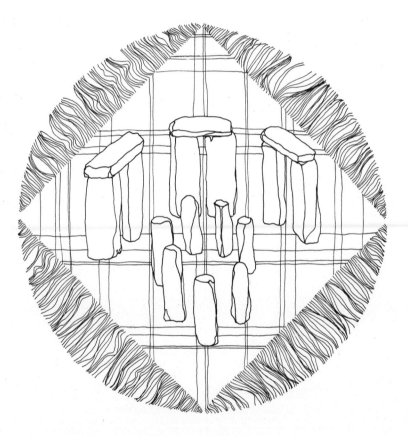

She crouched like a wild beast ready to spring.
She of the long nails, she of the long teeth,
she ran through the hills like thunder.

1

Her face had the black-blue shine of coal.
Her one bony tooth was red like rust.
Her hair was thick and dense and gray
like brushwood in a dying forest.
In her head was one eye like a pool,
swifter than a star in the winter sky.
That one stone eye in the hag's head
moved quicker than mackerel after a lure.

2

The old one crouched in the branches
of the old pollard oak, the last remnant
of her forest, the oak that grew in the cleft
of the rock over the mouth of her dark cave.
She made that cave, scratched it out
of the cold earth with her bony hands.
She crouched like a wild beast ready to spring.
She of the long nails, she of the long teeth,
she ran through the hills like thunder.

~

Myth and Meaning of the Cailleach

The Cailleach is a sort of mystery: a goddess who survived eons after her worship died out. She is vastly ancient, so ancient that we know virtually nothing of her original myth and ritual. She can be found in Ireland and Scotland and England—traced through folklore, through the names of ancient monuments and natural wonders, and through enigmatic verses and stories.

It is impossible to know how long she was worshiped, or by whom. The Celts came to the lands of the Cailleach some 2,000 years ago, bringing their own pantheon of gods and goddesses. The new arrivals recognized the Cailleach as already ancient, for as a famous Irish poem says, "There are three great ages: the age of the yew tree, the age of the eagle, the age of the Cailleach." It is utterly impossible to know what this goddess meant to her original worshipers, just as it is impossible—barring invention of a time machine—to know what language they spoke, how they lived, or how women were viewed within her society. What we know about her is scanty; what we can imagine is vast.

But the Cailleach must have been very important, for she did not disappear as countless other divinities have. As late as the last century, songs like our first invocation were sung about her; she was even sighted abroad in the land, as the second invocation shows, for it is derived from an eyewitness report in a nineteenth-century newspaper. If nothing is truly known about her, paradoxically she is still alive, still a power in the lands once dedicated to her. And from those vestiges, we can reconstruct something of the powerful original figure of ancient times.

She went by many names: Cailleach Bheur or Carlin in Scotland; Cally Berry in northern Ireland; Cailleach ny Groamch on the Isle of Man; Black Annis in Britain; the Hag of Beare or Digne in Ireland. She was of fearsome appearance, with only one eye—an eye of preternatural keenness—in the middle of a blue-black face. She had red teeth and hair white as a frosted apron. Over it she wore a kerchief and over her gray clothing, a faded plaid shawl.

It is hard to know whether she was already an aged goddess when the Celts arrived, or whether she was converted by them to a crone in recognition of her great antiquity. Similarly, it is hard to know whether the stories that refer to her as an aged woman were part of her original mythology or later inventions. Whatever the reason, her myths show her as old beyond measure.

An old woman she might have been, but she was still strong and vigorous. She owned a farm, for which she hired workers. Their contracts lasted six months, with the stipulation that none would be paid who could not outwork her. Looking at the hunched old thing, many a man fell for the trick and paid with his life, dying of overwork while trying to keep the pace she set. She was similarly vigorous sexually. All the men she loved—and they were countless—died of old age as she went on, always finding another pretty youth to share her bed.

The Cailleach was so strong that she carried boulders around in her apron; the ones she dropped became mountain ranges. Her name is attached to many prominent landscape features. She was the goddess of the famous Cliffs of Moher in the west of Ireland, especially of the one called Hag's Head, and of the mountains that stand inland from the ocean there, Sliabh Echghte, the Mountains of the Hag. Mountains were often named for her; "hag hills" like Beinn na Chailleach in Scotland are usually cloud-covered or stormy. When she needed to sit down, she clawed a chair into solid rock; these gigantic seat-like structures can still be seen in places like the Hag's Chair in Loughcrew in Ireland.

She was a spinner, sometimes known as the Spinning Hag. Like the Germanic winter goddesses Holda and Perchta, she tested women on their spinning abilities, punishing them if they were lazy or sloppy. Because of her, it was important never to take a spinning wheel out of the house after nightfall or to spin at night. Similarly, she might appear at your doorstep, looking for all the world like a little old granny, only to torment you and force you to do her bidding—usually spinning impossible amounts of some unlikely substance into fine thread.

She controlled the seasons and the weather. Specifically, she controlled wintery chill and storms and high winds. As a seasonal goddess, she was sometimes connected with a younger figure, named Brigid in Celtic times. The Cailleach, Scottish stories say, kept a maiden of that name imprisoned in the high mountains of Ben Nevis. But her own son fell in love with Brigid and, at winter's end, he eloped with her. The hag chased them across the landscape, causing fierce storms as she went. But winter cannot hold us perpetually in her grip, so the Cailleach was finally turned to stone and Brigid, the springtime weather, was freed.

These myths suggest that the Cailleach was originally a cosmic goddess of earth and sky, a goddess whose power was so vast that she could send storms or withhold them, could bring on the seasons or stall them in their progress. She was essentially creative—she made the mountains—but had a destructive aspect as well: she made these mountains, after all, by dropping huge boulders onto the earth without warning any of the tiny people who might have been in her way. The Cailleach's creativity is stern and even ruthless. She represents all those aspects of life we must honor because we cannot avoid or deny them.

Symbols of the Cailleach

Because of her great antiquity, it is hard to know what symbols her original worshipers connected with the Cailleach. Reading the vestiges of her worship that remain, however, we can safely speculate that rocks and mountains were connected with her from ancient times. Many high, rocky, cloud-swept hills in Ireland and Scotland bear her name; there are many legends, as well, which relate how she created mountains by dropping the contents of her apron on the ground. Other rocky outcrops, such as those at Loughcrew, are also named for her. There, as on other rock monuments of the megalithic people, we find superlative spiral imagery that has been tied to a goddess—though it is impossible to know if she is the Cailleach.

To understand the Cailleach, we can examine the symbolic resonance of rock. Rock is hard and adamant, persevering and permanent. It is also connected with the earth—although not the earth in her fertile aspect. The Cailleach is the barren and severe earth goddess, the earth at its most primitive and strong. Without rock, there would be no support for the soil on which we grow our food. Thus rock is a vital image of the deepest support the mother goddess can provide.

In addition to this primary symbol, we find some mythic traces that suggest a connection between the Cailleach and the cat. In one story from Scotland, the Cailleach appears in the form of a cat who tests the morality of a hunter in the middle of a stormy night. Black Annis, an English form of the Cailleach, was said to appear in spring in the form of a black cat. In the far west of Ireland, there are traces of a vestigial cat goddess who lived in a cave and answered questions like a prophet. However slight these traces, the connection of the hag goddess with the cat in other lands (Egypt and Korea, for instance) supports the use of the cat as a symbol for the Cailleach.

Feasts of the Cailleach

As with the symbols appropriate to her, it is difficult if not impossible to be certain what feasts were originally sacred to the Cailleach. However, it is likely that she was honored when winter loosed its grip on the land and spring breezes began to blow. In many stories, the Cailleach appears as the winter hag who attempts to keep the young spring goddess (perhaps a double of her, the Cailleach's younger self) confined. A struggle ensues, in which humanity has a part—dancing or holding mock combats between winter and summer. Invariably, the Cailleach is bested and the new goddess rules. But she, in turn, ages into the crone of winter, and the next year fights and loses to a new budding spring goddess.

The dual goddess is, in many lands, seen as a single woman who endlessly renews herself. Thus the spring goddess who ages is, magically, the same winter goddess whom she fought to bring warm weather to the earth. Thus the hag is one part of an endlessly repeating cycle. As such, while she may be fearsome, she must not be avoided or ignored. Bedrock might appear less pleasant than a green and blooming pasture but, without bedrock, the soil cannot sustain life. Without its winter rest, the world would not continue to provide for us.

The power of the hag is vast, and her opposition strengthens the vigor of spring. Symbolically, this was enacted in spring festivals in the Cailleach's lands. On May 1, on the Isle of Man, the hag goddess fought with her sister over possession of the land; mock combats were staged between the forces of winter and summer, with summer always winning. In Scotland, right through the beginning of the seventeenth century, March 25 was celebrated as New Year's Day, with contests being held to drive out the winter hag.

The connection of the crone with winter and with the change of seasons is also found in Spain where, on February 5, the feast of St. Agatha was celebrated. Clearly descended from an ancient goddess, the "saint" was depicted as an old woman who takes winter away by stuffing it into a sack she carries for the purpose. Here the winter hag controls the weather, but she herself decides to bring spring and does not need to be driven away, as is common in other countries.

Similarly, in Russia we find a springtime festival honoring a hag goddess similar to the Cailleach. Called Mokosh, she was said to wander through the countryside at this time of year, taking bits of fleece from sheep for her own spinning and critiquing the work of human women. In her honor, strands of wool were laid next to the fireplace every evening—an everyday ritual that also suggests the goddess was seen as fiery, possibly solar.

Suggestions for Invoking the Cailleach

It is difficult, in this society, to embrace the crone. When women in their twenties begin saving for face lifts, when women in their thirties exercise and diet to exhaustion, when women in their forties hide their age for fear of being judged negatively—where is there room for the one-eyed wizened crone goddess of our foremothers?

It takes courage to be a woman, but it takes special courage to face aging in a society where, because women are only valued for youthful appearance, age makes women invisible. Often it does worse: women live in poverty in the United States at a greater rate than do men, and women of age live in poverty at a greater rate than younger women. The fear of growing old, alone, abandoned, is enough to make the most vigorous woman quail—and it is, alas, a fear that has grounding in social realities.

Difficult as it may be to embrace the hag, it is necessary—for women of all ages. For if we live long enough, we all grow up to be hags. And so long as we concur with our society's degradation of the older woman—by silence and by action—we make our own potential futures more difficult. Embracing the Cailleach can be a step toward embracing our own potentials as purple-clad, powerful crones ourselves.

There are no ancient rituals to guide us in this journey, for the rites of the Cailleach are lost in the mists of time. Perhaps two thousand years have passed since her people regularly performed the actions appropriate to her majesty and strength. But ritual is not only created out of historical artifact. Those ancient rituals were created by people who, knowing the goddess and her images and her power, acted in ways appropriate to express that. We can do the same thing today. It is even possible that we will, however unwittingly, recreate the original rituals themselves, for if there is some archetypal reality to which we, as humans, respond, then people in vastly different eras and geographical regions could create the same rituals with the same meaning. We cannot know how close our creations are to the originals, but we can follow the same process in creating them.

To create a ritual to the Cailleach, begin by collecting a variety of rocks with which to deck the altar. A good way to do this is through a "magic hike," a kind of walking meditation where you attend to the world around you and let its messages be clearly heard. Don't just go out and pick up a bunch of rocks! Let the process of selecting the rocks be part of the ritual.

Locate an area with a good supply of interesting rocks (lakeshores are excellent, as are rocky streambeds) then walk slowly around the area, examining the rocks carefully. Notice how different they are, one from the other. While from a distance, or when looked at casually, rocks seem all alike, closer inspection reveals them to be extraordinarily diverse in size, shape, color. Some will capture your attention. Perhaps they will be unusually shaped or colored rocks. Just as possibly, there will be nothing special that distinguishes them from the others that lie about them, but they will seem somehow unique and powerful. So it is with older women: often they seem colorless, anonymous, but when you take time to really see them, they are as unique as carefully cut diamonds.

When you have assembled the rocks, create an altar using them. This could be a permanent structure in your yard, if you have sufficient room and if the rocks you have gathered are of sufficient size. Or it could just be a tabletop with the rocks artfully arranged. In the latter case, it's a good idea to cover the table with several layers of fabric (red, like the color of the Cailleach's teeth; or plaid, for her Celtic heritage, are good choices) to avoid damaging the finish.

Participants in the ritual will create the remainder of the altar by placing on it photographs of older women who have been significant to them. Mothers, grandmothers, teachers, aunts, neighbors—even public figures like Eleanor Roosevelt—are candidates for inclusion. If no photo exists, the woman can be represented with a small card bearing her name. In creating the altar, each participant should silently remember and honor each woman who represents a positive vision of powerful age.

After invoking the goddess and recalling the meaning of her image, each participant should invoke the women she has selected for the altar, telling their stories, praising their strength and vitality. This is a chance to tell family stories (the way Great Aunt Regina used to demand we eat more cookies than we wanted, the way her namesake Aunt Reggie liked to tour graveyards to trace family names), as well as an opportunity to honor the strength of those who have embodied the crone in the public eye. For a group, this ritual offers a special opportunity to get to know each other's heritage and background. For an individual, it is a powerful celebration of the images the inner self holds dear.

After this sharing, each woman will begin the process of embracing herself as an aged woman. If the circle includes women who are already crones, they can decide whether they wish to create a more aged appearance or not. Younger women will at this point create a Cailleach mask from their own features. A good way to do this is to use stage makeup (or, in the absence of that, simple eyeliner pencils will do) to reveal the aged face of each participant. Find the natural lines that result from constant expressions, draw fine lines along them, then smear them slightly to create a deep "wrinkle." Within a few moments, each woman can age twenty to forty years. Putting talc powder in your hair will heighten the effect.

If there are men in the group, or if a man is creating this ritual alone, there is no need to rehearse the appearance of the aging self. For men, aging does not necessarily connect with invisibility. Look at Hollywood for proof: an aging actor is often paired with a nubile young actress, while the number of exciting parts for older actresses is not only smaller, but rarely includes a sexual connection with a young and attractive male. Men's struggle, in accessing and accepting the crone, is ultimately the same as women's: to find and honor the old woman within. For men, however, social conditioning is strong enough that accepting the outer crone is probably necessary before the inner crone will reveal herself. In myth, heroes are often challenged to embrace (literally) the Cailleach, who then reveals herself to be as exciting in bed as any younger woman. Meditating on this possibility may present difficulties to men, but the myths suggest that such a connection dramatically empowers the male hero.

When you have completed aging the participants, each woman should turn to the next and observe her carefully and without speaking. Because one of the most disempowering parts of aging for women is the invisibility that goes along with it, being truly seen, especially in a ritual context, can be very empowering. After each woman has been fully seen, share your fears and experiences of getting older. This may be a painful part of the ritual, but it is important to be honest in order to move into a more positive stage.

After this sharing, pass around a hand mirror so that each participant can observe in silence how she looks in her Cailleach disguise. As you do so, refrain from commenting in any way. Observe yourself just as you observed the other women in the circle, without judgement or rejection. See if you look like any of the female relatives you have praised. Ask yourself what strengths are written on the face you see in that mirror: intelligence, curiosity, serenity. Hold those ideas in silence.

Then, begin to praise the woman you will become. The qualities you saw written on your face—praise them, and yourself, for embodying them. The connections you saw with relatives who have gone before—acknowledge them. If a woman finds it difficult to affirm her older self, others in the circle can assist her by praising what they see.

Close the circle by embracing each other, then invoking the Cailleach again, praising her for the strength she has given you. Celebrate afterward with a feast of old wines and brandies, aged cheeses and Granny Smith apples—celebratory foods reminding us that age, at its best, is a time of refinement, good taste, and great power.

~

Questions and Activities

1. Make a list of women who, when you were younger, embodied the strength of women to you. What qualities do you associate with them?

2. Taking that list, describe the ways in which you yourself have those qualities. What could you do to enhance those qualities and their expression?

3. For a week, pay attention to the words you hear used to describe women. Make a list of them. You can find them in printed materials, in other media, or in conversation. Now divide them into two lists: positive and negative. What messages are you hearing about women from your environment?

4. Taking that list, circle the words you like as descriptions of yourself. Now draw a line under the words you would feel uncomfortable with if used to describe yourself. Are there decisions you make about your behavior based on those messages?

5. In what ways do you typically hide your age?

6. What fears do you have of growing older?

7. Do you fear death? What are your attitudes toward dying? What fears do you have? What do you fear more than death?

8. If you had to lose one sense as you age, which would you most willingly give up? Which would be most painful to lose?

9. Have you made plans to support yourself in your old age? What will you need to be happy and healthy as you age? How can you start now to provide for that?

10. Have you made a will? A living will? Have you dealt with the technical details of inevitable aging?

Paivatar

Release

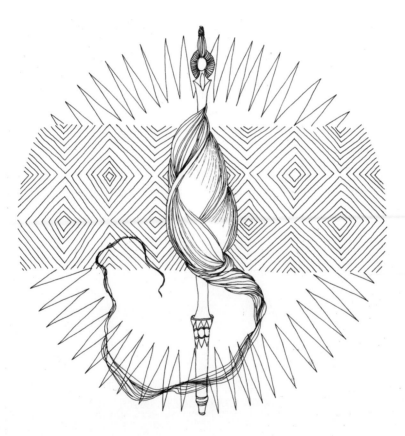

Journey now in peace, go around the earth
in safety, travel in joy, oh goddess!

Hail, lovely sun! Praise you for rising!
Praise you for dawning! Yesterday
we shivered in darkness while
you were trapped in the mountains.
Now you rise light as a silver bird.
Always rise like this, goddess,
always come back to us like this,
bringing us health and safety,
bringing the game to our arrows,
the fish to our fishhooks. Journey
now in peace, go around the earth
in safety, travel in joy, oh goddess!

Myth and Meaning of Paivatar

In the nineteenth century, a Finnish folklorist named Elias Lonnrot traveled around his native land, collecting stories from the residents of rural farms and homesteads. Finland had long since been Christianized, but old myths of ancestral gods and goddesses remained in the oral tradition. On long winter nights, storytellers would still weave the ancient tales of heroic deeds and epic struggles. It was these stories—soon to die out, as modernization reached even the remotest villages of the north—that Lonnrot wove into the Kalevala, a massive collection more than 22,000 verses long, one of the most impressive feats of individual scholarship ever known.

The myths reflect the wisdom and culture of a people who, though they have lived for hundreds of years next door to the Scandinavians and the Slavs and the Balts, speak an unrelated non-Indo-European language and tell of a different pantheon of divinities. There is a certain amount of mystery about who the Finns are and how they got to their lands, for they are linguistically related to the Hungarians and the Basques. Their myths, too, refer to different divinities than those found nearby. One of these is the sun maiden Paivatar, of whom an extremely significant myth is told.

Paivatar lived in the sky, we learn from the Kalevala, where she wove the golden light of day; her sister, the moon, wove a silver thread, the pale light of the shining moon. One day, the sun was stolen away from the sky by the crafty witch Louhi, gap-toothed mistress of icy North Farm, who used a magical song to freeze the sun inside a metal mountain. For five years it was night; for ten more years there was not even the glimmer of stars.

At last even the gods could not stand the cold and the dark. They called on the poet Vainomaoien and the smith Ilmarinen to free the sun maiden. They started by forging a new sun with heat provided by the sun's baby, fire. This child had been lost by Paivatar. One day, she was rocking her child's cradle at the edge of a rainbow, singing to him. But because the fire baby was so hot, he burned right through the cradle and fell through the six vaults of the sky. The falling spark was swallowed by a fish, which was followed by another fish, which was followed by yet another fish. And so fire lived on earth, hidden from the people there.

To free the sun, the heroes had to find and free the child. The only way was to catch a magical fish, which could only be done with a net made of flax sown and grown and spun within two days. The heroes managed to pull off that feat, but it took another of Paivatar's other children to catch the fish. The boy prodded the fish into the net, knifed it, removed a fish from its belly, and another fish from that one, until the spark of fire flew out of the final fish and across the world, right into the home of the smith Ilmarinen.

The smith was a magician, so he sang magical chants to subdue fire and make him useful. Then he set about forging a new sun and moon. No smith was more qualified for the task than Ilmarinen, who had already forged the magical tool called the Sampo, which created all riches. And indeed, Ilmarinen forged a new moon and sun, which he lifted up through the six vaults of the sky, placing them overhead where they would shine down on the world.

Sweat poured off Ilmarinen's beard from the difficulty of lifting the huge metal discs into the sky, but alas! even his skill was not enough. For the sun did not shine, nor did the moon. They hung there in the sky, flat plates of metal, and the world remained dark.

The gods and heroes stood together in that cold darkness.

Then Vainomaoien, the poet, lost his temper. He stormed over to gloomy North Farm and pounded on the door of Louhi's home, demanding to know where the goddess was hidden. The evil crew that tended Louhi taunted him: "The sun got into the crag, the moon vanished into the rock, and they will never get free, never, never at all!" At these words, Vainomaoien lost his temper again, and struck at Louhi's men with his short sun-hilted sword, a mere barleycorn longer than the swords of his opponents. With two strokes, like cutting off the heads of turnips, he lopped off the heads of the North Farm lads.

Then he went off to collect the sun. He found nine doors, each with three locks, to prevent his entry. Vainomaoien went back to Ilmarinen's smithy, where he ordered his friend to forge a three-tined hoe, a dozen ice picks, and a bunch of keys. Ilmarinen set immediately to work. Louhi, made nervous by the battle at her farm and by the knowledge that Vainomaoien was planning to return, flew to the window of Ilmarinen's smithy. Disguised as a bird, she flattered him, then asked what he was doing. The smith, who had seen through the witch's disguise, answered coolly, "Making a neck ring for that dame of North Farm." Terrified, Louhi flew home at once. She knew she was trapped. Freeing the sun, she flew back to the smithy in the shape of a pigeon. There she casually remarked to Ilmarinen that the sun was rising.

And so she was. The sky maiden was ascending the heavens and warming the earth once more. When the poet Vainomaoien saw the welcome sight, he burst into the happy poem on page 220. And the sun has remained with us ever since, lighting and warming our days on this earth.

Symbols of Paivatar

The symbols of Paivatar are connected with spinning and weaving: a batten, a heddle, and a golden shuttle. In earlier times in her homeland, textile crafts were predominantly a female activity. It is perhaps difficult today to realize just how omnipresent spinning was in earlier cultures. Every inch of every thread to weave every garment had to be spun by hand. Imagine how long it would take to spin enough fine yarn to make cloth to keep an entire village warm each year. Imagine how many hours it took to spin enough thread to string a loom to weave a sail for an oceangoing boat!

At any moment of the day, a woman of the household was likely to be spinning. All evening, and especially during the long winter nights in the north, women sat with their textile tools by the fireside, listening to one of the family "spin yarns" to entertain them while they spun thread, then knit or wove it into fabric, then assembled it into clothing and useful household objects. Thus the tools of the textile crafts indicated Paivatar's feminine industry and skill. And her power, too, for the women's work produced a major part of the wealth of each household. Skillful and energetic women would be able to not only clothe their own families, but produce enough quality thread and fabric to trade for other necessities. Is it any wonder that the image of competence in this mythic tradition was a spinner?

Feasts of Paivatar

The feast of winter solstice is the appropriate time to celebrate the release of the sun from its imprisonment in the grip of winter. The solstices and equinoxes were marked by most ancient peoples as significant milestones on the sun's annual journey around the earth. In far northern climates like Finland, the light and darkness of the seasons is extreme. The sun virtually disappears for several months in winter, while in the summer the sky never darkens into night; the sun, resting just below the horizon, turns the entire sky a sort of pearly gray, the famous "white nights" of the northland. With such dramatic changes, it is little wonder that the solstices were important feasts, while the spring and autumn equinoxes were recognized as moments of brief balance.

Paivatar's myth clearly connects with the winter solstice, when the sun seems to be deliberately hidden from those of us on earth who need her light and heat. Thus it is appropriate to invoke her on the year's longest night, which usually falls on December 21. Summer solstice, June 21, when the sun is in the sky for the longest number of hours each year, is another good time to invoke the power of the weaving sun maiden. As with any goddess, the inner seasons also determine appropriate times for invocation; thus any "winter of discontent" should be considered a likely time to pray to Paivatar.

Suggestions for Invoking Paivatar

Entrapment and release: these are the themes of Paivatar's story. And are they not themes to which we can all relate? Have we not all endured periods where we felt trapped, only to be finally freed into joy and movement again?

Perhaps it was a negative relationship from which we could not extricate ourselves. Perhaps it was a job that barely paid our bills and kept us chronically depressed, but which seemed to be the only thing available. Perhaps it was a period of budgetary crisis that threatened to be self-perpetuating.

Some unpleasant experiences are clearly time-limited. Like a bad patch of weather, we know that they'll eventually end. Even while the storm rages, we have hope, because we know that hurricanes blow away, tornadoes dissipate, and thunderclouds pass over.

But there are times when everything seems to have been bad for so long that hope begins to die away. It feels different from life's normal cycles. The sun seems not to have gone away for a few months but to be frozen in a metal mountain. As the Kalevala says, this is no normal winter: there is no sun for five years, then even the light of the stars disappears for another ten.

Drastic action is called for to break such an impasse. It's not enough, in these times, to just wait for change to naturally occur. In the vocabulary of the Kalevala, an evil force is holding hope and light away from us—and heroic action is needed to get them back.

When one is depressed by apparently endless bad fortune, action seems impossible. Lethargy is the usual reaction to long-lasting stress. Physically, emotionally, mentally, we shut down. We become, ourselves, the dame of North Farm. We assist in keeping the sun away—keeping change from our lives—in large part because we're too exhausted and hopeless to think of anything to change our situation. We go through the motions of our lives, but there is no joy or delight to be found.

Paivatar's story is like a dream, with each character representing some of the parts of the beleaguered self. There is the hopeful self, frozen into immobility. There is the hopeless self, the witch Louhi. And, happily, there are two heroes, each with different skills—and it takes them both to break the lock of the crafty witch. It takes both poetry and smithcraft, the myth tells us: both words and actions. Without the poet, the smith would not have been able to free the sun; without the smith, the poet would have been hopeless. Forging the link between words and actions—that is the magic that breaks the icy grip of endless winter.

A ritual invoking Paivatar is something that can readily be done alone, for it is within the power of the inner self to break through once again to hope. In order to mobilize the efforts of the inner self, both words and actions are necessary. Thus this ritual breaks down into two parts.

Firstly, visualize a happy future. Write down exactly what that future would look like. If the problem is work, write a want ad describing the perfect job, either at your current place of employment or somewhere else. If the problem is a conflicted relationship, write a description of a pleasant change in your love life. If the problem is money, make a list of all your bills and write the total needed to eliminate your debt in big letters at the bottom of that list.

Take your time in this part of the process; be as specific as possible. You are more likely to get exactly what you want if you know what it is. Fill in as much detail as you can. There is no limit to the length of your imagined future. Write it in whatever way makes you comfortable: on the computer, in your journal, on a yellow tablet.

You will undoubtedly find yourself negating your desires as you write. "Oh, there are no jobs like that," or "oh, right, with my qualifications, I don't think so," or "don't be silly, you'll never get something like that" may resound through your mind as you work. Notice and acknowledge the voice of Louhi, who keeps your hopefulness frozen in the metal mountain. Every time you hear this voice, write down its comments on a separate sheet of paper. Try to get all of them, in as bitter a tone as they are expressed.

Then, when you have completed writing down your ideal future and your negative responses to its likelihood on separate pieces of paper, destroy the second, negative paper. Tear it into tiny shreds, put the shreds in a kitchen pot, and burn them. Or tear them up and throw them out your window, flush them down the toilet, or toss them into the garbage disposal.

Put the ideal future up somewhere where you can see it: a bulletin board, the refrigerator door, the bathroom mirror. Pause when you notice it to read at least one section of it. You will be surprised at how much of it will, finally, come true.

But the poet Vainomaoien cannot free the sun without the actions of the smith Ilmarinen. And so you, too, must act.

There is a simple and yet very powerful ritual for changing your life. It is to do one new thing, something that you have never done, each day for a month. This can be as simple as driving a new route to work one morning. But it's better if you select something truly new, activities in which you have never taken part. Take a belly-dancing class. Go to a stable and watch the horses being groomed. Ask your friends to teach you crafts they practice. Sing aloud in public in a grocery store (one outside your own neighborhood will make you feel bolder).

This is an extraordinarily difficult discipline to follow. We all prefer to do things the way we've always done them. But doing things the way you've always done them has resulted in your being stuck. And our psyches tend to cling very tightly to outmoded and outworn behavior patterns, so trying to attack the source of your problems directly won't work. To solve your financial problems by working on your finances—hey, haven't you already tried that? It hasn't worked before; why should it work now? It's like Ilmarinen trying to get the sun out of the mountain by making a dull metal sun. By doing new things, you give a message to your deepest self that you need a change. (And while you're doing this, specialize in cheap and free things; it's easier on the budget. If you've previously been a spendthrift, you can even count as "one new thing" not accumulating new debt!)

It's fairly easy to come up with two or three or even a half-dozen new things to do. But by the end of a week or so, you'll be running out of ideas. Call your friends and tell them what you're doing. Ask what they'd suggest. Then follow up on their suggestions. Write a group poem over lunch. Take a walk through a public garden you've never visited. Tour a musical instrument factory. Make an ethnic dish you've never tried.

It won't take long before your inner self hears the strong message that change is needed. Your life may begin to change during your month of adventures. But it will certainly change within a short time thereafter. The deep self hears the message in your action. Like the sun coming out from the crag, you'll find hope returning to your life as its paralysis begins to depart. Be ready for hope and life and laughter to return to you!

∼

Questions and Activities

1. In your life now, what aspects are stuck or frozen? How long have you felt that way?

2. How do you feel about change? Do you cling to the old because you fear the new? Or do you chase after the new, forgetting the old?

3. When you hear a discouraging voice within you, does it sound like anyone you know or have known?

4. How do you respond to that discouraging voice? Do you argue with it? Ignore it and hope it will go away? Deal with it in some other way?

5. What would a perfect day look like for you? Describe it in complete detail.

6. For one week, observe yourself. How much of your life is controlled by habit?

7. Write a short sentence expressing your desire for change. Before you go to bed every night for a week, copy that sentence out in your journal. Let it seed your dreams.

8. If you had to express your deepest desire in one word, what would it be?

9. Write the word above on small pieces of paper and place them around your house. When you see them, breathe deeply and imagine your desire coming to fruition.

10. Find a photograph of yourself looking very happy. Carry that photograph around with you; when you feel distressed, look at it and imagine that happiness coming back to you.

The Maenads

Ecstasy

Yes! I will be there
for the revels—
tossing my head
and dancing on the dew.

1

Yes! I will be there
for the revels—
tossing my head
and dancing on the dew.
I will be there, yes! free
in the glad greenwood,
leaping like a deer
who fears no hunter.
There I will dance
with no man watching,
there I will find wisdom
in forest shadows.
Is there any gift greater
than feeling such joy?

2

Euoi, euoi!
How happy I am
running through the hills,
the skin of a fawn
my only cloak, eating
only the meat I kill—
this is such sweetness!
Euoi, euoi!
Come with me to the mountains,
sister! Come with me there!
We'll find honey there, and milk
and nectar and incense,
and women reveling, singing
euoi! euoi!
Join me and follow him,
follow the god of ecstasy,
that raucous boy—
euoi! euoi! euoi!

Myth and Meaning of the Maenads

The Maenads are the only figures in this book who were not goddesses. They are not even known to have worshiped a goddess, following as they did the god of ecstasy, Dionysus. Yet they deserve to be included here as the most important feminine representative of the idea of immanent divinity. For the Maenads, although they were not considered goddesses by the Greeks among whom they lived, seem to have found divinity within themselves during their wilderness rituals.

What were those rituals? We do not know, and probably never will. Followers of an ecstatic all-women's religion practiced for several centuries before 500 B.C.E., the Maenads kept their rituals utterly secret. All that we really know of them is that they departed their homes, accompanied by other Maenads—never in the company of men—and returned some days later. Apparently they were very tired on their return, for there are stories of Maenads collapsing in the village square, too exhausted to make the final steps to their homes, and waking to find themselves guarded by other village women who had not accompanied them to the mountaintop. But what did they do to weary them so? We will probably never know.

The secrecy surrounding their rites did not stop the Greeks from spreading rumors about their activities, or Greek dramatists from writing down these rumors, as did Euripides in his play *The Bacchae*, in which the above songs appeared (the name comes from an alternative name for Maenads, Bacchantes or Bacchae, derived from Dionysus's other name, Bacchus). The Maenads danced themselves into mania, so the stories went, possibly imbibing excesses of the wine their god had created. Reaching a state of intense intoxication, they then set about tearing living animals limb from limb. They drank the blood, devoured the meat, and wore the hides around their shoulders. Their ecstasy was so deep that they were no longer really conscious; thus they sometimes mistook family members for animals and tore them to shreds.

Fierce and frightening, these Maenads were irresistible to Greek artists, who painted and sculpted the women, hair flowing and unbound, draped in the skins of their prey, bearing wands of fennel decked with ivy. And dancing. Dancing with their heads thrown back and their mouths slack, throwing their arms out behind them. Women in ecstasy—what a subject! And so, though we have no actual record of the Maenads' rituals, we have hundreds of artistic visions of them. Whether these paintings have anything at all to do with the original worship, we cannot know.

But the hold of the Maenads on observers' imaginations is as strong today as it was more than twenty-five-hundred years ago. What did the Maenads do? Why did they do it? And why did their religion die out? These probably unanswerable questions have given rise to much speculation about these ancient women. They were insane, some speculate, prey to a sort of group psychosis. Or they were just mad, furious at their husbands and fathers for holding women in subservient roles. They were proto-feminists, striking back at the patriarchal religion by embracing a foreign and outlandish god. Or perhaps they were driven by a deep psychic need to embrace their own divine nature, which they realized in the ecstasy of their woodland rituals.

Of the Maenad's god, Dionysus, we have more information. Born of Zeus and Semele, an ancient mother goddess of whom little is known, Dionysus grew to young manhood nursed only by women, then began his triumphal procession across Greece. Resisted at first by the priests of conventional religion and mocked as "the women's Zeus," Dionysus was finally recognized as a full-fledged god in the seventh century B.C.E. This late addition of the god to the official pantheon was, for many years, interpreted to mean that he had literally just arrived; his usual homeland was given as wild Thrace, to the north of Greece. Yet recent excavations show him to have been in Greece before the Greeks—the Hellenic tribes—arrived. Thus there is mystery about the Maenad's god as well as the women themselves.

At the head of his procession of women he paraded, this intoxicated god, clad in women's robes and beautiful to see. Perhaps Dionysus was once "the shoot" (the meaning of one of his names), a god of vegetation destined to be destroyed as a human symbol of growth and death. According to this interpretation, the Maenads embodied the goddess of life and death, the nurse of life and then its devourer. The myths connecting Dionysus with Ariadne (originally a Cretan goddess whose name means "the very holy one") as his wife and chief Maenad support this identity of worshiper with goddess.

It is unclear how the Maenad religion was finally destroyed. But after approximately 200 years, it disappears from the historical record. Perhaps it had simply run its course, and women turned their attention to other matters. If the religion was appealing enough to last for centuries, however, it seems strange that it should so thoroughly fall out of favor. More likely is the co-opting of the religion by those who wished to bring the Maenads back to town. Embracing their god as one of the Olympians and establishing "Dionysian" rituals, which included drama, an art that grew quickly in popularity—these seem to have been the strategies that finally tamed the mad, manic women of the hills. But they live on in poetry and in art, their heads cast back and their limbs loose in the dance of ecstatic communion with the divine.

Symbols of the Maenads

In art, Maenads are readily recognizable by the ivy-covered staff they bear. Called a thyrsus, the staff was topped with a pine cone and draped with evergreen vines. In other cultures, the ivy has meanings consistent with the image of the ecstatic woman: it indicates protection of the feminine force, eternal life, intoxication. Thus the ivy can be said to be the most significant symbol of the Maenad.

Wine, too, is important in Maenad symbolism. Among the many things not known about these women is whether they employed intoxicating substances in their rituals. Assuming, as many do, that the point of their efforts was to transcend normal consciousness, and given Dionysus' rulership over wine, it may be that they used plant products to achieve an altered state. The connection of intoxicating beverages and religion is still found in the use of wine in Christian communion to represent the blood of the savior, and we still speak of "spirits" to mean both liquor and disembodied powers. Thus wine is an apt image for the power the Maenads sought to bring within themselves.

The hand-held frame drum or tambourine is also a common symbol for the dancing Maenad, who is often shown creating her own music with a percussion instrument. Flutes, too, sometimes appear in Maenad hands in Greek art, suggesting that the ecstatic ritual dances were performed to their melody. Animal hides, shown as part of typical Maenad attire in ancient art, have significance in representing the woman's tie to her animal body even as she moves into another realm of consciousness. But these symbols are much less important, in denoting a Maenad, than the ivy-covered staff or thyrsus.

Feasts of the Maenads

In Athens even into historical times, the City Dionysia was celebrated in mid-March—still, intriguingly, the time of a Dionysian festival in many cities, although the austere St. Patrick has replaced the divine boy as patron of the wine-besotted revels. On the night of the last full moon of winter, a festival procession of Maenads accompanied their god through the city, riding in a ship, throwing figs and nuts to the cheering crowds. This was the day to celebrate the last year's harvest, for the new wine was opened and people drank until they were satiated.

Another Greek festival connected with the Maenads was the Oschophoria on October 18, when Ariadne was invoked by processions of people bearing grape boughs in her honor. In its original homeland of Crete, it has been proposed, the festival was the initiation ritual for both girls and boys, announcing to the community that, like the new crop of grapes, they were now mature.

Finally, a festival called Lenaia, held during the full moon of January, was celebrated in late historic times in Athens and other Greek cities. The festival was said to be in honor of Dionysus Lenaia—"lenai" being another word for the Maenads. Women did not figure prominently in this festival, which focused on a king elected from the lower classes; this suggests the feast arose late, perhaps during the time of the taming of the wild women. At the Lenaia, parties were held, as were dramatic contests in which role reversals were jokingly celebrated. The connection of the full moon with this festival, as well as with the other Greek festivals for Dionysus, suggests that the original secret Maenad festivities were likely held at that phase of the moon, making it an appropriate time for invoking these powers.

Suggestions for Invoking the Maenads

It could be argued that the Maenads are still alive and well, hanging out in dim-lit bars and at boozy parties everywhere. They're honkytonk angels, swallowers of bitter little pills, positively-fourth-street junkies. They find their ecstasy at raves now, and their spirits are trapped in bottles. Why invoke them? Aren't they already here?

Today's smoky hangouts seem a far cry from the mountaintops where, in the safety of women's company, the original Maenads could dance (or drink, or even drug) themselves into an altered state in order to encounter the divine within. Yet the energy that drives these fallen Maenads may well be the same as that which led their foremothers to follow the raucous wine god. With no social context for intoxication as a religious ritual, those who yearn for ecstasy find it wherever they can. In a culture that denies the spiritual value of Dionysian ways, the Maenads are driven underground, revealing only the dark sides of their longing to incarnate divinity. And it is a rarely spoken truth about intoxication: it can make you feel divine. And because we do not speak about it, those hooked on ecstasy furtively return, again and again, to their divine connection.

Contemporary religion is generally more at ease with transcendent divinity, with god out-there (preferably up-there) rather than god in-here. Yet, in ecstatic states, mystics know that they do more than connect with an external divine force. They sense it inside themselves, feel themselves to be godlike—or goddesslike, in the case of Maenad women. But where there is no vocabulary that admits the desirability of such a state, where there are no rituals and no initiations, few can learn to experience ecstasy without risking psychological, physical, or psychic harm.

Addictive behaviors and substance abuse are damaging to men's lives, but social prescriptions about what is appropriately feminine mean that women who have followed a negative Maenad path are usually severely castigated and criticized. When such a woman ends her search for artificially induced intoxication and ecstasy, she is usually unwilling to examine the possible spiritual implications of that search. She may spend years fighting the impulse to return to that path. Yet only by embracing and affirming her desire for communion with the divine can such a woman be truly healed. Invoking the Maenad, that brave woman of ecstasy who found a safe way to celebrate her inner divinity, can be a way to such healing.

Women who have never permitted themselves to search for ecstasy through intoxication may find the image of the Maenads frightening or repellent. Such a woman may feel threatened or uncomfortable with the idea of invoking the wild women of our collective past; she may also be, or have been, judgmental about women who engage in Maenad-like behavior. Yet there is nothing shameful or abhorrent about the human desire for ecstatic communion with the goddess within. Acknowledging the archetypal power of the Maenad can open doors for such a woman.

Invoking the Maenad today is extraordinarily difficult. This chapter gives no specific ritual suggestions because each person on the goddess path must do substantial self-analysis on the subject of ecstasy and addiction before choosing any action. Women in recovery from addiction may wish to explore their spiritual hungers and to find nondestructive ways of meeting them, such as drumming or trance-dancing. Women in relationship to addicted people, whether as partners or friends or family, may examine the possibility of spiritual hungers driving such behavior, as well as examining their own addictive processes—for a relationship can be an addiction as well as any substance. Women who are fearful of ecstatic experiences can take this opportunity to evaluate the sources of that fear. Thus the struggle to celebrate the ancient followers of Dionysus will be the most challenging of any figure discussed in this book. The desire for ecstacy and the transformation that can accompany it is an important human drive. Driving it into the shadows, attempting to deny its power, may lead to destructive manifestations; to banish the Maenad is not, paradoxically, to diminish her power. She remains with us and within us. Let us find a way to free her again, to make again some mountain sanctuary for her wild desires, and to protect her in that brave search for the goddess within.

~

Questions and Activities

1. What addictive behaviors (drinking, drugging, spending to excess, eating, exercising, caring for others to the detriment of your own wholeness) have you engaged in or been tempted to engage in?

2. If you currently practice an addictive behavior, when does the urge seem strongest? What emotional benefit do you seek from the behavior? How does it make you feel when you have acted excessively?

3. If you formerly practiced addictive behaviors, what made you stop? How do you feel about the behaviors now?

4. If you have not practiced addictive behaviors, how does it make you feel when you become aware that others do? How do you act toward them?

5. What spiritual values might your own, or another's, excessive behavior hide?

6. People often speak of controlling addictive tendencies. If you have struggled with this, how does that struggle for control feel to you?

7. For a week, pay attention to one media (newspaper, television, movies). Do you see images of out-of-control women in that media? What messages do these images give you?

8. Do you think of some addictive behaviors as more appropriate for women than others? Why?

9. Have you ever experienced an ecstatic moment in nature? Describe it.

10. What does ecstasy or transcendence feel like for you?

Pomona

Joy

Oh! how Pomona loved her orchards!
Oh! to live among Pomona's trees!
Oh! to be loved as much as that!

Pomona lived in ancient times,
a nymph whose merest touch would green
an orchard, would fill its boughs with fruit.
Oh, how Pomona loved her orchards!
The rest of nature left her cold, but
fruit trees! apples! pears! These were
Pomona's great delight, her fiercest joy.
She bore a knife, but not for hunting—
no, hers was used to trim a hedge
of rose or cherry-wood, or to prune
a fruitless tree, or graft an aged apple
so that it burst forth fresh and new.
Orchards were her secret nurseries
and trees were her beloved ones
who never thirsted, never withered.
Oh! to live among Pomona's trees!
Oh! to be loved as much as that!

~

Myth and Meaning of Pomona

In ancient Rome, there were innumerable agricultural goddesses, ruling both plants and the activities needed to nurture them. Pomona's speciality was fruit, especially those borne on trees. Apples, plums, cherries, peaches—all these sweet and nourishing splendors—fell under her rulership.

The great Roman poet Ovid penned the poem on page 240 to Pomona as part of his great work called *Metamorphoses*. Like the other poems in the series, Pomona's tells the story of a shapeshifting divinity. In Pomona's case, it was the fertility god Vertumnus, who changed himself into a woman to court the goddess.

Here's how the story went: Pomona, as we learn in Ovid's poem, was extremely happy among her fruit trees, working as hard as ever an orchard-tender could, and loving every moment of it. But the great love goddess—called Venus on that boot-shaped peninsula, and Aphrodite in Greece—felt slighted by the nymph, who seemed to feel no call to mate.

And so she sent gods to court her. Well, perhaps not gods, for Pomona was just a nymph. Demi-gods, it would be better to say. All the woodland spirits crowded around Pomona, trying to catch her fancy. Satyrs came, those half-goat creatures, but she ignored them. Horned Pan came wearing a pine-wreath, and weary Silenus his companion, but they got the same treatment. Priapus came (Ovid winces at this phallic energy, and won't name him); Pomona did not even glance at his enormous endowment.

Then Vertumnus came, an ancient god of the fields. Seeing how tenderly Pomona cared for her trees, he yearned after her so strongly that he determined he would win her. But he got the same results as those interested only in carnal joys: nothing.

He refused to be discouraged. Thinking perhaps he was too old to please the goddess, he dressed up as a young farmer, bringing a basket of new-harvested barley to her door. He even remembered to sprinkle his hair with hayseeds, the better to look the part.

But nothing.

He tried being a handyman, carrying a ladder and a pruning knife. Nothing. He tried coming as a soldier, in full battle dress. As a fisherman, bearing creels and tackle.

Nothing.

Then he hit upon the ultimate disguise. Wrapping himself in a woman's shawl and powdering his long hair gray, he took up a stick and limped into Pomona's orchard. Acting as though he was nearsighted with age, he stumbled about, drawing close to the fruits and breathing in their fragrances. "These are very pretty," he said in a thin, old-lady voice, "but you are prettier, my dear."

Pomona, to his surprise, did not pull back. Vertumnus grew bolder. He kissed her.

And she did not draw away.

Having caught Pomona's attention, Vertumnus began to work toward his goal. Pointing out how the goddess's trees bloomed only because they were pollinated by roving bands of bees, he asked why she wasted her youth, refusing all offers to mate. When she could make no answer, Vertumnus began to play matchmaker, telling Pomona of a god who loved her dearly. How kind he was, how good a husband he would be. How well he would tend the orchards with her.

Pomona listened carefully, rapt in the old woman's eyes. The god could tell she was falling in love. And so he took her in his arms, and they were one.

It is of course difficult to say how much of this charming tale was Ovid's own invention, how much came from the religious tradition of ancient Rome. It is known that Pomona was a very ancient goddess, served by one of the dozen priestly brotherhoods called the flamines. In her shrine a few miles out of the city, called the Pomonal, no festival was celebrated, and little is known about her ancient worship.

Rome's relation to Greece is unusual; most conquering nations eliminated the worship of native divinities, replacing them with new ones from the home country. But the pantheon of Greece was so powerfully appealing that the Romans imported it back home, identifying local gods and goddesses with the great Olympians in what is called syncretism. Thus Juno, ancient goddess of woman's individuality, was associated with queen Hera; the maiden goddess Diana was assimilated to the rather different Artemis; and Minerva was linked to Athena because of their warrior nature, although the former had a healing aspect the latter lacked.

But there were many goddesses who had no corollary figure in Greek myth. Some of these were limited in their function, as for example the goddess of the door hinge, or the one who ruled a child's first trip away from home. Pomona was, however, not one of those; her function was far too vital to be a mere abstraction of an event in human life. She may well have come from pre-Roman times, having been the goddess of one of the peoples who occupied Italy in earlier times when, as the Roman author Pliny the Elder said, "the forests were the temples of the gods." In those early times, divinities were not pictured in human form but as "the most beautiful tree in the countryside" (Pliny again).

Her ancient significance is hinted at by her being assigned one of the priests (flamines) of the Arval Brotherhood. A dozen flamines served as many gods—all of them related to the fertility of the fields and orchards that surrounded the city. Membership was extremely prestigious; the emperor himself was always an honorary member in the brotherhood, as were senators and other prominent men. Their original job seems to have been to parade ceremoniously around the fields, invoking fertility upon them, in festivals from May 17–20 each year. Once Rome's territory grew larger than a three-day's walk, a single site was selected to represent the whole land.

Significant as Pomona originally was, she had faded to a dim shadow by imperial times, when Roman writers transcribed and codified the myths and rituals of the goddesses and gods. Pomona's connection to trees and fruit-raising remained, as well as the location of her shrine and the myth of her courtship. But for the rest, it is lost in the mists of time.

Symbols of Pomona

There is one preeminent symbol of Pomona: fruit. Even though so much of her ritual and tradition is lost, it is clear that this goddess was represented by the fruit she tended. She may have even been originally seen as embodied in the fruit tree itself, bearing its ripe sweet boons.

Contemporary use defines fruit as any sweet-tasting seed container. Plants born on shrubby bushes (blueberries and currents) as well as on vines (grapes, melons, kiwi) are considered fruit as well as those born on trees. The latter, however, seems most clearly Pomona's preserve. Thus cherries, peaches, apples, pears, oranges, lemons, and bananas could all be used to symbolize the goddess.

Feasts of Pomona

Although the ancient feast of Pomona has been lost, she may well have been invoked during Rome's harvest festival weeks in July and August. The festivals began with the Lucaria, on July 19 and 21, followed by the Neptunalia on July 23 and the Furrinalia on July 25. After a break—probably to work on the land—the next series of festivals began: Portunalia on August 17, Consualia on August 21, Volcanalia on August 23, Opiconsivia on August 25, and Volturnalia on August 27. Any fall festival date would be appropriate to Pomona, as would Arbor Day, May 25, when trees are planted.

Suggestions for Invoking Pomona

Following the goddess path sometimes feels like balancing on a razorblade. On the one hand, we wish to honor the insights of those who have worshiped the goddess before us; on the other hand, we yearn to create rituals appropriate to our current needs. Often we dip in a conservative direction. Where there are plentiful extant records showing how the people who named her viewed a goddess, we find ourselves imaginatively constricted. Having seen how Hera was reinvented to serve the purpose of patriarchy, why would we want to do the same thing? When we can hear the prayers of contemporary Hindus to their goddess Kali, why should we invent new ones?

Yet we live in our own times, with our own needs. And thus goddesses like Pomona, of whom little is known, are special gifts. We have enough of the goddess's story and her symbolism to begin designing a ritual, but not enough to limit how it should be celebrated. Pomona, and goddesses like her, allow us to become aware of the process of ritual design—a process that is very likely similar to those used by the goddess's original worshipers.

Using Pomona as an example, then, let us go through the process of understanding how ritual is created. Ritual, as mentioned in an early chapter, is an action taken with intent. One useful insight is to see ritual as the opposite of dreaming. Dreaming conveys messages from our unconscious mind into consciousness; if we can learn to read dream symbolism, we can gain insights into our inner selves. Ritual uses the language of dreaming in order to change the deep mind; it uses symbol and action to encode an intention that then is heard and, presumably, worked on by the unconscious mind.

Often, in ritual, one starts with intention. Perhaps your intention is to grow more respectful of yourself, to allow your boundaries to be violated less frequently by others. How would you form that into a ritual? You would find images (fences, perhaps, or armor) that convey your intention. You would also think of appropriate actions, such as wrapping your arms around yourself protectively. From these you might invent a story—or you might find one already in literature or myth that you can use, like the story of Athena's making a sacrifice of her own father after he attempted to violate her. From intention is drawn image and action; from action, narrative grows. With these three ingredients, a ritual can be developed.

In the case of Pomona, we already have an image—the fruit tree, laden with fruit. And we have a story, which includes action—disguise, in this case, and courtship. What we do not have is intention. We can, of course, guess at it. Doesn't it seem obvious? Wouldn't you, if you relied on your apple trees to provide sweetness all through the winter, want a ritual that encouraged the tree to bear lots of fruit?

But wait. Something is wrong with this logic. For a ritual to encourage lots of fruit would best be held in spring, when the trees are blooming; it would better be symbolized by sprigs of flowers than by fruit. Yet we know that Pomona is symbolized by fruit, not flowers. Thus we must explore the symbolic significance of fruit.

We can use encyclopedias and dictionaries, but our own associations will lead us in the right direction just as surely. Fruit: it is something that offers us pleasure and delight, and that also nourishes us. It is something we can store, something that doesn't have to be eaten immediately—far different from, for example, meat. It is a food that might last awhile.

Fruit is, our associations begin to show us, a great deal like an old woman!

The old woman who appears in the story is therefore an image similar to that of the fruit. She has weathered many seasons; she is no bud, no blossom. She has gained knowledge, which ripens within her like the seeds within a fruit. And she can be both sweet and nourishing.

We find in what little is left of Pomona's story, then, a doubling of meaning—two images that convey the same inner intent. Pomona, goddess of fruit, is both young and old at once, just as the fruit is both the end of the season's growth and the beginning of the next season. A ritual to her would acknowledge both endings and beginnings—or rather, the beginnings implicit in any ending, as well as the ending hidden in every beginning. Like Janus, Roman god of the year's hinge, Pomona looks both ways.

Thus rituals that invoke her could be located at points of change: when leaving an old job to take on a new one, when moving from one location to another, when graduating from college, when retiring from the working world. She is a perfect goddess to call on for a croning ritual, welcoming women to their elder years, but she is just as appropriate to a girl graduating from junior high and moving into the intensity of high school. The intention of such a ritual would be to acknowledge and celebrate past growth, and to remind the deep self that life is not over because change, like autumn chill, is in the air.

A ritual to Pomona could be as simple as placing an apple on a plate and cutting it ceremoniously, looking in careful awe at the moist flesh that surrounds the central star of seeds, then slowly eating the apple, savoring each tart bite.

But the ritual could not end there, for Pomona's message is not just that there is beauty and value in memory. The ritual must conclude with planting one or more of the apple's seeds, because the second part of Pomona's gift to us is awareness of the great potential we bear within us, like fertile seeds. At any given moment, we stand at the cusp of our future, bearing our past as we move into it. In the rich complexity of the simple image of Pomona's fruit, we can find spiritual messages that can sustain us as truly as any well-tended orchard.

∼

Questions and Activities

1. What traditional rituals did your family celebrate?

2. What religious rituals did you celebrate as a child? As an adult?

3. What feelings do holiday rituals evoke for you?

4. What feelings do religious rituals not associated with holidays evoke for you?

5. Are you aware of experiencing differences of mood during different seasons?

6. What habits do you have that are similar to rituals? Especially examine your daily habits of cooking, eating, cleaning. Where did you get these habits?

7. What habits of speech and thought do you have that are ritualistic? Do you ever stop yourself or someone from saying something out of a sense that "bad luck" comes from such speech?

8. What crafts did your family practice that might be connected to your heritage and its values? Do you know any songs or dances from your heritage? Do you practice them today?

9. How do you feel about rituals other than those you grew up with? Do you feel uncomfortable with rituals that are strange to you? What feelings are evoked by such rituals?

10. Do you prefer private or public ritual? What experiences have you had with each? What different benefits do you experience with each?

Afterword

Further Along the Goddess Path

This book has offered only the briefest of introductions to twenty goddesses. There are many excellent works available that will further introduce you to the ways of the goddess. In addition, many dedicated teachers can assist you in discovering your own inner connection to the figures discussed here and the many, many others that world culture offers.

In traveling further along the goddess path, remember to use both inner and outer resources. You will find a dazzling array of possibilities for further reading in bookshops and libraries. Read carefully and with respect, for the insights of generations are often distilled into a few spare words or a simple prayer. Similarly, be wary of making quick generalizations ("the goddess is always a mother," for instance), which are more likely to be based in your emotional needs than in the material itself. Research in libraries is likely to take you into the fields of anthropology, folklore, mythology, art history, and religion—all of which are categorized differently. When researching, don't forget to read bibliographies, for the perfect source of information may lie hidden therein. A single author may mention a book that turns out to be vital to your personal search. It is thrilling to find an out-of-print book containing a beautiful invocation to your favorite goddess—a prayer that might have been lost to history without your personal attention.

You may well find yourself drawn to travel to locations you read about in your armchair sojourns in the lands of the goddess. Many tour operators now offer goddess-oriented excursions to Greece, Ireland, and other important sites. Visiting an ancient temple or stone circle may become one of your most cherished memories. Similarly, make it a point to visit all museums in your own town and in areas you visit.

Many of the remaining goddesses in the world are displayed as art, not as the religious figures they are. Anthropological and natural history museums often offer treasuries of non-European goddess figures.

Individuals, too, are great resources for your continued growth in goddess spirituality. You may find someone at a nearby community college or university, and frequently you can connect with teachers through spirituality centers and bookstores in your area. Publications and organizations devoted to the goddess are similarly useful in locating teachers who approach the goddess in a way with which you feel comfortable.

As important as research is the creative process, which can be called "insearch." Insearch means examining your dreams and visions for information about how the immanent goddess manifests herself in your own psyche, your own life. Similarly, creating artworks inspired by goddess traditions is a valuable way both to discover more about your inner goddess and to introduce others to her image.

As part of insearch, you may wish to examine ways you can incorporate goddess traditions into your daily life. In many ancient cultures, honoring the goddess with a nod to the rising sun or with a small prayer before preparing food was an integral part of community life and personal worship. Finding your own ways to bring goddess energy into your everyday life can be a vital link between your studies, your more formal worship, and your inner development.

The goddess path is not always an easy one to travel. There are some who deeply fear the rising power of the feminine; they can create disturbances at the workplace, at home, in the neighborhood. It is unfortunate when people who preach love find it so difficult to practice. But be aware that the very power you find so sustaining can be, to those invested in monotheistic religions centered on gods, extremely threatening. Judicious silence is in order when confronted by such people. Should they be family members or close friends, however, attempting dialogue can be a potentially rewarding challenge. It may, on the contrary (or in addition), be extraordinarily painful. Not everything about this emerging religion is easy.

Similarly, you may find yourself led to take on difficult social tasks as a result of your study of the goddess. Unacknowledged talents may be called upon; you may need to make some changes in the patterns of your daily life; you may find yourself going back to school, organizing a center, working in a hospice, writing a book. You cannot predict, at any point in this journey, where the next part of it will lead.

But you will have company as you travel. Not only are there increasing numbers of people who will joyously accompany you, but there is the goddess herself. She surrounds you: she is the air, the water, the soil beneath your feet, the stars over your head. And she is within you: she is your passion and your joy, your inspiration and your challenge. Walk this path with her. You may not know where it will lead, but you can be assured that the journey will be one you will never regret.

~

Sources

The prayers and invocations in this book are adapted from the following translations of the originals:

Amaterasu

Nihon, Shoi. *Nihongi.* Charles Tuttle, 1972.

Philippi, Donald L. *Norito: A Translation of the Ancient Japanese Ritual Prayers.* Princeton University Press, 1991.

———. *Kojiki.* Columbia University Press, 1977.

Wheeler, Post, translator. *The Sacred Scriptures of the Japanese.* H. Schuman, 1952.

Aphrodite

Boer, Charles, translator. *The Homeric Hymns.* Swallow, 1970.

Evelyn-White, H. G., trans. *The Homeric Hymns and Homerica/Loeb 57.* Harvard University Press, 1936.

Friedrich, Paul. *The Meaning of Aphrodite.* University of Chicago Press, 1978.

Lang, Andrew, trans. *Homeric Hymns.* Reprint: Ayer Co Pub, 1972.

Sargent, Thelma. *Homeric Hymns: A Verse Translation.* W.W. Norton, 1975.

Artemis

Boer, Charles, trans. *The Homeric Hymns.* Swallow, 1970.

Evelyn-White, H. G., trans. *The Homeric Hymns and Homerica/Loeb 57.* Harvard University Press, 1936.

Ferry, David, trans. *The Odes of Horace.* Farrar Strauss and Giroux, 1997.

Godolphin, F. R. B., ed. and trans. *Great Classical Myths.* The Modern Library, 1964.

Horace. *The Odes and Epodes of Horace.* A Modern English Verse Translation Joseph P. Clancy, tr. University of Chicago Press, 1960.

Lang, Andrew, trans. *Homeric Hymns.* Reprint: Ayer Co Pub, 1972.

Sargent, Thelma. *Homeric Hymns: A Verse Translation.* W.W. Norton, 1975.

Shepherd, W. G., trans. *The Complete Odes and Epodes: With the Centennial Hymn.* Penguin, 1983.

West, David, trans. *The Complete Odes and Epodes.* Oxford University Press, 1997.

Athena

Boer, Charles, trans. *The Homeric Hymns.* Swallow, 1970.

Evelyn-White, H. G., trans. *The Homeric Hymns and Homerica/Loeb 57.* Harvard University Press, 1936.

Godolphin, F. R. B., ed. and trans. *Great Classical Myths.* The Modern Library, 1964.

Lang, Andrew, trans. *Homeric Hymns.* Reprint: Ayer Co Pub, 1972.

Sargent, Thelma. *Homeric Hymns: A Verse Translation.* W. W. Norton, 1975.

Brigid

Carmichael, Alexander. *Carmina Gadelica: Hymns and Incantations Collected in the Highlands and Islands of Scotland in the Last Century.* Lindisfarne Press, 1992.

Jackson, Kenneth Hurlstone. *A Celtic Miscellany: Translations from the Celtic Literatures.* Penguin Books, 1971.

The Cailleach

Billson, Charles J., collector and editor. *Folk-Lore of Leichestershire and Rutland. County Folk-Lore, Vol I.* David Nutt, 1895.

MacKenzie, Donald A. *Scottish Folk-Lore and Folk Life.* Blackie & Son Ltd., 1935.

Demeter

Foley, Helen P., ed. *The Homeric Hymn to Demeter: Translation, Commentary, and Interpretive Essays.* Princeton University Press, 1998.

Meagher, Robert Emmet. *Helen.* University of Massachusetts Press, 1986.

Mylonas, George E. *Eleusis and the Eleusinian Mysteries.* Princeton University Press, 1961.

Richardson, Nicholas James. *The Homeric Hymn to Demeter.* Oxford University Press, 1974.

Gaia

Aeschylus. *The Plays.* Trans. John Herrington. Yale University Press, 1986.

Boer, Charles, trans. *The Homeric Hymns.* Swallow, 1970.

Evelyn-White, H. G., trans. *The Homeric Hymns and Homerica/Loeb 57.* Harvard University Press, 1936.

Getty, Adele. *Goddess: Mother of Living Nature.* Thames and Hudson, 1990.

Godolphin, F. R. B., ed. and trans. *Great Classical Myths.* The Modern Library, 1964.

Lang, Andrew, trans. *Homeric Hymns.* Reprint: Ayer Co Pub, 1972.

Sargent, Thelma. *Homeric Hymns: A Verse Translation.* W. W. Norton, 1975.

Hathor

Bleeker, C. J. *Hathor and Thoth.* E.J.Brill, 1973.

Olson, Carl, ed. *The Book of the Goddess, Past and Present.* Crossroad, 1985.

Young, Serinity, ed. *An Anthology of Sacred Texts by and about Women.* New York: Crossroad, 1994.

Hera

Evelyn-White, H. G., trans. *The Homeric Hymns and Homerica/Loeb 57.* Harvard University Press, 1936.

Lang, Andrew, trans. *Homeric Hymns.* Reprint: Ayer Co Pub, 1972.

Sargent, Thelma. *Homeric Hymns: A Verse Translation.* W. W. Norton, 1975.

Inanna

Poems of Heaven and Hell from Ancient Mesopotamia. Translated and
Introduced by N. K. Sandars. Penguin Books,1971.

Wolkstein, Diane and Samuel Noah Kramer. *Inanna: Queen of Heaven and
Earth, Her Stories and Hymns from Sumer.* Harper and Row, 1983.

Isis

Apuleius, Lucius. *The Transformations of Lucius, or The Golden Ass.* Translated
by Robert Graves. London: Penguin, 1951.

Taylor, Thomas. *Metamorphosis or Golden Ass of Apuleius.* Kessinger Publishing,
1997.

Walsh, P.G., trans. *The Golden Ass.* Oxford University Press, 1995.

Kali

Avalon, Arthur and Ellen, trans. *Hymns to the Goddess, translated from the Sanscrit.*
Luzac and Co, 1913.

Harding, Elizabeth. *Kali.* Weiser, 1993.

McLean, Malcolm. *The Life and Work of Ramprasad.* State University of New York
Press, 1998.

Mookerjee, Ajit. *Kali: The Feminine Force.* Destiny Books, 1988.

Kuan-Yin

Blofeld, John. *Bodhisattva of Compassion: The Mystical Tradition of Kuan-Yin.*
Shambhala, 1978.

Yu, Anthony C., translator and editor. *The Journey to the West.* University of
Chicago Press, 1977-83.

The Maenads
Millman, Henry H., trans. *The Bacchae.* Dover, 1997.

Rudall, Nicholas, trans. *The Bacchae.* Ivan R. Dee, 1996.

Williams, C. K. *The Bacchae of Euripedes: A New Version.* Noonday, 1990.

Muses
Ferry, David, trans. *The Odes of Horace.* Farrar Strauss and Giroux, 1997.

Horace. *The Odes and Epodes of Horace: A Modern English Verse Translation.* Joseph P. Clancy, tr. University of Chicago Press, 1960.

Shepherd, W. G., trans. *The Complete Odes and Epodes: With the Centennial Hymn.* Penguin, 1983.

West, David, trans. *The Complete Odes and Epodes.* Oxford University Press, 1997.

Oshun
Beier, Ulli, ed. *Yoruba Poetry: An Anthology of Traditional Poems.* Cambridge University Press, 1970.

Nicholson, Shirley. *The Goddess Reawakening: The Feminine Principle Today.* Theosophical Publishing House, 1989.

Pomona
Innes, Mary, trans. *Ovid's Metamorphosis.* Viking Press, 1987.

Mandelbaum, Allen, trans. *The Metamorphosis of Ovid: A New Verse Translation.* Harcourt Brace, 1993.

Ovid. *The Metamorphoses, A Complete New Version.* Horace Gregory, trans. New American Library, The Viking Press, NY, 1958.

Paivatar

Bossley, Keith, ed. *The Kalevala (World's Classics)*. Oxford University Press, 1989.

Lonnrot, Elias. *The Old Kalevala and Certain Antecedents*. Prose translations with forward and appendices by Francis Peabody Magoun, Jr. Harvard University Press, 1969.

Saule

Benjamins, Eso. *Dearest Goddess*. Current Nine Publications, 1985.

Jonval, Michel. *Les Chansons Mythologiques Lettones*. Librarie Picart, n.d.

Katzenelenbogen, Uriah. *The Daina: An Anthology of Lilthuanian and Latvian Folksongs*. Latvian News Publishing Company, 1935.

Bibliography

In addition to the above, the following are good basic sources for information about goddess religions, old and new:

Ardinger, Barbara. *Goddess Meditations.* Llewellyn, 1998.

Athena Center Goddess Graduate School, P. O. Box 439014, Chicago, Illinois 60643.

Beltane Papers, quarterly magazine, P. O.Box 29694, Bellingham, Washington 98228-1694.

Budapest, Zsuzsanna E. *The Grandmother of Time: A Women's Book of Celebrations, Spells and Sacred Objects for Every Month of the Year.* HarperSanFrancisco, 1989.

Bullfinch, Thomas. *Bulfinch's Mythology.* Hamlyn Publishing Group, 1964.

Christ, Carol. *Rebirth of the Goddess: Finding Meaning in Feminist Spirituality.* Routledge, 1998.

Colgrave, Sukie. *The Spirit of the Valley: The Masculine and Feminine in Human Consciousness.* J. P. Tarcher Inc. 1979.

Crawford, O. G. S. *The Eye Goddess.* Phoenix House, 1957.

Daly, Mary. *Beyond God the Father: Towards a Philosophy of Women's Liberation.* Beacon Press, 1985.

———. *Gyecology, The Metaethics of Radical Feminism.* Beacon Press, 1990.

Dames, Michael. *The Silbury Treasure: The Great Goddess Rediscovered.* Thames and Hudson, 1976.

Dexter, Miriam Robbins. *Whence the Goddesses: A Sourcebook.* Pergamon Press, 1990.

Eisler, Riane. *The Chalice and the Blade: Our History, our Future.* Harper & Row, 1987.

Ellis, Normandi. *Dreams of Isis: A Woman's Spiritual Sojourn.* Quest Books, 1995.

Ellis, Peter Berresford. *Celtic Women: Women in Celtic Society and Literature.* Eerdmans, 1995.

Galland, China. *Longing for Darkness: Tara and the Black Madonna.* Viking, 1990.

Gantz, Jeffrey, trans. *The Mabinogion.* Barnes & Noble Books, 1976.

Gimbutas, Marija. *The Language of the Goddess.* HarperSanFrancisco, 1991.

———. Miriam Robbins Dexter, editor. *The Living Goddesses.* University of California Press, 1999.

———. *Goddesses and Gods of Old Europe, 6500-3500 B.C.: Myths and Cult Images.* University of California Press, 1990.

———. *The Language of the Goddess.* HarperSanFrancisco, 1995.

Goddessing, newspaper, P. O. Box 269, Valrico, Florida 33595.

Grace, Patricia. *Wahine Toa: Women of Maori Myth.* Paintings and Drawings by Robyn Kahukiwa. Collins, 1984.

Graves, Robert. *The White Goddess.* Farrar, Strauss and Giroux, 1948.

Green Egg, magazine, #22B, 212 S. Main Street, Willits, California 95490.

Green, Miranda. *The Gods of the Celts.* Barnes & Noble Books, 1986.

Griffin, Susan. *Woman and Nature; The Roaring Inside Her.* Harper & Row, 1978.

Grimm, John and Jacob. *The Complete Grimm's Fairy Tales.* Pantheon, 1944.

Hall, Nor. *The Moon and the Virgin: Reflections on the Archetypal Feminine.* Harper Colophon, 1980.

Hawley, John Stratton and Donna Marie Wulff. *Devi: Goddesses of India.* University of California Press, 1996.

Highwater, Jamake. *Myth and Sexuality.* New American Library, 1990.

Hollander, Lee M., trans. *The Poetic Edda.* University of Texas Press, 1988.

Hurbon, Laennec. *Voodoo: Search for the Spirit.* Harry N. Abrams, Inc. Publishers, n.d.

Husain, Shahrukh. *The Goddess: An Illustrated Guide to the Divine Feminine.* One Spirit, 1997.

Jade. *To Know: A Guide to Women's Magic and Spirituality.* Delphi Press, 1991.

Johnson, Buffie. *Lady of the Beasts: Ancient Images of the Goddess and her Sacred Animals.* Harper & Row, 1988.

Johnston, Basil. *The Manitous: The Spiritual World of the Ojibway.* Harper Collins, 1995.

Kerenyi, Karl. *Goddesses of Sun and Moon.* Spring Publications, 1979.

Knappert, Jan. *The Aquarian Guide to African Mythology.* The Aquarian Press, 1990.

Markale, Jean. *Women of the Celts.* Translated by A. Mygind, C. Hauch and P. Henry. Inner Traditions, Inc., 1986.

Monaghan, Patricia. *O Mother Sun: A New View of the Cosmic Feminine.* Crossing Press, 1994.

———. *The New Book of Goddesses & Heroines.* Llewellyn, 1997.

Morrison, Dorothy. *In Praise of the Crone.* Llewellyn, 1999.

Obeyesekere, Gananath. *The Cult of the Goddess Pattini.* University of Chicago Press, 1984.

Of a Like Mind, quarterly newsletter, P. O.Box 644, Madison, WI 53716.

Onassis, Jacqueline, ed. *The Firebird and other Russian Fairy Tales.* The Viking Press, 1978.

Orenstein, Gloria Feman. *The Reflowering of the Goddess.* Pergamon Press, 1990.

Patai, Raphael. *The Hebrew Goddess.* KTAV Publications, 1967.

Peradotto, John, and J. P. Sullivan, eds. *Women in the Ancient World: The Arethusa Papers.* State University of New York Press, 1984.

Pomeroy, Sarah B. *Women in Hellenistic Egypt: From Alexander to Cleopatra.* Wayne State University Press, 1990.

Preston, James J., ed. *Mother Worship: Theme and Variations.* University of North Carolina Press, 1982.

Redgrove, Peter. *The Black Goddess and the Unseen Real.* Grove Press, 1987.

Sandars, N.K., trans. *Poems of Heaven and Hell from Ancient Mesopotamia.* Penguin Books,1971.

Spender, Dale. *Writing or the Sex? Or Why You Don't Have to Read Women's Writing to Know It's No Good.* Elsevier Science, 1989.

Starhawk. *The Spiral Dance: A Rebirth of the Ancient Religion of the Great Goddess.* Harper & Row, 1979

Stone, Merlin. *When God Was A Woman.* Harcourt Brace Jovanovich, 1976.

Teish, Luisah. *Jambalaya: The Natural Woman's Books of Personal Charms and Practical Rituals.* Harper & Row, 1985.

von Franz, Marie-Louise. *Problems of the Feminine in Fairy Tales.* Spring Publications, 1972.

Waters, Frank. *The Book of the Hopi.* Drawings and source material recorded by Oswald White Bear Fredericks. Penguin Books, 1977.

Whitmont, Edward C. *Return of the Goddess: Femininity, Aggression and the Modern Grail Quest.* Routledge and Kegan Paul, 1983.

Index

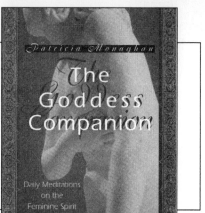

The Goddess Companion
Daily Meditations on the Goddess

PATRICIA MONAGHAN

Engage your feminine spirit each day of the year! Here are hundreds of authentic goddess prayers, invocations, chants and songs—one for each day of the year. They come from dozens of sources, ranging from the great classical European authors Ovid and Horace, to the marvelously passionate Hindu poets Ramprasad and Ramakrishna, to the anonymous gifted poets who first composed the folksongs of Lithuania, west Africa and Alaska. In fresh, contemporary language that maintains the spirit of the originals, these prayers can be used for personal meditation, for private or public ritual, or for your own creative inspiration. They capture the depth of feeling, the philosophical complexity, and the ecological awareness of goddess cultures the world over.

Organized as a daily meditation book, *The Goddess Companion* is also indexed by culture, goddess, and subject, so you can easily find prayers for specific purposes. Following each prayer is a thoughtfully written piece of prose by Patricia Monaghan that illustrates the aspects of the goddess working in our everyday lives.

1-56718-463-4
7½ x 9⅛, 312 pp., bibliography, index $17.95

To order, call 1-800 THE MOON
Prices subject to change without notice

The New Book of Goddesses & Heroines

PATRICIA MONAGHAN

They come out in your dreams, your creativity, your passion, and in all of your relationships. They represent you in all your glory and complexity, and you represent them. They are the goddesses and heroines that form our true history. Your history. Let these mythic stories nourish your soul as they speak to you on a level as deep and mysterious as the source of life itself.

The third edition of this classic reference offers a complete, shining collection of goddess myths from around the globe. Discover more than 1,500 goddesses in Australia, Africa, North and South America, Asia, Europe—and experience her as she truly is. This new edition also adds hundreds of new entries to the original text—information found only in rare or limited editions and obscure sources.

There is a new section on Cultures of the Goddess, which provides the location, time and general features of the major religious system detailed in the myths. A comprehensive index, titled "Names of the Goddess," provides all available names, with variants. Stories, rites, invocations, and prayers are recorded in the Myths section, as well as a list of common symbols. Never before has such a vast panorama of female divinity been recorded in one source.

1-56718-465-0
8½ x 11, 384 pp., illus., photos, softcover $19.95

To order, call 1-800 THE MOON
Prices subject to change without notice

Magical Gardens
Myth, Mulch & Marigolds

PATRICIA MONAGHAN

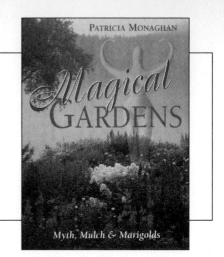

Like ancient alchemists, gardeners transform common materials—seed, soil, sun and water—into the gold of beauty and nourishment. In the process, gardeners transform their own souls as well; time spent in the garden is a sacred time, a time of meditation and worship. For such gardeners, *Magical Gardens* offers insights in making a more conscious connection between soul and soil, between humus and the human spirit.

Plant an Angel Garden, which comes into its own in the moonlight, shining with its own secret radiance . . . or an Aphrodite's Bower, abundant with flowers and passion, crowded and dense with bloom . . . or a Sorcerer's Secret Garden, where in voluptuous privacy you can feel secure enough to envision utter freedom. Myths, meditations and magical rituals are combined with garden plans that honor the old divinities and the old ways.

1-56718-466-9
8½ x 11, 208 pp., softcover $17.95

The Office Oracle
Wisdom at Work

PATRICIA MONAGHAN

A strategy manual in the tradition of Machiavelli, Sun Tzu's *The Art of War*, and Tom Peters's *In Pursuit of Excellence, The Office Oracle* provides fast, savvy advice to help you skillfully master all of work's challenges.

With three quick tosses of four coins, you can become a workplace wizard. *The Office Oracle* will lead you to the appropriate lesson you need to ponder. Learn when you should smile and when to attack, when to take advantage of career opportunities, how to make money in the gray areas, and 197 other shrewd strategies for success.

Refuse to sleep through the marvelous flow and flux that surrounds you. Open your eyes to the multiple possibilities of every occasion. Learn to detect change as it is about to occur and use it to your advantage. Become one of the wise with the help of *The Office Oracle.*

1-56718-464-2
5¼ x 6, 224 pp. $7.95

The Mysteries of Isis
Her Worship & Magick

DE TRACI REGULA

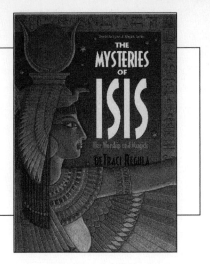

For 6,000 years, Isis has been worshiped as a powerful yet benevolent goddess who loves and cares for those who call on Her. Here, for the first time, Her secrets and mysteries are revealed in an easy-to-understand form so you can bring the power of this great and glorious goddess into your life.

Mysteries of Isis is filled with practical information on the modern practice of Isis' worship. Other books about Isis treat Her as an entirely Egyptian goddess, but this book reveals that she is a universal goddess with many faces, who has been present in all places and in all times. Simple yet effective rituals and exercises will show you how to forge your unique personal alliance with Isis: prepare for initiation into Her four key mysteries, divine the future using the Sacred Scarabs, perform purification and healing rites, celebrate Her holy days, travel to your own inner temple, cast love spells, create your own tools and amulets, and much more. Take Isis as your personal goddess and your worship and connection with the divine will be immeasurably enriched.

1-56178-560-6
320 pp., 7 x 10, illus., softcover $19.95

Goddess Meditations
BARBARA ARDINGER, H.Ð.

Bring the presence of the Goddess into your daily spiritual practice with *Goddess Meditations,* a book of 73 unique guided meditations created for women and men who want to find a place of centeredness and serenity in their lives, both alone and in groups, either in rituals or informally.

Call on a Hestia for a house blessing . . . the White Buffalo Calf Woman for help in learning from your mistakes . . . Aphrodite for love and pleasure . . . Kuan Yin for compassion. Although it's directed toward experienced meditators, this book includes guidelines for beginners about breathing, safety, and grounding, as well as instructions for rituals and constructing an altar.

Also featured is the powerful "Goddess Pillar Meditation," based on the Qabalistic Middle Pillar Meditation; nine Great Goddess meditations that address issues such as protection, community, and priestess power; and seven meditations that link goddesses to the chakras.

1-56718-034-5
256 pp., 7 x 10, softcover $17.95

Maiden, Mother, Crone

The Myth and Reality of the Triple Goddess

D. J. CONWAY

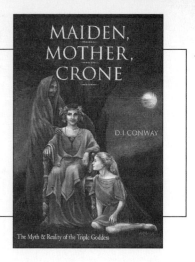

The Triple Goddess is with every one of us each day of our lives. In our inner journeys toward spiritual evolution, each woman and man goes through the stages of Maiden (infant to puberty), Mother (adult and parent) and Crone (aging elder). *Maiden, Mother, Crone* is a guide to the myths and interpretations of the Great Goddess archetype and her three faces, so that we may better understand and more peacefully accept the cycle of birth and death.

Learning to interpret the symbolic language of the myths is important to spiritual growth, for the symbols are part of the map that guides each of us to the Divine Center. Through learning the true meaning of the ancient symbols, through facing the cycles of life, and by following the meditations and simple rituals provided in this book, women and men alike can translate these ancient teachings into personal revelations.

Not all goddesses can be conveniently divided into the clear aspects of Maiden, Mother, and Crone. This book covers these as well, including the Fates, the Muses, Valkyries and others.

0-87542-171-7
240 pp., 6 x 9, softcover $12.95

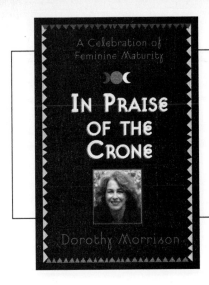

In Praise of the Crone
A Celebration of Feminine Maturity

DOROTHY MORRISON

When Dorothy Morrison began her menopausal metamorphosis at the early age of 32, she thought her life was over. Then she discovered a reason to celebrate: she'd been invited to the Crone's party!

Meet your hostess and mentor, your Personal Crone. Mingle a bit and find your Spirit Self. Discover why the three of you belong together. Learn to balance yourself, gather wisdom, reclaim your life, and make the most of your natural beauty. Then meander into the Crone's kitchen and find home remedies that can take the edge off minor menopausal aggravations without the use of hormone replacement therapy or prescription drugs.

Written with humor and compassion from someone who's been there, *In Praise of the Crone* alleviates the negativity and fear surrounding menopause with a wealth of meditations, invocations, rituals, spells, chants, songs, recipes and other tips that will help you successfully face your own emotional and spiritual challenges.

1-56718-468-5
288 pp., 6 x 9 $14.95

To order, call 1-800 THE MOON
Prices subject to change without notice

Celtic Women's Spirituality
Accessing the Cauldron of Life

EDAIN MCCOY

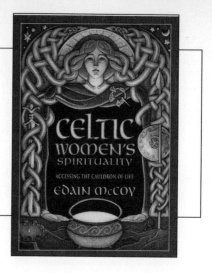

Every year, more and more women turn away from orthodox religions, searching for an image of the divine that is more like themselves—feminine, strong and compelling. Likewise, each year the ranks of the Pagan religions swell, with a great many of these newcomers attracted to Celtic traditions.

The Celts provide some of the strongest, most archetypally accessible images of strong women onto which you can focus your spiritual impulses. Warriors and queens, mothers and crones, sovereigns and shapeshifters all have important lessons to teach us about ourselves and the universe.

This book shows how you can successfully create a personalized pathway linking two important aspects of the self—the feminine and the hereditary (or adopted) Celtic—and as a result become a whole, powerful woman, awake to the new realities previously untapped by your subconscious mind.

1-56718-672-6
352 pp., 7 x 10, illus.

$16.95